IN THIS GREENHOUSE OF GARDENING SECRETS, anyone who has ever tried to raise plants will find numerous ways to avoid pitfalls, save money, and create a garden of greenery indoors. Here are easy-to-follow instructions for potting, feeding, pruning; handy hints on recognizing the symptoms of a sick plant: brown spots, bud blasting, dropped leaves; the perils as well as the pluses of watering, sunshine, and plant food—and everything you need to know about plants in the captivity of your apartment.

STAN AND FLOSS DWORKIN are well known to America's gardening audience, locally and nationally, because of their weekly "Garden Spot" segments on WNBC-TV's NewsCenter 4 and the NBC network's TODAY SHOW. In the metropolitan New York area they are the hosts of two radio shows on WRVR-FM: "The Apartment Gardeners" and "The Apartment Gardeners' Sunday Show." They are frequently teachers and lecturers in horticulture at plant societies, horticultural societies, and botanical gardens. Their magazine articles have appeared nationally, and they are the authors of three cookbooks including BAKE YOUR OWN BREAD, available in Signet edition.

SIGNET Books on Gardening

THE APARTMENT GARDENER

Stan and Floss Dworkin

ILLUSTRATED BY
Floss Dworkin

A SIGNET BOOK
NEW AMERICAN LIBRARY
TIMES MIRROR

SIGNET TRADEMARK REG. U.S. PAT. OFF. AND FOREIGN COUNTRIES
REGISTERED TRADEMARK—MARCA REGISTRADA
HECHO EN CHICAGO, U.S.A.

**SIGNET, SIGNET CLASSICS, MENTOR,
PLUME and MERIDIAN BOOKS**
are published by The New American Library, Inc.,
1301 Avenue of the Americas, New York, New York 10019

FIRST PRINTING, APRIL, 1974

9 10 11 12

PRINTED IN THE UNITED STATES OF AMERICA

Contents

Preface

This is a book to tell you how we do it. It tells where and why we failed, and where and how we made it. It comes from our own experiences, except for a few places, and we'll say so when those come up.

The whole back of the book tells you where to find plants and supplies and plant societies, and it even tells you where you can go to talk to a living, breathing horticulturist.

We had to write this book. All the books we liked were far out of date, and it seemed to us that most of the more modern writers we read (and we read every plant book in the New York Public Library system before moving on to the library of the Horticultural Society of New York) were writing from experiences so different from ours as to have little relevance for us. We live in an apartment. We have no house, no greenhouse, no sunporch, no basement, no coldframes, just a steam-heated apartment and windows covered with city soot.

While older plant books had many good ideas, the technology of growing has made such strides recently that even books written only twenty years ago seem far out of touch. Plastic for propagation and terrariums, the availability of sterile mediums and soil-less mixes, indoor plant lighting, all kinds of gardening aids put into every gardener's hands, at low cost, techniques previously available only to the rich or to those who worked for the rich.

Apartment gardeners have problems particular to apartments, and for years we've tried to solve those problems, and at the same time to make our city apartment fit for human habitation. So, to all of you who've cornered us at our lectures and courses, to all of you who've telephoned us at home or on our radio show, and to those of you who don't know us from Adam and Eve but have been trying to grow in an overheated and underlit apartment—hang in there, help is on the way.

PART I

BUYING PLANTS

1. Buying Plants: Where and From Whom?

It's easy to buy a plant, right? You just walk into a florist, pick out the one you want, put your money or your charge plate on the counter, and either walk out with it or have it delivered. Right?

Well, that's an interesting approach.

First of all, most "florist's" are probably the worst place to buy a plant. Few know anything about houseplants, however much they may know about cut flowers.

Nowadays, there are some stores that do specialize in houseplants, but they, too, are usually run by people who look for the buck first, and service to the customer last. Most of them have gone into the business because it looked like a growing field (it is), not because they knew anything about plants and wanted to put their knowledge to work for them.

There are some plant stores that are run by people who know plants. If you hear of one, cherish it.

DO WE EVER BUY FROM A FLORIST?

We can't honestly say that we never buy a plant from a florist shop. One of our favorites came from a florist who knew neither what it was nor what it needed. We asked, "What is this?" and he answered, "Four dollars."

Would it grow in an apartment? Absolutely!

We paid the $4 and today have a shiny, luxuriant *Pandanus veitchii*—because we later found out what it was and how to give it proper culture. You can be sure that most of the others that florist sold died from overwatering.

WHAT ABOUT PLANT STORES?

We have students who are in the plant business. We like to think that anyone who cares enough to take courses in horticulture cares enough to sell a plant into the right environment. At least, in a plant store, you don't have to worry about the owner's prime concern: it's plants, not American Beauty roses.

SUPERMARKETS

We've examined a lot of plants sold in supermarkets, and spoken to a lot of people who have bought them there. From our experience, a supermarket is a bad place to buy a large plant. The small ones for around 39¢ are okay, but then almost any place is a possible place to buy a 39¢ plant. But look at the big plants in your neighborhood supermarket window. We don't mean the first few days they're in, but after a week or so. Are the plants still looking healthy (after all, the first day out of the greenhouse, any plant will look healthy), or are the lower leaves starting to yellow? There are always problems in buying big plants (see Chapter 3) and those apply in spades to big supermarket plants: a plant going from a warm greenhouse to an air-cooled supermarket to a warm apartment just *has* to suffer.

WOOLWORTH'S

Recently we went browsing through the plant department at a local Woolworth's. It looked like a disaster area: some plants were rotting, leaves were off; other plants were wilted beyond recall; others had been in the low-light of the store long enough to get leggy.

In the past, that department had been beautifully kept and watered, the plants moved in and out so fast there was no chance for them to get leggy.

If you know your onions, you may get a good buy at Woolworth's—especially if you get the first pick of the shipment. Get on your bike and visit the big and busy branches.

In fine, it depends on who's taking care of the department, and when you go. But Woolworth's does offer a moneyback guarantee. We've used it: a succulent died on us very quickly and we brought the pot back and got our money back. Try to do that with your local florist.

GREENHOUSES AND GARDEN CENTERS

At a greenhouse there is usually someone who can give you intelligent advice about houseplants. But for the city dweller, they are not easy to get to.

Garden centers carry mostly outdoor plants. The few good exotic houseplants we've found there, though, were often at a good price. Also, one can sometimes get a very good buy on supplies.

Do remember, though, that florists, plant stores, Woolworth's, garden centers, and most greenhouses all get their plants from the same places—southern or western greenhouses and plantsmen.

Most of the plant material sold in the eastern United States comes from Florida and makes the long trip up in trucks, which means that they are used to that higher humidity, and the intense Florida sun, etc. (In the West, they come mostly from California.) So, however easy a plant is supposed to be to care for, we must remember that it has spent the early part of its life (like a child's formative years) in conditions very different from those of our apartment.

However, it should be said that some greenhouses do hold plants a while before selling them in order to "harden them off" to northern conditions.

AMATEURS TURNED PROFESSIONAL

There is a group of growers we're always happy to buy from, or just to visit; those are the amateur growers who have let their hobby run away with them and turned professional.

We give the names of several of these plant friends in the back of the book among other recommended plant people. Generally speaking, the plants they sell aren't as expensive or "high-strung" as the plants grown by the larger commercial outfits, because they themselves propagate the plants they sell. If you have such a grower in your area, use him, for the plants he raises are *adjusted to your area*.

These growers are usually members and mainstays of the amateur plant societies, and love to talk to you about their plants.

PLANTS FOR FREE

Some of our best plants we didn't buy at all. If you belong to a plant society, or just have friends who grow plants, you have a great source of free or inexpensive plants, grown by people in conditions similar to yours (mostly), who are not only able but overjoyed to tell you how they treated them, what they fed them, how often they watered them, what light they gave them, whether or not they talked to them, and so on. Cuttings from friends are often more successful than large bought plants.

Part VII contains a listing of some houseplant society addresses. If you can join them, do it. You won't be sorry.

PLANTS BY MAIL

We'll give you an absolute: don't buy tender, soft plants from far away. The Post Office Department seems to take a special joy in taking boxes marked "LIVE PLANTS" and giving them the roughest and slowest treatment. Especially if they must be routed through the Chicago system.

Having said this, let us assure you that we are in favor of buying plants through mail order. For one thing, you know where they came from: California sun, New England greenhouse, etc. Also, mail-order buying gives you access to individual growers who are good but too small to travel great distances to the city for flower shows and the like. Their plants are generally cheaper and usually come insured (or can be for a few cents extra), so that any loss due to Post Office mishandling can be adjusted.

Seeds, bulbs, tubers, and the like are especially satisfactory bought through the mail. Here, the Post Office can do little to hurt your purchases, and any reputable, well-established seedsman will make an order good, no matter who's to blame.

With bromeliads, orchids, and cacti, you need have no qualms about distance. They can live quite a while out of their pots and survive quite bad treatment in the shuffle, and still turn into excellent plants.

PLANT SALES

We're lucky here in New York City. We have major and minor botanic gardens, most of which have regular plant sales once or twice a year (and some of which have permanent plant shops). Sometimes the plants are specially grown by the gardens themselves; sometimes they are "excess" plants; sometimes they are grown by volunteers; sometimes they are bought from commercial growers in the area. This past year we bought a group of bromeliads from the Brooklyn Botanic plant sale; they had been bought as pups (for bromeliad offsets, see Chapter 23), from a famous Florida grower, and rooted and potted by the Garden staff. They are lovely plants now.

Some of the most unusual succulents in our collection come from the Wave Hill Center for Environmental Studies, which has two sales a year.

If you have a botanic garden or horticultural society in your area (check Part VII), give them a call and ask about their sales. Or call the garden editor of your local newspaper.

Block parties or other local fund-raising activities often include a plant sale as part of the festivities, and sometimes you can find something quite nice there, but do examine those plants carefully for bugs. Most commercial growers and botanic gardens spray their plants before they sell them (though at the Brooklyn Botanic sale we also saw trays of annuals loaded with aphids), but block-party sellers usually don't.

CAVEAT EMPTOR?

The general run of plant sellers seems to believe it is indeed up to the buyer to beware. And many plant buyers seem curiously willing to accept that. When they buy a plant and it dies on them, they assume that it is somehow *their fault*, and never think of complaining to the person who sold it to them.

Before we knew anything about bugs we bought a fuchsia infested with white fly. We returned the plant to the florist and he was astounded. No one had ever returned a plant before. As it was, he refused to give us our money back so we took a clean plant in exchange. But even that was a victory. (However, though the plant was gone, the white fly lingered on in our apartment.)

You too have to realize that, as with anything else, from eggs to refrigerators, both buyer and seller have their responsibilities. And a seller who hasn't told the truth as to the conditions a plant requires (even through ignorance) hasn't lived up to his.

When you are buying, *do* be wary. But remember, if you make a mistake, you are not guilty of anything that cannot be adjusted by a trip back to the store, corpse or invalid in hand.

LOOKING FOR TROUBLE

If we've seen a plant that we want, unusual, inexpensive (we won't spend a lot of money for a plant—we can't afford it), desirable (from what we've read about it, perhaps, or been told about it), and appropriate to our growing conditions, it won't matter where we see it; what matters is what we see *on* it.

First of all, is the plant of a good, healthy color and appearance? We don't want to buy an unhealthy plant and then nurse it back to health. We have no stray-kitten complex. We like healthy plants—at least to buy.

Does it have all its leaves? We look for places where leaves may have dropped off. If a plant has lost its leaves, there's a reason. Even if it has lost leaves from trauma, why should we take an injured plant into our home when the world is full of uninjured ones?

We look at the tips of leaves (of frondy plants) to see if the florist's scissors have been at work. It is common practice, especially with a plant such as *Dracaena marginata*, to cut off the tips of leaves as they brown. (They can turn brown for many reasons, but they never grow back.)

And then we look for bugs. We examine the undersides of leaves, the axils, the growing tips: all the places where bugs like to congregate.

We'll look to see if roots are coming out of the bottom of the pot. If they are, the plant may be so potbound that it may have trouble being successfully repotted.

And we'll examine the surface of the soil to see if there are any bugs crawling around. Once the plant is out of the shop, it can be very difficult to get a store to make an adjustment—mostly they insist *you* were to blame.

TRAUMA

When we were answering telephone questions for the Horticultural Society of New York, trauma was at the root of a good third of the questions.

Trauma is shock.

Once plants have matured in some particular niche of the world, they do not want to move. Like all true conservatives they resent change.

If a plant is raised in a greenhouse and brought into your apartment it will go into shock and, in an effort to survive, will drop the expendable parts of itself: flowers, leaves, stems, etc.

Trauma is usually caused by temperature change, humidity change, light change, or most frequently a combination of these factors. It generally appears anywhere from a few days to a week or so after the plant is brought home. It won't happen all at once, but you'll see that those gloxinia flowers are dying very quickly and the other buds aren't opening; that after a week, the rubber-tree leaves are falling; or your asparagus fern fronds are turning yellow. (See Chapter 3.)

A certain amount of trauma is to be expected. If you're prepared for it, perhaps you can combat it with mistings of water, and other ways to raise humidity; with additional light; or with better air circulation.

But what do you do if you have no choice of light location? And no air conditioner to lower the summer temperature of your apartment? Or no way to turn down the steam heat to cool off your winter apartment? Then you've got real problems.

Try not to bring plants into your apartment in the middle of the summer. Especially if they've come from an air-conditioned store.

Try not to bring high-humidity plants into your apartment unless you can provide high humidity (see Chapter 5, RAISING HUMIDITY).

Don't bring cacti or other sun lovers into your home unless you have a bright location in which to grow them. It's true that cacti suffer less from shock than any plant we know, but they can suffer a long and lingering decline.

[16]

But don't despair. There are so many plants that fit into so many niches of the world that no matter what your conditions (within reason) you can find plants you can grow successfully. All you need is to know something about the life needs of the plants you will see for sale.

2. Buying Plants: What?

How long should a plant last? No plant is forever, though the joy of it should last longer than a vase of cut flowers.

Is the one season of ageratum worth the price you pay for it? Sure, if you know it. But too often these are sold next to the philodendrons and there is no sign saying that they are annuals.

When you buy a pot of tulips, you get some flowers which will probably be blown in a few days, leaving you with foliage and some bulbs you can't carry over in an apartment. But you do have those few lovely days.

When you buy an amaryllis, you get a few exciting winter weeks of watching the flower stalk and buds and flowering (spectacular) and a bulb you *can* carry over from year to year (see Chapter 27) at a price probably no higher than you would pay for the tulips.

Marigolds will give you a full summer and half a fall of flowers, but you'll have to throw the plant out at the end of its season. And is it really a good *house*plant? Aren't the best houseplants those we can enjoy year round?

A cattleya orchid in flower is an expensive plant. But the flowers can last for a month in an apartment. The plant itself is tough, although the likelihood of its flowering again without a window greenhouse is small (see Chapter 26).

Bromeliads are also expensive, but their flower spikes can last for months, and when the spike goes, you'll very likely get offsets to carry on (see Chapter 23), which can be quite exciting.

A gloxinia requires a good deal of humidity to keep it coming back into flower (see GESNERIADS, Chapter 22), but once you know how, you can keep a gloxinia for 10 years, with more blossoms every year. And this from a tuber that may cost you $1.

And what about a foliage plant, such as a dracaena? With care, dracaenas can come close to living forever, lasting for years and years, into a decade or more in an apartment and even after they get too big or leggy for beauty, you can start the same plant anew by air-layering (see Chapter 17, VEGE-TATIVE PROPAGATION).

Do you want to begin big or small? Big plants are impressive but small ones have a longer life ahead of them. We advise everyone to buy small plants and grow them up.

But what plants should you buy in the first place? That's what we're trying to answer in this chapter.

A SHOPPING TRIP

To help you choose, let's go shopping together. The list that follows is the result of a shopping trip among the florists and plant stores and supermarkets in our New York City neighborhood. All the plants you'll see in the list were for sale in our local stores.

What we say about the plants we found on that shopping trip are things we wish we had known when we began buying plants for our apartment garden.

The remarks given here on culture are just to help you choose. After all, a cactus is a great apartment plant, but only if you have a sunny window; a gloxinia is gorgeous if you have the humidity, but a disaster otherwise. We haven't tried to give you the last word on culture for every plant in cultivation, so if your favorite isn't listed here, read on: most of this book is about culture.

And, please remember, we are not bringing the gospel, we are expressing our opinions and prejudices, our experiences and those of a few of our plant friends. If you've got a plant that we say is a poor apartment plant and you've grown it up to be a prizewinner, more power to you; drop us a note and we'll try to include it in the next edition. And if you see something you *must* try, don't let what we say stop you. Heaven knows we learned a lot from our mistakes—and for you, it may turn out to be the best plant you ever owned.

So, let's go shopping.

ABUTILON hybrids (flowering maple)

This is *not* a maple, though some forms have maple-shaped leaves.

Bought in bud, you'll often find some of the flowers will open, then the rest of the buds blast (shrivel and fall off before opening). But this plant can be grown successfully for a season if you give it good light, with some direct sun, and fair humidity. Don't allow it to dry out completely or you'll eventually lose it. Keep it well potted, "moving it up," that is, transplanting it to a larger pot, as soon as it shows any sign of being underpotted.

Available in many colors, and in variegated and green leaves of different shape. Easily grown from seed or from tip cuttings.

Quite an interesting plant, but it requires attention.

ADIANTUM species and hybrids (maidenhair fern)

Really inappropriate to apartment culture because it requires high humidity and constant moisture at the roots. Its light requirements are modest. Direct sun will burn it. If you can, try it in a protected environment (see Chapter 18).

There are several species and hybrids available, including a few miniatures.

AECHMEA fasciata

A good apartment plant, this bromeliad is widely available year round. Its pink-purple-and-blue flower spike can last for months, and the plant itself will stay in dramatically presentable condition for quite a while after. You'll have to pay $12 to $15—or as high as $35 at a fancy store—for one in spike, but it's worth it. Look down the "vase" formed by its leaves and choose one where the spike is just coming out.

Keep water in the "vase"; mist the foliage whenever you can; but soak the bottom only once a week. See Chapter 23 for more bromel information.

AEONIUM various species

This is a good apartment plant for a moderately bright

window (not the full southern or western exposure you might need for true cacti). This succulent grows in rosette form, the edges of the leaves sometimes gently spined. They often redden in the sun, and make a handsome display in a bulb pan. (See Chapter 10, POTS.)

Allow to dry well between waterings and feed seldom with a weak solution of any plant food. Does well in any humidity. Propagate from seed or from cuttings of the rosettes.

AESCHYNANTHUS species and hybrids (lipstick plant)

This glossy-leafed trailing gesneriad is available in most shops only as large mature plants in hanging baskets. In flower, they are most spectacular and tempting, with bright flowers coming from dark calyces (the darker part at the base of the flower). However, unless you can give the plant the high-ish (40–50%) relative humidity it has been getting in the greenhouse, you'll find it losing flowers quickly, blasting buds, and getting straggly. If you've bought one already, take several cuttings for propagation (see Chapter 17) and make your own hanging basket. The young plant you make yourself will have a better chance of surviving in your apartment.

Give good bright light in an eastern exposure and allow to go barely surface-dry between waterings. Feed frequently at half-strength with 15-30-15 plant food while the plant is in active growth. See GESNERIADS, Chapter 22.

African violet, see SAINTPAULIA

AGERATUM houstonianum hybrids

These small annual plants flower in pale-blue puffs; they can be bought in flower and will continue to flower on your sunny windowsill or outdoor terrace or fire escape for the remainder of the summer season.

Heavy drinkers, they must be kept well watered or you will lose them. Feed weekly while in flower.

AGLAONEMA hybrids (Chinese evergreen)

Excellent for apartments, this plant doesn't seem to mind

low humidity and even grows well in that very modestly lit corner over *there*. Don't expect it to flower for you unless it is quite a mature plant and your conditions are ideal.

Allow to dry out somewhat between waterings, and feed with fish emulsion at long intervals.

We've kept its long, paddle-shaped foliage alive for three years (so far) in a vase of water.

The plant is available in some extremely handsome variegations.

ALLIUM schoenoprasum (chives)

Of course you can buy and grow chives in pots from your supermarket but only if you separate out the overcrowded bulbs and replant them immediately; otherwise they have little chance to survive. (See Chapter 21.)

Allow to dry out well between waterings, and don't bother trying to carry them over to next spring unless you're willing to give the bulbs a very cool window. Kept in the sun, they will flower for you, but the foliage will get rather stringy.

ALOE vera (burn plant)

We have a friend, accident-prone at the charcoal grill, who keeps at least three *Aloe veras* around through the summer, to treat the many burns he inflicts on himself. He breaks off one of the long, thin pale-green stems and rubs the juice on his wound. He, and many others, swear by it.

We've found aloes to be fine for a very bright window, but a little weak growing in many dimmer apartment locations.

Allow to go quite dry between waterings, as with most desert succulents, and feed sparingly. Propagate by cutting out an offset and rooting it in an open propagation box (see Chapter 15).

Aluminum plant, **see** *PILEA cadierei*

Amaryllis, **see** HIPPEASTRUM

ANANAS comosus species (pineapple)

This is *the* pineapple, though many bromeliads seem to be called pineapple. It's found with green or variegated foliage, with and without fruit. The fruit will ripen, but usually it's not worth the eating (there are many generations of hybrids between this and what Dole cans), and no, you cannot expect more than one fruit from it. That's not the way bromeliads work (see Chapter 23).

Since this is a terrestrial bromeliad, you should keep the soil moister than you would with epiphytic bromeliads. (Terrestrial plants have their roots in the soil; epiphytic plants have their roots in organic matter, say, in the crotch of a tree. With epiphytic plants the roots are mostly for support, the plant taking its nourishment largely from the damp jungle air.)

We find some varieties too spiny for comfort in the apartment, and the plant tends to take up quite a bit of room, but in good light, it should survive.

Spray the foliage with water whenever you think of it.

APHELANDRA squarrosa hybrids (zebra plant)

This is really a tempting plant: the dark green foliage with its striking pale stripes and startlingly yellow inflorescence (flower spike). But we don't know anyone who grows it successfully in an apartment; certainly no one who flowers it again.

In nature this plant grows as a large shrub. The tips of the stems are cut off and rooted, and that's what you get in the city: those tips in flower. But the plant keeps trying to become a shrub again, and so grows quite leggy. To keep a compact plant, you might keep making tip cuttings. They root easily.

Keep well watered and in as much humidity as you can manage. Feed well, and give bright light, though not direct sun. Only you can figure if it's worth it.

ARAUCARIA excelsa hybrids (Norfolk Island pine)

In its native South Pacific, this lookalike for a true pine can grow over 200 feet tall.

With effort, it can be grown well in an apartment, but most aren't. The most successful apartment grower of these we know has a room with bright light on two sides, and he hoses down the walls every day! The room has a drain, brick walls, and a tile floor, so no harm comes to his apartment, but we certainly couldn't make it in ours.

If you want to try, start small and train your plant to your conditions. These trees can be quite expensive and finicky bought large.

Keep well watered; feed with fish emulsion at half strength every few weeks and keep the humidity as high as possible. Set in a bright location, but watch out for direct sun if your plant has become used to living indoors.

ARDISIA crispa (coral berry)

This plant, too, is a shrub. We keep ours small in a small pot, which means that it doesn't flower, but we have apartment friends who let theirs grow more and get sweet-scented flowers and handsome red berries.

It doesn't require your brightest window, and it wants to go a bit dry between waterings. Feed moderately. Humidity doesn't seem important, but winter it in a cool, bright window.

ASPARAGUS plumosus, A. meyeri, A. sprengeri (asparagus fern)

Although these 3 plants are all called asparagus fern, they aren't ferns at all, but the tender cousins of the hardy edible asparagus.

They make better apartment plants than ferns. First of all, their humidity requirements are less than ferns—though they need some spraying and other humidity help in the average apartment; they won't die if you accidentally allow them to go a bit dry—though they prefer constant damp; and they flower, leaving little red berries, if conditions are favorable. (Ferns never flower: they have a different sex life.)

Asparagus ferns do require some direct sun, and more feeding than true ferns. We feed ferns with fish emulsion, but give asparagus ferns a balanced food (15-30-15). See Chapter 8, FEEDING.

ASPIDISTRA elatior (cast-iron plant)

This broad, pointed-leaf plant was enormously popular a generation ago, but it's hard to find now.

The culture is, apparently, virtually anything you want to give it, short of leaving it soaking. Allow it to go dry, put it in your dim corner, feed it only twice a year—and this foliage plant will still go on. Of course, if you want it to thrive, give it a bit more food and light.

ASPLENIUM nidus (bird's-nest fern)

The long, pale, leathery leaves of this true fern radiate from a dark feathery center that *is* a little like a bird's nest.

It has a chance in your apartment if you have decent humidity and can keep the plant well watered. Feed with fish emulsion at half strength every few weeks and give it a little sun. If you get burn, pull it away from the sun.

You'll see bird's-nest ferns with fronds as long as 3' for sale. Avoid them. You have very little chance of one this large doing well for you. But you may be able to grow a small one into a sizable plant successfully yourself.

AUCUBA japonica

This shrub makes a very nice window plant; you can see large versions of it in many bank lobbies. Its yellow-mottled foliage makes a nice color accent and it is easy to care for.

Give it good light, allow to go a bit dry (but not too dry), between waterings, feed once a month when in active growth, and don't worry about humidity.

AZALEA hybrids

These plants are often quite sad. After Easter one sees so many of them with their brown leaves and bare stems abandoned on the street, aluminum foil still on the pots.

In an apartment, azalea plants require constant moisture at the roots, fair humidity, and an acid soil. Feed with an iron-rich, high-acid food at half strength every 2 or 3 weeks. Direct sun may redden the leaves, so be prepared to pull the plant back, but it needs as much light as it can get to thrive.

Be sure to remove the aluminum foil from the pot and scrub off the algae.

Baby's tears, see HELXINE

Basil, see OCIMUM

BEGONIAS

Begonias are among the best apartment plants you can find, and no houseplant collection should be without some. We grow literally scores, and many of them we got by trading cuttings with friends; they propagate very easily.

It is a huge and varied plant family and certain types are easier than others, while certain ones aren't really well suited to apartments at all. Probably more semperflorens begonias are sold than any other kind, but these aren't the most desirable for an apartment grower. They require too much sun to do their best, and, quite frankly, they just aren't interesting enough. They do best as outdoor bedding plants, grown as annuals and started fresh each year. If you have that very bright window or sunny balcony or fire escape, they can make a nice display provided you keep them bushy by frequent pinching back (see Chapter 9, GROOMING).

We prefer the rhizome types ourselves (see *B. erythrophylla* and *B. 'Maphi'* below, and for a discussion of what rhizomes are, see Chapter 27, BULBS, TUBERS . . .). You can propagate these by 8 or 9 different means, and if you get even a bit of a leaf from someone, you can expect to get a plant (see VEGATATIVE PROPAGATION, Chapter 17). Their foliage is often handsomely mottled, their stems hairy and spotted, their rhizomes . . . well, unusual is a good word. Best of all, they are happy, for the most part, in apartment conditions. They don't demand the front places on that one bright windowsill; if they go dry between waterings it's all to the good; they are not heavy feeders; for the most part they don't require high humidity; and they'll do very well under fluorescent lights.

However, there are some rhizome types we don't recommend for beginners. For example, we've never had success with rexes or with *B. 'Rajah,' B. 'Gogoensis,'* or *B. 'Universe'* outside of a protected environment. But there are so many others, both very tiny and very large, that you have a wide choice.

We also grow joyfully several cane-type and a few upright-type begonias. See below.

Calla types. This is an interesting development in begonia hybridizing, the most famous example being *Begonia* 'Charm.' The leaf shape is very similar to semperflorens begonias, but the foliage is variegated: streaked, spotted, white, green, cream, red, in various combinations. They are sometimes quite difficult to grow because the variegations means a shortage of chlorophyll (present only in the green). Also, they require relatively high humidity. Callas are not recommended for beginners, but if you're growing other begonias successfully, you may want to try one.

Cane types (angel-wing begonias). Cane-type begonias (the stems look a bit like thin bamboo stalks) can run from a quite small *Begonia* 'Preussen' to a very large *B.* 'Corallina de Lucerna.' They can be excellent apartment plants, if you have the sun and the space. Some of them are very easy to flower in a bright window. Their blossoms hang down in beautiful clusters, making a most spectacular display. Others are a bit shyer of bloom ('Sophie Cecile' for example), but have handsome foliage. Belva Kusler's hybrids are especially recommended: they are durable and they grow.

Growing all the canes well depends largely on your light; they want some direct sun. They like to go a bit dry between waterings and want to be fed a balanced food (15-30-15), and a high humidity isn't necessary. But they can grow quite large. If you have room, fine; if you don't, either stick to the rhizomatous begonias or keep the canes cut back. The cuttings root well in an open propagation box (see Chapter 15, PROPAGATION BOXES).

B. erythrophylla (beefsteak begonia). A good apartment plant, this is probably the most popular of the rhizome-type begonias; the rubbery leaves have a pale green front and a red back. It flowers in very early spring or late winter under natural light. For us, it doesn't flower under fluorescent light because it requires long nights and we don't have the space to give it a separate set-up. Demanding only moderate light, it does prefer a slightly higher humidity than do the cane types, and does best when allowed to dry out very slightly between waterings. Feed as you would the canes.

Begonia 'Preussen' has been in bloom for 5 months and should now be pruned back.

B. leptotricha (woolly bear). This is a semperflorenslike begonia that is much more difficult to grow. We've never had much luck with it, but the fuzzy foliage makes it a very interesting and attractive plant if you can keep it going. Try a higher humidity than with the semps and less light. Allow it to go barely dry between waterings.

B. hiemalis (winter flowering). These are interesting begonias because of their different appearance and the large size of their flowers, which will flourish in the cold weather—if in a steam-heated apartment you can keep the plant cool. So this is a maybe plant. And some of them do present special problems: 'Schwabenland Red' for example is genetically quite prone to fungus—a problem we can live without. If fungus occurs, scissor off the affected parts.

Allow these winter flowerers to run a bit on the dry side, and give a good deal of bright light.

They are also available as "elatior" begonias or under the trade name "Rieger."

B. 'Maphil' ('Cleopatra'). One of the oldest and one of the loveliest of the hybrid "miniatures," this is a rhizome type that gets treated just like *B. erythrophylla*. Its lovely star-shaped leaves are mottled with chartreuse.

B. rex. Rex types are a rhizomatous group grown for their gorgeous leaves. Don't buy one unless you know what you are doing because you will have trouble knowing whether it has died or gone dormant. And it may go dormant just because you've removed it from its nice greenhouse.

Rexes require high humidity, constant watering, and very diffuse light. Even then, they are still chancy in an apartment. Once they begin to go dormant, watering may cause them to rot. Really not for apartment culture except in a protected environment.

B. semperflorens (wax begonias). The Latin name "ever-flowering" is quite literal; these flower so easily and continuously that it's almost boring. The more light, the more flowers. They want more sun than any other begonia, but they will flower even under fluorescent lights. They prefer going dry between waterings (but not to the point of wilting), don't care about humidity, and will take whatever food you give them. In the fall, take cuttings from your terrace plants and, when rooted, pot them up for your brightest winter window.

Tuberous begonias. Poor in an apartment. See Chapter 27, BULBS, TUBERS . . . .

Upright types. This is a group of begonias with stems less woody than the canes, more upright habit than the semps, no rhizome, and usually somewhat hairy leaves. *B. scharffii* is a beautiful example, with pink flowers dotted with dark-red hairs. They want good light, with some sun, if you have it. Allow to go a bit dry between waterings or you risk rot.

Bird's-nest fern, **see** ASPLENIUM

Boston fern, **see** NEPHROLEPSIS

BOWL GARDENS

Generally speaking, planted bowls or brandy snifters are better and much less expensive if you can make them yourself. The ones you'll find planted in most florist's are so over-grown that they'll be unsightly in a very short while. See Chapter 18, GROWING IN A PROTECTED ENVIRONMENT.

If you must try a bowl garden, use plants that require roughly similar conditions.

Burn plant, see ALOE

Burro's tail, see *SEDUM morganianum*

CACTI

This is a huge subject to cover in a few words, and we have a chapter on them later on (Chapter 24). About buying, let's just say that, in general, we feel safe buying any small cactus not obviously desiccated, sick, or injured, even if not named, virtually anywhere. They are tough and great for a bright sunny window, but if you have no sun, just sigh and pass on to another counter.

CALADIUM hybrids

Caladiums are beautiful foliage plants. Their large heart-shaped leaves may be variegated with red or pink or white or other colors in many combinations. They make a good houseplant, but they are of tropical origin and if you let them get too dry or too cool they will drop their leaves and go dormant. If you then continue to water them well, you'll rot the tuber. So, keep them warm and happy, and you'll have a good long season before they go dormant. (See Chapter 27, BULBS, TUBERS . . .)

Quite undemanding as to light. Provide a slightly higher humidity by misting the leaves occasionally, and feed once a month with dilute fish emulsion. Once the plant begins to go into dormancy, stop feeding and slowly reduce watering.

In florist shops and dime stores, only the plants in leaf are offered, but you can buy dormant tubers from some garden centers and by mail from most general seedsmen.

Calamondin orange, see CITRUS

CALCEOLARIA herbeohybrida (pocketbook plant)

This cool-greenhouse plant is completely unsuited to apartment culture: we wouldn't have it on a bet. Bought in flower, you can expect all the flowers to collapse by the next day.

CAMELLIA japonica hybrids

Believe it or not, camellias can make excellent apartment or balcony or fire-escape plants. They will flower in a moderately bright window even as a plant less than 2 feet tall.

Give them good bright light, feed regularly while in growth, and don't allow to run completely dry. (That's how we lost a beauty.) Keep them cool and bright during the winter, and in the spring put them outside as soon as you can. In the south, of course, they can live outdoors year round.

Candy-corn plant, see HYPOCYRTA

CAPSICUM frutescens hybrids

These are real hot peppers, and edible. There are similar-looking genuses which aren't edible, so be careful. Usually bought already in fruit, they make very decorative plants with their red or yellow peppers. But they are grown as annuals and so not worth a large investment. (They *may* survive the winter, cut back, on a cool, bright window.)

Keep on a bright windowsill and water only as the top of the soil goes dry. Feed lightly. Humidity doesn't seem relevant.

Cast-iron plant, see ASPIDISTRA

CELOSIA argentea varieties (cockscomb)

One look at the startlingly red or orange flowers tells you where this plant gets its common name.

This is a tender annual, so don't expect to carry it over the winter. The small plants available in early summer will give you handsome flowers all summer and into the fall, provided you give it some sun, don't let it really dry out, and provided the bugs, to which all annuals are prone, don't eat it up.

CHAMAEDOREA elegans bella (also sold as Neanthe bella)

This is a lovely miniature palm, and fine for apartment culture, but don't put it into a bottle garden. The tiny ones you see for sale are not dwarfs but babies. They will soon grow out of any container. We have one several years old that is almost 4' tall—very dwarf as mature palms go.

Here's a plant that we almost killed by putting into direct sun one spring. It burned so badly that we lost fronds and thought we'd lose the whole plant. In a location where most plants cry out for more light, our palm is nearly always in flower (though you may not at first recognize those skinny sticks as flower stalks).

Water well, and then wait until the soil is barely dry on top. Humidity doesn't seem to matter. We feed ours once a month (or less) with a dilute fish emulsion. That may seem like very little food, but the plant is big enough.

Occasionally, we haul our palm friend into the shower with us.

Chinese evergreen, see AGLAONEMA

Chives, see ALLIUM

CHLOROPHYTUM species and varieties (spider plant)

We don't know a more satisfying apartment plant, but it won't do well in the dark. Many spider plants seem to be sold as reduced-light plants, and it's just not so. Set it in a good bright light, with some direct sun, and come late spring you can expect the long flower stalks to come out with weeks and weeks of little white flowers, followed on the same stalks by plantlets. When the plantlets develop roots, cut them off and pot them up directly in soil. (See Chapter 17.)

Spider plants will grow well in "normal" apartment humidity but the tips of their leaves will tend to brown. An occasional misting will help keep the leaves green. Allow the soil to dry out between waterings and feed with half-strength fertilizer (15-30-15) as soon as growth starts in the spring.

Another reason for browning tips is crowded roots. Now, don't protest that you just repotted your plant 3 months ago: chlorophytums grow very quickly (which means you can buy a small plant and in a few months grow it quite large).

Examine the tips of the leaves to see if the florist has been trimming them; *you* get trimmed if you buy a trimmed plant.

CHRYSANTHEMUM hybrids

These plants are lovely if bought just for their flowers because the flowers last quite well. But unless you're willing to take cuttings for propagation, don't expect to do anything else with them. You've very little chance of carrying them over: they're just too crowded in the pot. They are great perennials for *outdoor* gardens.

Cineraria, see *SENECIO cruentus*

CISSUS antarctica (kangaroo vine), C. rhombifolia (grape ivy)

Terrific apartment plants, both of them, making excellent hanging baskets, although the stems, with their leathery dark-green leaves, do tend to go *up* more than down.

They don't mind going dry between waterings, although they don't require it. They will survive in a dull window, though they do best in a bright one. Any humidity above desert air and any feeding schedule will keep them happy. These rate among the best apartment plants.

C. discolor. This is another hill of beans altogether. We sometimes see this one sold as a terrarium plant without any warning that the plant grows too large for terrariums. The leaf colors are exquisite, but it requires very high humidity, constantly moist soil, and diffuse light. Unless you have a high-humidity spot in your apartment, we just don't see this doing well for you.

CITRUS mitis (Calamondin orange)

The first plant we ever bought was a Calamondin orange. The seller told us not to worry if a few of those green balls fell off, that was natural. Well, we listened to a few fall, then a few more, then a whole bunch, and got very nervous. The seller lied; those balls (fruit) weren't supposed to fall off, but our apartment was then just too dry to keep a citrus plant. Since then we've raised our humidity and have flowered the same plant quite successfully.

We feed it well, with acid plant food, give it plenty of sun and water, and it's content with the humidity we manage to provide. The flowers smell heavenly. Never allow it to dry out completely or you'll lose it.

This charming plant can be in flower and fruit at the same time, and the little oranges are edible.

There are many excellent citrus fruits available by mail order: lemons, limes, and other oranges. Try whatever you can find, but water them well and mist the leaves daily.

Cockscomb, see CELOSIA

CODIAEUM hybrids (croton)

There's a lot of this bright-leafed foliage plant sold in New York, and most of it dies very quickly. This is not an apartment plant because it requires a high humidity and good diffuse sun. If you must buy it, don't let it dry out, mist the foliage often, and give a bright location.

COFFEA arabica (coffee)

You can't really expect to get coffee from this plant but you can enjoy its shiny dark foliage. However, it wants a bit higher humidity than most apartment shrubs, and strong diffuse light.

If you do grow it, don't allow it to go dry and use a very rich humusy soil—our standard soil mixture with an extra helping of humus (see Chapter 7), and feed every 2 weeks with a half-strength solution of fish emulsion. Do not allow it to get potbound or you can expect to lose leaves.

COLEUS varieties and hybrids

Coleus are excellent apartment plants for color, available in greens, yellows, reds, pinks, all mixed. Their foliage is matched by no other plant but croton, and as we've said, you can't grow croton in an apartment. It's very easy to grow from seed or from cuttings, so it's not even necessary to buy plants.

Don't allow it to go dry, though it will come back if you do. Feed moderately with a balanced food, and pinch off the flower buds as they form. Humidity doesn't seem crucial to its well-being.

Since coleus grows so rapidly, it is susceptible to bug problems, so examine the undersides of the leaves often. It is usually grown as an annual but we've never had any trouble keeping it happy over the winter by cutting it back and keeping it in a bright window. The plant does extremely well under fluorescent light, but as it grows tall, you'll have to cut it back to keep it under your lights.

It seems a shame to recommend buying this plant, since one packet of Bellevue Hybrid seeds from Stokes (see page 390) provided enough coleus for ourselves and 50 of our students.

COLUMNEA hybrids and species (flying-goldfish plant)

If you've got the conditions, this trailer is a great plant, and if you see the bright arching flowers, it's easy to understand how it gets its name. For culture, see AESCHYNANTHUS. The trailing GESNERIADS are more thoroughly discussed in Chapter 22.

Coral berry, see ARDISIA

CORDYLINE terminalis (ti plant)

These plants are quite palmlike, except for the bright red of the leaves. They had quite a vogue a number of years ago, and they can still be found around. You were sold a piece of stem and were told to put it in water where it would sprout into a plant. Well, usually it did. Cordyline is closely related to dracaena, but it isn't quite as durable a plant. It's quite susceptible to spider mites, and requires a higher-than-apartment humidity. However, a daily misting helps.

Give moderate sun and keep well watered. A monthly feeding with a dilute solution of fish emulsion will be enough.

The one thing that makes the plant desirable is the highly-colored foliage (bright reds mixed with greens). If you've got the conditions, go ahead. We've found that a planting of 3 small plants in an 8″ pot makes for a handsome display.

Corn plant, see *DRACAENA fragrans*

COTYLEDON tomentosa

This succulent is hairy (as the name would tell you, if you knew horticultural Latin), very handsome, and compact—if you can give it bright sun. If not, pass it by. Allow to go quite dry between waterings.

CRASSULA argentea (jade tree)

This succulent is a beauty, but it requires a lot of sun. It does look like a tiny tree, with branchlike stems and a brown, barky trunk. It will flower for you if you have a mature enough plant and can give it enough sun (difficult in apartments).

Feed with fish emulsion when it starts growth in the spring. Allow to go somewhat dry between waterings. Sometimes a leaf falling to the soil will propagate itself.

There are also other attractive crassulas available from succulent specialists—any of which could be a good apartment plant if you have sun. (See Chapter 25.)

CROCUS (potted) various species and hybrids

We're not talking about buying crocus corms here (see Chapter 27), but rather the potted croci, ready to flower.

If you buy them, do so with the understanding that you're going to throw the corms out after flowering and use the pot for something else. You have two chances of reflowering those crocus for next year: little and none. The corms have been forced to get them to flower before the season, and they haven't been fed or treated for survival. You may save them if you have an outdoor garden and can put them in the ground for a season, without worrying about flowering them until the *following* year. And then it's not terribly likely.

Croton, see CODIAEUM

Crown of thorns, see *EUPHORBIA splendens*

CRYPTANTHUS bivitattus (earth star)

An excellent apartment plant, as are all the smaller-growing species of cryptanthus, this gem looks something like a starfish. They seem to adapt quite readily to the lower humidity of an apartment and even flower in low light (though the flowers are not much—the name means "hidden flower").

This is a terrestrial bromeliad, and so should be watered from the top, wetting the foliage when you do. Spray now and then, and feed very seldom with any dilute plant food.

Propagate by breaking off some of the offsets, and rooting them in an open propagation box (see Chapter 15).

CYCLAMEN persicum hybrids

Cyclamen are beautiful plants with flowers like butterflies. They are tender tuberous plants. They are also cool-culture plants, and we hope you know what that means in an apartment. If you can keep the temperature about 50° and give the plant a very bright window after flowering, you may just have a chance of carrying it through. If you can't, forget it. At any rate, you'll never have as good a plant as the commercial growers get from seed.

If you are given one, don't ever let it go dry. Good luck.

Cyclamen (as if the culture weren't tough enough) are also susceptible to cyclamen mite (see PESTS AND PROBLEMS, Chapter 13). We look at them in windows and don't buy them.

Daffodils, see NARCISSUS

DIEFFENBACHIA hybrids, species, varieties, (dumb cane)

These are among the loveliest of houseplants, both for ease of culture and attractive foliage. The huge broad leaves are speckled or streaked in green and cream or white, and the plants will grow quite tall (we had one 7' tall).

It is called "dumb cane" because the leaves and stem contain a compound to which some people are violently allergic and all people are somewhat sensitive. Chewing on the leaf (as a child or animal might) can well cause swelling of the tongue and constriction of the throat. One of our students was made seriously ill by reaction to the plant's juices.

Normal apartment humidity will do for this plant; but put it in some sun; don't treat it like a dark-corner plant. Also, don't allow it to go too dry or it will start throwing leaves. Feed every 3 or 4 weeks with dilute fish emulsion. For propagation, see Chapter 17.

DISH GARDENS

The same holds for dish gardens that was said for BOWL GARDENS. Make, don't buy them.

DIZYGOTHECA elegantissima (false aralia)

A graceful plant, with thin, dark, leathery leaves. It is lovely, but prone to spider mite. The foliage is quite lacy in young plants (the only kind you should have in your apartment). This juvenile form of the foliage coarsens as the plant matures.

Do not allow to dry out, and mist daily. The plant prefers filtered sun. Propagate mature plants by air-layering (see Chapter 17).

DRACAENA

These plants are enormously popular as apartment and office plants, and justly so; on the whole they require minimal care and minimal light, making them perfect for those dimmer locations. We have a beauty (*D. fragrans*) growing in our bedroom, on a stand some 6' from the nearest window, over to the side where it gets no direct sun at all. It thrives.

Altogether, we grow now about 6 species and hybrids, and they are among the least demanding plants in our collection.

D. fragrans (corn plant). A handsome and hearty plant, with long glossy leaves, which will do well in almost any environment.

Water when the leaves begin to droop, but don't allow to get too dry or you may get root problems. Feed once a month with a dilute fish emulsion.

D. fragrans massangiana is sometimes sold as just "massangiana," in case there is anyone who isn't confused yet. The central stripe of the leaf is quite pronounced. It is often offered with its large canes bare and only a fringe of leaves on top. We prefer the plant with most of its leaves.

D. godseffiana. A real charmer with spotted leaves; a slow grower, though not really a miniature. You could use it for terrariums, but it doesn't require the higher humidity. Filtered light is best.

D. marginata. A plant with slim, dark-green leaves edged in dark red. Very dramatic up close. Be sure you don't let this one get too dry. It will droop easily and quickly start throwing leaves (which is why you see so many looking like palms: with a tuft of leaves on a long, thin, bare stem). This can be very discouraging, especially in a plant that's really quite tough otherwise. Keep from direct sun or it's likely to burn. We bought a baby plant from the dime store 4 years ago and now have a 6' tree.

D. sandersiana. Here's a dracaena with lovely markings, pale cream on green. Treat it like the others (though it seems to mind less going dry). It grows slowly and makes a much smaller plant than does *D. marginata*.

Dumb cane, see DIEFFENBACHIA

Earth star, see CRYPTANTHUS

Easter cactus, see SCHLUMBERGERA

Easter lily, see LILIUM

EPISCIA species, varieties, hybrids, sports

This gesneriad is an excellent plant for humid, not-too-bright conditions. Its quilted and variegated foliage (green mixed variously with purple, red, brown, cream, etc.) makes it a real sensation. Also, it flowers (with variable ease in various kinds), which is not so readily true with many foliage plants. Episcia flowers range from white with purple specks (*Episcia* 'Cygnet') to yellow (*E.* 'Tropical Topaz') to pink (*E.* 'Pinkiscia') to red (*E.* 'Acajou'), with shades in between. It spreads by sending out stolons (runners) and can make a lovely hanging basket.

See GROWING IN A PROTECTED ENVIRONMENT, Chapter 18, for episcias in flying saucers.

Humidity requirements are fairly high, but light requirements are quite modest: the foliage colors are brought out beautifully under fluorescent light. Don't allow the soil to dry out, and, if not in a protected environment, mist daily. Feed every 2 weeks with a balanced food (15-30-15) at half strength.

This is a plant we'd really like to see in more plant stores. It has many of the desirable qualities of the widely popular African violets, and is even beautiful when *out* of flower. Except for some of the more exotic low-chlorophyll sports, it will flourish under approximately the same conditions as African violets. By all means, if you find one, buy it. For more recommendations, see GESNERIADS, Chapter 22.

EUONYMUS japonicus

This shrub is available in both green and variegated foliage. (The variegated kind is called blond euonymus.) It is a very simple thing to keep small; just keep cutting it back and root the cuttings (see Chapter 17, VEGETATIVE PROPAGATION). For a large and bushy plant, put the rooted cuttings back into a larger pot with the original plant.

Allow to go barely dry on the soil's surface before watering, but not really dry. Mist the foliage with water occasionally or give it a shower to keep it shiny. Feed with dilute fish emulsion every month, and give good light but not much direct sun. Try to keep it cool in the winter or you'll get weak growth.

EUPHORBIA splendens hybrids (crown of thorns)

This can be a really lovely plant or it can be a disaster. It is not a cactus, despite the thorns, and if you treat it like one, you'll lose all those leaves.

So, give it all the sun you can, but don't allow it to go really dry between waterings. Feed occasionally with 15-30-15 plant food at half strength. Humidity doesn't matter, but watering does. (See EASIER SUCCULENTS, Chapter 25.)

This plant is available in pink-flowered and white-flowered hybrids as well as red, and in thick-stemmed or miniature hybrids, too.

E. pulcherrima (poinsettia). Though very decorative and Christmasy, this is a poor houseplant, difficult to carry over, and then not really worth the trouble. If you must, buy it for the season, but unless you're willing to grow it as a foliage plant, give it away to someone with a greenhouse.

The poinsettia's flowers are quite tiny. Those colorful parts—usually red but also available in pink or white—are *bracts*, adapted leaves, which color up as flowering comes on.

False aralia, see DIZYGOTHECA

FATSHEDRA lizei

This is an intergeneric hybrid between fatsia (a shrub) and hedera (ivy). It retains the upright habit of the fatsia and has taken some leaf shape and texture from the ivy. There is one important thing to remember about this plant: it doesn't care too much about feeding or humidity, and it doesn't even require much light, but it must never be allowed to really dry out, or you'll lose it.

FICUS benjamani (weeping fig)

This makes one of the most handsome trees you can keep indoors, but it requires some special attention. It needs good light, but not much direct sun. It needs to be rather well watered and fed (fish emulsion in dilute solution most of the time, but an occasional shot of dilute 15-30-15), and it needs misting if your apartment humidity is "normal."

This is one of those trees that one sees as very large plants for very large prices. If you can get cuttings from a friend, try to start your own; the mortality rate among just-purchased adult trees of this kind is rather high. (See the next chapter.)

F. diversifolia (mistletoe fig). From the biggest and most difficult to the smallest and easiest. The common name refers to the tiny fruits it bears. We've found this fig very adaptable to most apartment conditions, even thriving under fluorescent light. And it will stay small for a long time.

F. elastica hybrids (rubber tree). This tree usually dislikes drying out, but if yours is used to going dry, don't start watering it every day. It requires high-ish humidity and frequent feeding with dilute plant food. And keep it out of direct sun.

They make for tricky houseplants: most die quickly; but, if you can keep one alive for a while, after that period of adjustment, they become almost indestructible apartment plants.

F. lyrata (fiddle-leaf fig). Really beautiful, but, while it requires the same culture as *F. elastica,* it is often the most difficult of the ficuses to grow. What it really wants to be is a 50' tree.

FITTONIA verschafeltii, F. v. argyroneura, F. v. pearcei

The first has red-veined leaves, the second has silver-veined leaves, the third has pink-veined leaves. All are gorgeous. These are terrarium plants, with all that implies: high humidity and even moisture. Under good fluorescent light they will stay compact and spread over the ground. With poor light they will start to climb out of the terrarium.

Flowering maple, see ABUTILON

Flying-goldfish plant, see COLUMNEA

FREESIA hybrids

Forget these as houseplants, though they are lovely to see
and smell—especially the new tetraploid hybrids. They require cool-greenhouse culture. Even buying them in bloom
can be disappointing because the flowers go so fast in an
overheated apartment.

FUCHSIA hybrids

Fuchsias have truly spectacular flowers: two-tone or
three-tone, in purple, red, and white, hanging down like big
psychedelic raindrops.

These plants can be grown in a bright window, but we
wouldn't: they are just too attractive to white fly. If you have
fuchsia, you're going to have white fly, and it's just not worth
it.

However, if you've got a somewhat protected spot on your
balcony, well away from your other plants, and you're willing
to throw the plant away in the fall—give it a try. But don't
blame us if you spend the next 3 years fighting white fly.

GARDENIA jasminoides hybrids

Think you can't flower a gardenia on your windowsill?
You can. Just give it the best light you have, feed it with a
dilute acid plant food every 2 weeks (when in growth), keep
it as cool as you can, and *never let the soil dry out.* A daily
misting helps, too. That's all there is to it. You can expect 2
bloomings a year on a mature plant.

For a heart-rending discussion of bud drop, see Chapter
14.

Geranium, see PELARGONIUM

German ivy, see *SENECIO mikanioides*

Gloxinia, see SINNINGIA

GRAFTED CACTI (moon cacti)

The name "moon" is given to these interesting creatures by the florists. The first came (and many still do come) from Japan. No, they are not born that way, with the head colored one way and the body another; they are the result of one kind of cactus having been grafted onto another body. This is done because the stock cactus (the body) is a sturdy, fast grower, while the scion (top) may be a slow grower or have trouble (because of its color) making its own chlorophyll.

They should be treated just like any other cacti, and are just as prone to rot if you keep them in too clayey a soil, and require just as much sun to stay healthy and thrifty.

Grape ivy see CISSUS rhombifolia

GYNURA aurantiaca (velvet plant)

The purple velvet foliage of this charming plant makes it look like a difficult exotic, but it's really quite easy. If you have a bright window it's an excellent apartment plant, flowering freely in small orange daisies, and setting seed, and interesting at every stage.

Give plenty of sun, allow to go barely surface-dry between waterings, and feed sparingly with dilute plant food.

At the end of the season, you may find the plant looking a bit straggly. Cut back sharply and root the cuttings. The original plant will resprout and the cuttings will root easily. We like to hang this one.

Heart-leaf philodendron, see PHILODENDRON oxycardium

HEDERA species and hybrids

Only hedera is true ivy. German ivy, Swedish ivy, grape ivy are not true ivies, and get treated differently.

Ivy is a plant that everyone insists is a good apartment plant but it isn't. It is too attractive to red spider and scale, for one thing. And it needs too cool an environment for wintering well. It's also too finicky about watering (it will just shrivel and die if allowed to go really dry). Any one draw-back we might overlook, but all three?

You might try it outdoors on a semi-sunny terrace, but don't bring those mites indoors.

HELXINE soleirolii (baby tears)

We've never liked this creeper as a houseplant. It makes a good terrarium plant, if you don't mind it taking over the world. It does require good humidity, lots of moisture, and fairly intense light to keep it from getting leggy. There is nothing so silly-looking as those tiny-leafed stems reaching for the light.

Hens-and-chicks, see SEMPERVIVUM

HIPPEASTRUM varieties and hybrids

This is a very satisfying plant, if you don't mind caring for a bunch of straplike foliage for months to get a few weeks of spectacular budding and flower. The star-shaped flowers can be 8″ across. See Chapter 27, BULBS, TUBERS . . . for amaryllis culture.

You'll find these in the stores in early winter, often prepotted, and coming into bud.

HOYA carnosa varieties and hybrids (wax plant)

Not only waxy leaves, but sweet-scented waxy flowers, too, make it truly a "wax plant."

There are other species of hoya, if you look for them, just as easy to grow, but not as widely available.

This is one of our favorite plants. In fact, in different varieties and hybrids the hoya is *several* of our favorite plants. It is easy to culture, undemanding, and beautiful to look at. What more can you ask for in a houseplant? Flowers? Well . . .

We have a friend who flowers hoya in New York City: she has a brilliant unblocked Eastern exposure and grows inside an air-conditioned apartment. She lets us come over and smell whenever we want.

Give the plant a good bright window (even under fluorescent lights they do well), and allow it to dry well between waterings. Humidity is irrelevant. Feed every few weeks when in active growth with dilute 15-30-15.

It flowers on short "spurs" which, after the flowers die, stay on the plant from year to year. Don't cut off these spurs or you have no chance of flowering at all.

HYACINTH hybrids (potted)

These will do a lot better for you than CROCUS, TULIPS, or NARCISSUS. And then there is that marvelous smell! Water them well in whatever pots they come, don't bother to feed, keep them cool, and throw them out after they've finished blooming.

HYDRANGEA hybrids

There is a rumor around that these are good pot plants: they're not. Don't buy them for an apartment, except to enjoy the flowers briefly. They are large, hardy shrubs and go weak and leggy in an apartment's warmth and poor light.

When you get one as an Easter gift, enjoy the blooms, keep it evenly moist, give it coolth, good humidity, and, if you have it, an hour or two of sunshine every day, and then pass it on to a friend with a house in the country.

Ice plant, see LAMPRANTHUS

IMPATIENS varieties and hybrids (patience plant)

Succulent stems and spurred flowers make this a handsome windowsill bloomer, if you don't get spider mite and aphids. Don't allow it to go too dry, feed every week with dilute 15-30-15, and give it a sunny spot.

To keep the plant over the winter (in a bright window), take cuttings in the fall and start from scratch. The sugary crystals formed on the edges of the leaves are a natural phenomenon.

Ivy, see HEDERA

Jade tree, see CRASSULA

Japanese yew, **see** PODOCARPUS

KALANCHOE species and hybrids

These handsome bloomers are available almost year-round nowadays, in very striking flower colors: reds, oranges, and yellows. They require a lot of sun to bring them back into flower, but they will grow and thrive in less.

Let this succulent go moderately dry between waterings in warm weather, but water very sparingly and keep cool during the winter months. See EASIER SUCCULENTS, Chapter 25.

Kangaroo vine, **see** *CISSUS antarctica*

LAMPRANTHUS species (ice plant)

This plant with its very narrow leaves and pink, daisylike flower, is a strange succulent, because it will die quite easily if allowed to go dry for any time at all. It requires good light to stay compact, and a great deal of sun to flower, which, all in all, doesn't make it a desirable apartment plant, in our opinion.

LANTANA camara

This is a delightful plant, with roundish flowerheads, usually opening yellow and turning red in sun—but it has problems. It flowers freely on an east windowsill (we have friends who flower the dwarfest kinds under lights), but it is quite susceptible to white fly and aphids, so be warned.

Keep well watered and lit, and feed every few weeks when in active growth (15-30-15, half strength). Given some sun, they'll flower year round. When in flower, don't move the plant around, as the flowers fall off easily. Sometimes, attractive black berries are set.

Because of the bugs, we don't buy it any more. We enjoy visiting the big lantana standards and the hanging lantanas at the New York Botanic Garden. In Bermuda it grows as a weed.

[46]

LILIUM longiflorum (Easter lily)

Enjoy the scent and the flowers, but don't expect to carry the bulb over to next year. (Greenhouse and outdoor gardeners may get a second set of blooms in the fall.) If you insist on trying, keep the plant in full sun after flowering, and feed with 15-30-15 every 2 weeks until late fall. Allow the foliage to dry off before the first frost, and keep the bulb in a dark location, at a cool temperature (about 50–55°). Water only enough to keep the bulb from drying out. When new growth starts again, water and feed. And let us know how you make out.

Lipstick plant, **see** AESCHYNANTHUS

Live-ever, **see** SEMPERVIVUM

Maidenhair fern, **see** ADIANTUM

MARANTA leuconeura kerchoveana, M. l. massangeana (prayer plant)

A very nice spreading apartment plant, which closes its oval variegated leaves each night in "prayer," but prefers a slightly higher than "normal" humidity. Try a daily misting. Water well and give a location with diffuse light. Propagate by dividing the clumps.

Marigold, **see** TAGETES

Massangeana. We had a lot of calls about this, and it turned out our callers had bought *DRACAENA fragrans massangeana*, which see.

Miniature rose, **see** ROSA

Mistletoe fig, **see** *FICUS diversifolia*

MONSTERA deliciosa

This plant is sometimes wrongly identified as split-leaf phil-odendron. It is a close relative, though, and requires the same culture.

Monstera is a jungle plant, and though it is sold as being an ideal houseplant, it must make a real adaptation before it's happy in the normally-low apartment humidity, so mist daily or more often when you first get the plant. It likes a very rich soil and feeding every few weeks with dilute fish emulsion. It will also take a good deal of diffuse light, though not direct sun. Don't allow it to go really dry between water-ings.

The leaves only split when the plant is mature, so hang on. Those aerial roots the plant puts out will, if given the chance, dig right into your carpet and either they or the carpet have to be cut away.

Moon cacti, see GRAFTED CACTI

Moses-in-the-cradle, see RHOEO

Moss rose, see PORTULACA

NARCISSUS hybrids (potted)
Turn back and see CROCUS.

Neanthe bella palm, see CHAMAEDOREA

NEPHROLEPSIS exaltata hybrids (Boston fern)

There are many hybrids that are identified by florists as Boston fern.

Some time ago, ferns were very popular as houseplants, and the idea has lingered on, though indoor conditions have changed. We now have lots of steam heating and lots of dry apartments and houses, and ferns just can't stand the dryness.

They require humid air and damp feet all the time, and a humusy soil, and filtered light.

If you can provide that, go right ahead and buy this or other ferns. We wish you luck. (For ferns that may stand a better chance in your apartment, see ASPLENIUM and PTERIS.)

NEPHTHYTIS afzelii

One of the easiest apartment plants there is, and almost infallible. We have grown this one in plain pots, in hanging baskets, attached to a totem, and flopping free, and it always works. Cut off a bit to stick in a vase of water and it roots for you; the spearhead-shaped foliage can be quite decorative.

As to culture, we have let them go almost as dry as cacti and kept them even darker than SANSEVERIA. We have forgotten to feed them and kept them in our dryest air. If we had to choose a few plants to give as a gift to someone with a black thumb, this, and its close cousin SYNGONIUM, would be among them.

For best culture, though, allow to go only moderately dry between waterings and set in filtered light.

Norway spruce, see PINUS

OCIMUM basilicum (basil)

This is sweet basil, a delightful herb and a good houseplant, except that, as with many annuals, it is prone to bugs—all bugs. We always grow it and always eat it. See SALAD ON YOUR WINDOWSILL, Chapter 21, for cultural details, but briefly, give it plenty of sun and water.

ORCHIDS

We wish the florists and plant stores would drop their cattleyas and cymbidiums and carry some paphiopedilums, for example—orchids that an apartment grower has a chance of flowering. We've also had luck with phalaenopsis (moth orchids), though that's supposed to be a warmer orchid.

For more on orchids, see Chapter 26.

PANDANUS veitchii (screw pine)

This tropical shrub, with its long, prickly-margined, sword-shaped leaves, can grow to quite a respectable size (we've seen one 4' tall in an industrial loft) and make excellent houseplants. They are content with modest light and humidity, and prefer to go slightly dry between waterings. Aerial roots, for balance, may grow from the stem.

The shiny green foliage can be mistaken for a bromeliad (and watch out for the spines). We've been happy with ours for years. For propagation, see "Offsets" in Chapter 17.

Patience plant, see IMPATIENS

PELARGONIUM

These are, of course, what the catalogs and florist shops call "geraniums." And if you have enough sun to grow happy cacti and succulents, you should flower them beautifully.

Geraniums are sometimes easy to propagate, and sometimes difficult. We have found the Jiffy-7 to be a great step forward that way (see VEGETATIVE PROPAGATION, Chapter 17). In fact, we gave a few to Floss's mother, and when we visited found she had put a geranium cutting into a Jiffy, and sat the thing in a saucer of water, to keep it constantly moist. She got incredibly rapid rooting and had great success with transplanting.

Pelargonium domesticum—"Martha Washington." This is a very popular geranium because of its beautiful flowers (dark centers and lighter toward the edges of the petal), but they are seldom successful in an apartment. They require too cool conditions for a good apartment plant.

P. hortorum—zonals. These are called "zonal" geraniums because of the horseshoe-shaped zone of darker green on the leaves. Zonals are what we call standard geraniums and they are certainly popular. If you have the light, they make good apartment plants through the spring and summer, though you may have trouble wintering them. We no longer grow the standard-size plants because they take up so much of our limited sunny space. We much prefer the miniatures which we can keep in leaf all winter.

For the standards, do keep them cool and drying through the winter, though they can be watered as often as any other houseplant through the growing season. We don't know where the idea came from that they prefer to be kept dry while in growth. Feed occasionally with a balanced plant food.

P. hortorum—miniatures. These are our favorite flowering geraniums (the scented kinds are our real passion) and we grow more than a dozen of them. Their flowers are almost as large as the flowers on the standard plants, but they will flower from stems sometimes only 3" or 4" long. Great.

They vary in their sun requirements, with some demanding as much as the standard kinds and some a bit less, but don't try these beauties unless you have a bright window. Winter them on a cool windowsill, but don't let them go completely dry. Feed every 2 weeks while in growth with a dilute solution of 15-30-15.

P. hortorum—fancy-leafed. These variegated plants are found in both standard and miniature sizes and they can be most attractive and even startling. Their culture is the same as the standard or miniature, but we have found them shyer to flower.

P. peltatum—ivy-leafed. This is a poor apartment plant, and we no longer grow it. It needs a higher humidity than the others, and bright light, and seems susceptible to every pest going. The trailing stems are handsome, but leave them to folks with sun porches.

Scented-leaf geraniums, various species. These are marvelous apartment plants, if you have the sun for them. Their flowers are less spectacular than the other types, but we don't care about flowers with these gems—the scent of the leaves is often so pleasing that it's a delight to grow them where you can reach out and finger a leaf as you go by. Sometimes, just watering them will release the scent, or a breeze will rustle a group of them and the room will be filled with mixed scents. They come in many scents: rose, lemon, oak, nutmeg, apple, and others, in standard and miniature sizes, in various leaf shapes, and even in variegated leaf (we have a lovely lime-scented hybrid called 'Snowflake').

Cut them back in the spring and you'll get good new growth. The culture is the same as for the standards and miniatures.

PELLIONIA daveauana

With handsome muted, silvery, creeping foliage, this is an excellent plant for terrariums (it's slow-growing) or for a 40% humidity spot on a windowsill. It doesn't require much light, and no sun. Don't let it dry out, and feed it once in a great while with dilute fish emulsion. We like it because of the subdued variegations on the leaves.

PEPEROMIA various species and hybrids

Peperomias are basically high-humidity plants, and so require special treatment if you want to bring them into an apartment. Some of the smaller ones are good for terrariums. However, if you manage to keep one alive for a while on your windowsill or under lights (see RAISING HUMIDITY, Chapter 5), you can wind up with a very satisfying small plant. We do warn you though that most peperomias brought into most apartments lose leaf after leaf and die a lingering death.

They will propagate from a healthy leaf, but not from one that's fallen off—at least for us.

Keep well watered and in diffuse light. Feed occasionally with a dilute plant food.

Pepper, see CAPSICUM

PETUNIA hybrids

Of all the flowering annuals we no longer give space to on our windowsill, petunia was our favorite. But they just take up too much room for us. If you'd like to try this, just for the spring and summer, go right ahead. They flower freely with a minimum of sun (that's *sun*, not a dim corner), and require little care. Success with this annual may lead you to try some more challenging plants.

PHILODENDRON species, varieties, and hybrids

Members of this huge and varied genus can be great apartment plants or deceptively finicky ones, depending on the varieties you grow.

Some are vining and some are self-heading (that is, nonvining); some are cut-leaf and some are entire (uncut). In some species the young leaves are entire and the mature leaves are cut. For the vining types, a normally cut-leaf kind may grow entire if it has no support. (In the jungle, cut-leaves serve a purpose: they allow the torrential jungle rains and the jungle winds to go *through* the leaf without breaking it.) Whether the viners or self-headers are more desirable depends on what you want. We have one friend proud of his 30′ of philo vine (draped up and down over a curtain rod), and another whose 6′ wide self-header is her pride and joy. The self-headers usually need no support, while the viners do. But those self-headers do tend to grow *wide*.

If you've forgotten to water your philo or have left it in too dark a spot and get weak growth—chop that weak growth right off: the base of the plant will sprout new growth and be all the better for it.

Most kinds have the potential to grow quite large (the heart-leaf—the most popular kind—is an exception), and only space keeps us from growing more than 8 or 10 kinds at a time.

P. oxycardium—heart-leaf philodendron. Don't be a snob, this is one of the easiest houseplants you can find, responding well to many different conditions, and forming luxuriant plants if you treat it right. The only way you can really damage this plant is to give it too much sun or to leave it soaking in water all the time. Diffuse light and a moderate drying between waterings is best.

Make your plant look fuller by picking up a straggly stem and pinning the middle to a bare spot in the soil with hairpins. The nodes will root and send out new branches.

P. panduraeforme. This is a very handsomely-shaped viner which you can train to a totem (a standing board) without trouble by using rubber bands to hold the stems against the bark. A good apartment plant if you don't buy it too mature, and hence, too "high-strung." (See BUYING LARGE PLANTS,

Chapter 3.) Good diffuse light and constant moisture at the roots will keep it growing well, along with an occasional feeding with dilute fish emulsion.

P. selloum hybrids. This fast-growing self-header is usually sold as quite large plants, and we would be leery of them. They have all the faults of large plants (see BUYING LARGE PLANTS). If you can get a small one and grow it on, great, though it does require more than normal-apartment humidity. Mist it daily, and keep well watered in a rich soil. Feed with dilute fish emulsion every 3 weeks, and keep where it will get a bit of sun and a good deal of filtered light.

Jungle plants are often like that—preferring moisture at the roots and filtered light, as they get it on the floor of the jungle.

Philodendron pertusum. This is a mistaken name for the juvenile form of *Monstera deliciosa* (which see). At this stage, the leaves have holes, but the margins are entire (not split). As mature plants, if they live that long, the leaves will split.

Piggy-back plant, see TOLMIEA

PILEA

These are species of humidity-loving plants, requiring little direct light, and happiest, for the most part, in a terrarium.

Pilea involucrata. This plant, with interestingly crinkled dark oval leaves, makes tiny flowers at the growing tips. The muted variegations of the foliage can make it worth having but only if you can provide the necessary humidity.

P. cadeirei (aluminum plant). This was the first plant we ever identified by looking in reference books, so we have a special soft spot for it. It's sold widely, but it isn't really a good apartment plant, unless, as with other pileas, you can raise your humidity. Keep them all well watered. The plant apparently extracts a mineral from the soil to make the aluminumlike streaks on the leaf surfaces. Handsome, but not easy to keep.

Pineapple, see ANANAS

PINUS abies (Norway spruce)

It's hard to believe, but we really did see this on our shopping trip, right there among the impatiens and philodendrons. And although it's unlikely that anyone would try to take a pine tree home as a houseplant (Norfolk Island pine is *not* a pinus), in case anyone is tempted, pine trees are terrible apartment plants. If you have a penthouse and can keep it outdoors all winter, with some wind protection, you might want to give it a try; but pines are simply not for indoor or windowsill culture.

PITTOSPORUM tobira

As small plants, the leathery-leafed pittosporum makes a good apartment plant, especially if you can keep it grouped with a bunch of other plants to keep all their humidity a bit higher. But larger plants tend to get unmanageable in an apartment, making humidity demands that are hard to fulfill. Do prune it.

Allow the soil surface to go barely dry before watering again, keep in a rich, humusy soil, and feed occasionally with fish emulsion. Provide some early direct sun. We have heard that it can be flowered.

Also available in a variegated form.

PLATYCERIUM species (staghorn fern)

Though the large flat fronds are very handsome, this is a very poor apartment plant because it requires high humidity. There are some who grow them in houses or on porches, but unless you can manage semi-tropical conditions, forget about it in an apartment.

PLECTRANTHUS species (Swedish ivy)

This succulent, with its waxy scalloped leaves, makes an excellent houseplant in any of its several available species, variegated and green. The plain-leafed *Plectranthus australis* is the usual one in the shops, but look for *P. oertendahlii*, a smaller, almost miniature, plant with variegated leaves, and the pale-margined, upright *P. coleoides marginatus*. We grow and enjoy all three.

Swedish ivy is often sold in quite large hanging baskets. These are very handsome (and expensive) but in an apartment they soon get to look straggly. It's much better to buy a small plant and make cuttings (which root very easily)—see Chapter 17—and make your own bushy plant by potting up the rooted cuttings with the original plant. (This holds for many hanging plants—especially the wandering Jews.)

Allow to dry well between waterings (though *P. coleoides marginatus* seems to need more water), and keep in a good, though not your best, light.

PLEOMELE reflexa

A close relative of the dracaena and an excellent apartment plant, except for its habit of making one long, single stem. As the plant can grow quite tall, this looks rather odd. Pinch back the growing tip of a young plant (or take cuttings from a mature one) to stimulate branching. For culture, see *DRACAENA fragrans*.

Pocketbook plant, see CALCEOLARIA

PODOCARPUS macrophylla (Japanese yew)

These evergreens are sold widely as 6″ babies, but they will, on a terrace, get to be 4′ or 5′ tall. Culture is the same as for PITTOSPORUM, including the need for additional humidity.

Podocarpus seems oddly susceptible to scale.

Poinsettia, see EUPHORBIA pulcherrima

POLYSCIAS fruticosa 'Elegans,' P. guilfoylei victoriae

Not widely available, the fernlike lacy leaves of these

plants make them attractive, but their need for humidity and intense diffuse light make them rather poor apartment plants. When found they are usually for sale as large plants, and quite expensive. On the whole, its best to enjoy polyscias in a botanic garden.

PORTULACA grandiflora (moss rose)

Here's a charming miniature annual that's worth some pot space on your brightest windowsill; it's drought-resistant, too. The sun-loving flowers close at night and they won't open unless the day is bright.

The flowers come in singles and doubles and in many colors. Grow them for the season, then throw them out (or try cuttings—see Chapter 17).

PORTULACARIA afra

This is a delightful tiny-leaved succulent (also sold variegated) that will do well for you, even under lights. A good apartment plant, as long as you don't drown it or keep it in the dark. Feed it monthly with dilute fish emulsion.

Pothos, see SCINDAPSUS

Prayer plant, see MARANTA

PTERIS cretica 'albo-lineata,' P. ensiformis 'Victoriae, and other species

So you want to grow ferns in your apartment? Well, here's your chance, a group of ferns that require less humidity than most. Don't mistake us: these won't stand the dry air of a "normal" dry apartment. But if you can raise your humidity to, say, 40%, you can expect more success with these ferns than with almost any other.

They have very interesting forms, with the fertile fronds looking quite different from the sterile fronds.

Remember the humidity, keep their feet damp, and feed once a month with dilute fish emulsion or orchid feed (10-10-10). And don't put them into direct sun.

RHIPSALIS various species

This is a jungle cactus, and a very adaptable apartment plant that comes in many delightful shapes. These plants have been known to survive low humidity and long droughts, and still come back to thrive. Some will flower in an apartment with good, strong, diffuse light or an eastern exposure.

For best culture, water well and keep the humidity high. Pot them in a rich but light soil (like our standard soil mix—see Chapter 7) and feed monthly with dilute fish emulsion.

RHOEO spathacea (Moses-in-a-cradle)

You'll sometimes see this plant sold as *Rhoeo discolor*. Its handsome foliage is dark green above and purple underneath.

It is not really a good apartment plant unless you can provide good humidity. Also, we have never been able to get the light right for flowering: too much sun and it scorched, and when we pulled it back, no flowers. Not that the flowers are that great. They are interesting, though, forming in the axils of the leaves. If you are successfully growing other medium-high-humidity plants, you should be able to succeed with this one.

ROSA hybrids (miniature roses)

We won't say anything about standard roses except that they are terrible apartment plants.

The miniatures, however, are another story. On a bright windowsill (or under strong fluorescents) they will flower for you delightfully. They require feeding (15-30-15) at full strength during their growing season, every 2 weeks, but otherwise can be expected to do better than the standard geraniums in an apartment.

The one drawback to miniature roses is that they are very susceptible to spider mites, which can cause every leaf to drop before you're even certain the bugs are on the plant, and go on to infect your whole collection. Watch out for a paling of the leaf or for falling leaves. (See Chapter 13, PESTS AND PROBLEMS.)

They are deciduous, however, and drop their leaves in the fall. Do keep cool and on the dry side while waiting for new growth. If you're looking for an adventure, try miniature roses.

ROSEMARINUS officinalis (rosemary)

This herb is a shrub and must be treated like one, pruned back to insure bushy growth, and given plenty of light. But it will die if you let it dry out. We've lost a couple that way. Keep it where you keep your annuals, and water it as much as you would a basil plant.

Rubber tree see FICUS elastica

SAINTPAULIA various hybrids (African violets)

What? You don't even grow one African violet? How come?

African violets are members of the gesneriad family, the greatest flowering houseplant family there is. (For their culture, see Chapter 22, GESNERIADS.)

The ones you see for sale now are mostly "Rhapsodie hybrids." This is not a particular strain, but a group of plants selected for vigorous growth, which have been patented. They are more expensive than the more usual old-time hybrids, but they do hold their flowers well after they're bought, and they reflower quite abundantly. Watch out: some African violet nurseries are selling plants under made-up names, which means you don't really know what you have. If you don't care, so long as it flowers, fine. If the name matters to you, you may be disappointed. Growers who are members of the plant societies (see page 385ff.) don't do such unscrupulous things.

SANSEVERIA various varieties and hybrids (snake plant)

Here's another plant you almost have to *beat* to death to kill. It is a succulent with stiff swordlike leaves, undemanding as to light, feed, and water. It grows slowly, so it won't, as some houseplants do, take over your bedroom.

We admit we used to consider it a dull plant, but there have come onto the market several new kinds, both in form and color, which make it more interesting. Now, we recommend it highly, especially for beginners who can't find an AS-PIDISTRA to practice on. See EASIER SUCCULENTS, Chapter 25.

SAXIFRAGA sarmentosa (strawberry begonia)

This plant has the world's wrongest common name, being neither strawberry nor begonia (although, like a strawberry, it does spread by runners).

Saxifrage are lovely, but in most apartments they are difficult outside of a terrarium. We've said it before, about PILEA and PELLIONIA. What makes this plant desirable are the offsets that form at the ends of long stringlike stems. But without the humidity, it's unlikely to stay alive.

If you enjoy especially difficult plants, look for the tricolor variety.

SCHEFFLERA various species (umbrella tree)

Here's a plant that will survive in most apartments (as long as you can keep it bright without setting it on top of the radiator). It can become quite large but, again, don't start with a large plant that's already gotten used to a greenhouse: start small. The plant will grow, if it's healthy.

Give it good light, water thoroughly and allow to go dry, give an occasional misting with water, an occasional feeding with dilute fish emulsion, and an occasional prayer.

SCHLUMBERGERA gaertneri (Easter cactus)

We like this as an apartment plant, preferring it to its cousin, *Zygocactus truncatus*, the Christmas cactus. We give it moderate light with some direct sun, and don't let it go succulent-dry. Though this is a cactus, it is a jungle cactus and won't do its best if allowed to dry out, except during its dormant period.

Ours flowers in the spring, though not usually in time for Easter. We feed it seldom with dilute 15-30-15 plant food.

SCINDAPSUS aureus (variegated pothos)

This plant has the same leaf shape as the heart-leaf philodendron when young; but in the jungle, pothos grows up and has very large leaves that split.

We've been told that some people have trouble growing this plant, but we've always considered it a winner among houseplants, as easy as philo, but with a little variegation to make it interesting. Of course, too much variegation can make problems. The less green in the leaf, the less chlorophyll the leaf manufactures; too little chlorophyll and the plant can't live long. We've seen some varieties that were almost white, and can understand how these might be very difficult to grow, but the run of pothos you'll find for sale cheaply around the stores are simplicity itself.

Allow to dry out moderately between waterings, feed once a month or so with dilute fish emulsion, keep in diffuse light, and make cuttings when the vines get too long.

It does tend to grow in one long string; as an alternative to potting up several rooted cuttings in a pot, wind the string back to the soil and pin it down with hairpins to root.

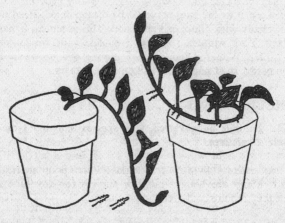

Young Scindapsus aureus, *called pothos, makes a single stem. Using hairpins, pin the stem around the soil and it will root at each node.*

Scorpion plant, see TRADESCANTIA

Screw pine, see PANDANUS

SEDUM morganianum (burro's tail)

The bluish blush on the small fleshy leaves makes this a handsome apartment plant, if you can keep it bright in the winter. This succulent should grow with its many leaves compactly against the stem. In our apartment, the winter sun is too dull and ours tends to show some bare stem.

Water well when in growth, and don't be afraid to cut back the straggly parts (see EASIER SUCCULENTS, Chapter 25).

SEMPERVIVUM species (live-ever, hens-and-chicks)

A great houseplant, it spreads by means of offsets which then root and make offsets of their own. Some are handsomely webbed, and some turn beautiful shades of red in the sun.

This is a succulent, so allow to go well-dry between waterings. Keep it in the sun, or you'll be disappointed. Feed only occasionally with dilute fish emulsion. This succulent is hardy in New York winters, so keep it outside your windows for the winter. Wintered indoors, the growth will be weak. For balcony use, see Chapter 25, EASIER SUCCULENTS.

SENECIO

This genus is quite varied, with species that aren't recognizable as relatives.

Senecio cruentus hybrids (cineraria). Poor, poor apartment plants. Many are bought but few survive for any time because they require cool-greenhouse culture.

S. mikanioides (German ivy). This shiny-leafed succulent is not at all related to ivy. A very good apartment plant, but keep it on the bright side. Allow to dry out somewhat between waterings. Cuttings root easily and several potted together make a nice hanging basket.

S. rowleyanus (gooseberry plant). A most unusual succulent with berrylike leaves strung like beads. Give it as much sun as you have and allow to dry well between waterings.

SETCREASEA purpurea

An excellent apartment plant, and closely related to the wandering Jews. The coloring on this trailer is quite lovely, purple on both sides of the somewhat hairy leaves. It flowers easily in a moderately-lit window and makes an excellent hanging basket, provided it's given periodic "haircuts" to keep it neat. The flowers are short-lived, but they do keep coming.

Allow to dry somewhat between waterings and feed once a month with any dilute plant food. (From our desk we can look over at a plant tray and see the splash of color the leaves make even under fluorescent lights. Very satisfying.)

SINNINGIA speciosa (gloxinia)

This is a tuberous gesneriad and is discussed in Chapter 27, BULBS, TUBERS . . . , and in Chapter 22, GESNERIADS.

A spectacularly-flowered plant, it is probably our favorite of all, but you have to have the conditions for it. It usually does better under lights than on a windowsill, though if you have a brilliant eastern exposure you may do quite well with it (don't forget to turn the plant frequently under natural light). Grow within 4″ of your fluorescent tubes.

It's usually humidity that determines whether or not you make it with this beauty. It requires from 50–60%, and that's a lot for an apartment (see RAISING HUMIDITY, Chapter 5). If you can make the conditions, there's no plant we'd recommend more highly.

From a buying point of view, you'll have more success with a good, plump *tuber* you get from a good gesneriad grower than with an expensive *plant* you buy in flower from a florist. Almost invariably, the bought plant drops its buds. But don't buy a poor "bargain" tuber for 25¢ when you can get a great tuber for $1 from Buell's (see page 386).

Snake plant, see SANSEVERIA

Spanish bayonet, see YUCCA

SPATHIPHYLLUM various species, varieties, and hybrids

Here is a perfect apartment plant: it does not require special care; it does not require good light; it doesn't even require high humidity. And with all that, it will flower for you, sending up months' worth of creamy white spathes (those hooded things that calla lilies have).

We keep ours on a dresser some 12' from an obstructed east window—it gets no direct sun at all (though the room is moderately bright for a while each day), and yet it flowers for us.

Allow to go slightly dry between waterings, give it good light in winter and diffuse light the rest of the year, and feed once a month with dilute plant food of any kind.

Spider plant, see CHLOROPHYTUM

Staghorn fern, see PLATYCERIUM

STREPTOCARPUS species and hybrids (rosette types)

This gesneriad does not make a good apartment plant: at least not for us. It requires room we can't give it and special care and very careful watering. There are other beautifully flowering gesneriads much more suitable for apartments. (See Chapter 22.)

Swedish ivy, see PLECTRANTHUS

SYNGONIUM podophyllum hybrids

Another excellent foliage plant, and one that can be

trained as a climber or to fill a hanging basket. The foliage is variegated in various quite interesting spearhead shapes.

All the wonderful things we've said about the easy culture of NEPHTHYTIS also hold true for syngonium.

TAGETES hybrids (marigolds)

Culture the same as for CELOSIA.

As with any annual, don't be afraid to throw it out at the end of the season—then you can give space to some lovely winter foliage plants.

Tahitian bridal veil, see TRIPOGANDRA

Ti plant, see CORDYLINE

TOLMIEA menziesii (piggy-back plant)

An unusual plant, and a fair apartment-grower with hairy leaves. On mature leaves, plantlets begin to grow out of the place where the leaf joins the petiole (leaf stem). These plantlets can be rooted and potted up.

Undemanding, tolmiea doesn't seem to care about humidity and doesn't need bright light. However, it does need frequent watering. Once those leaves really wilt, they won't come back. Also, the plant (perhaps because of the hairy leaf surfaces) seems quite sensitive to air pollution and appreciates an occasional shower to wash the leaves.

TRADESCANTIA blossfeldiana, T. fluminensis, T. albiflora 'albo-vittata,' etc. (wandering Jew)

Just about any tradescantia you can find will make a good, strong-growing houseplant. The thick stems are quite brittle, but any broken stems root readily—which makes it possible to grow your own hanging baskets instead of buying them.

Give them good light and they will reward you with free flowering at the ends of the stems. The flowers last only a day, but they are produced in succession. Feed very lightly occasionally, and allow to go somewhat dry between waterings.

Handsome foliage, strong growth, freely flowering: what more do you want in a houseplant?

Scorpion Plant. There is another tradescantia being sold widely as of this writing and we've been unable to identify it beyond the florists' name: scorpion plant. (Its stems curl up at the ends, supposedly like a scorpion's tail.) With small alternate leaves and segmented stems, this is a wonderful apartment plant, growing faster than any other we've ever seen, and rooting extremely easily. We haven't flowered ours yet (and we haven't seen it in flower in the plant stores or greenhouses either) but even as a foliage plant it is well worth having. Allow to go dry between waterings and give a bright location. Feed once a month with dilute fish emulsion. It doesn't seem to care about humidity.

TRIPOGANDRA multiflora (Tahitian bridal veil)

Another relative of the wandering Jews, this is a very small-leafed and delicate-looking plant, which isn't delicate at all. In moderate light it flowers freely with many tiny white flowers, which, along with its handsome hanging habit, makes it, for us, a desirable apartment plant.

Allow to go moderately dry between waterings, and feed like scorpion plant, above.

TULIPA hybrids, potted

Tulip flowers last a very short while. We've never considered them worth bringing indoors. If you want to see tulips, go to a botanical garden in spring—now *that's* tulips. See CROCUS.

Umbrella tree, see SCHEFFLERA

Velvet plant, see GYNURA

Wandering Jew, see ZEBRINA and TRADESCANTIA

Wax plant, **see** HOYA

Weeping fig, **see** *FICUS benjamani*

YUCCA aloifolia (Spanish bayonet)

This is a tender yucca, with very sharp points. (There are hardy species, but they do poorly indoors.) It is slow growing and needs a bright sunny window to do well. Allow to go very dry between waterings and keep cool and bright, and on the dry side in the winter.

If you come across *Yucca elephantipes*, remember that it wants to grow about two stories high.

Zebra plant, **see** APHELANDRA

ZEBRINA pendula varieties (wandering Jew)

An excellent houseplant, its culture is the same as for its close relative, TRADESCANTIA.

The flowers on zebrinas are purplish, the foliage is striped, and there is even a 4-colored variety available—*Zebrina pendula 'quadricolor.'*

ZINNIA elegans hybrids

A good flowerer on your sunniest windowsill, but with all the shortcomings of the other annuals. See CELOSIA.

ZYGOCACTUS truncatus (Christmas cactus)

Here we have another jungle cactus, and one that likes the same care as the other jungle cacti: some extra humidity and good watering, combined with moderately bright light.

But bringing this plant into flower can be quite a production. It is a long-night plant, which means that it demands about 12 to 14 hours of *uninterrupted darkness* during autumn and winter to set bud. If yours is in a room where any light is on, or even where a light goes on from time to time, the plant may fail to set bud. If you have a room that fills the darkness requirements (and this means that there is no street-light shining outside your window), fine. If not, try this:

Starting in mid-September, begin to reduce watering, and put the plant into a dark closet from 6:00 in the evening until 8:00 in the morning. Take the plant out during the day. Keep this up for about 3 months, then increase the watering to normal and return the plant to its accustomed position.

Naturally, we can't be bothered with this three-act play. Instead, we grow Easter cactus (SCHLUMBERGERA, which see).

3. Buying Large Plants, or How to Turn a Good Houseplant into a Difficult Exotic

We get calls from people asking us where to get *big* plants. If pressed, we give them a name—but we always give them a warning, too.

Very few of the big plants sold in and around New York City survive and thrive. And from what we've heard, it's no different in other major northern cities.

It is different in the South. We'll explain why later.

We tell people that if they want a large, dramatic plant, they should buy a small one and grow it on up. There are several large-growing plants that are well suited to apartment culture: dracaenas, monsteras, philodendrons, dieffenbachias, chamaedorea palms, scheffleras, pandanus, ficus, beaucarnea, etc. (These are the same plants the florists try to sell you large; after all, they are mostly fast growers.)

"But," people ask, "what's the difference between growing it from a baby and *buying* it large? If it's a good plant, it's a good plant—right?"

Wrong.

If you buy a small plant, it has a good chance of growing used to the conditions in your apartment: dry, dim, hot. (For one thing, a small plant is closer to its soil, and so gets a bit of extra humidity that way.) If it doesn't survive, all you've invested is the price of a small plant, and you can find another small one to try again, changing your conditions somewhat, if possible.

If you buy a large plant, it has already spent a good deal of its growing life in a greenhouse atmosphere, in a different part of the country, and it has little chance of making the adjustment to your dry, dim apartment. It may hang on for a while, but it will most likely begin losing leaves (and losing the struggle) almost as soon as you bring it into your apartment, and go downhill from there. And then what have you lost? A lot of money, plus trouble, guilt, discouragement, and even heartache.

So, the older and the larger the plant that you buy, the longer it has been growing in greenhouse conditions, and the more difficult it will be for the plant to make an adjustment. (Even plants that don't really require exotic treatment are forced along like this by the suppliers, because it's easier for these southern greenhousemen to get big plants quickly under jungle conditions.)

Now, the small plants we're recommending may also have been grown under the same exotic conditions—but the younger plant has a better chance to adapt. And if it doesn't, you've a lot less to lose.

Certainly, it takes time to grow a big plant from a little one: but often less time than you would think. A young dieffenbachia grew almost 3' for us in one year. A *Dracaena marginata* went from an 8" baby to a 5' beauty in about 2 years.

Palms are slower growing. It took almost 6 years for our *Chamaedorea elegans* to get to the point where we could really consider it a big plant, but we rarely fed it. Once you have grown a palm to that size and for that long, it's all but indestructible (as long as you don't give it any direct sun), and in flower virtually all the time. (Palms in the home have what are generally described as "insignificant" flowers; well, they may be insignificant, but they are certainly interesting.)

Philodendrons, monsteras, and scheffleras are also relatively fast growers, and also quite adaptable to home culture. Start it young, and you can have a *Philodendron selloum* with a spread of 6' within a year or so, provided you feed it well and give it as much water as it requires, and good, though filtered, light.

Buy one with a spread of 6', and you'll most likely find the leaves dying back from the tips because you can't provide it with the jungle humidity of its parent greenhouse.

Often, you'll find the sellers offering dieffenbachias and dracaenas potted with 3 plants of different heights to the pot. The effect is very pleasing. But you can achieve the same effect yourself by potting 3 plants together—plants that have been growing along in your conditions, and are therefore likely to survive.

The trouble with the three-in-one plants you buy—aside from the shock of bringing them into your apartment—is that the roots of the plants have often gone into competition for possession of the pot. If *you* pot the 3 plants up yourself, the roots have to do a lot of growing before they'll crowd each other; with the bought group, the struggle may already have reached a showdown where all 3 plants may lose.

HANGING BASKETS

Buying large hanging baskets can lead to a similar trouble. The grower makes hanging baskets by planting several rooted cuttings in one container, selling them at their fullest growth—which means they can only go downhill after you buy them. The pots are usually full of roots, and the top growth has gone as far as it can go without looking overblown. Once you get it home, even in decent conditions, it can only begin to look worse. Make it yourself, and you've got something to look forward to.

Tradescantia, zebrina (wandering Jews), plectranthus (Swedish ivy), cissus (grape ivy) are all great hangers and make gorgeous baskets; they root so quickly and grow so quickly that you can, within a few months, have a lovely hanging basket of your own making, accustomed to your conditions. In proper light, a few $1 cissus quickly grow to be as handsome as that $25 basket you passed up at the florist's.

Chlorophytum (spider plant) is another popular hanger. A small plant grows so fast that all you have to do is repot it into a larger pot once a month, feed it with very dilute 15-30-15 at every watering, give it the good light it prefers, and in a few months you can have something quite lovely. Chlorophytums grow so fast that they may suffer from underwatering and/or crowded roots in pots that are already too small for them.

We haven't said anything about bringing baskets of ferns into the apartment because we're against it unless you can provide high humidity. If your air is that moist, buy a few small plants and pot them into a large, shallow hanging basket. They will shortly make a good display.

With virtually any hanging plant, you can grow your own handsome basketful with little trouble—and it's likely to survive.

BUYING LARGE CACTI

Cacti fall into a class by themselves. In general, the true cacti are so slow growing that a large cactus plant is likely to be anywhere from 10 to 25 years old. This represents a large investment on the grower's part, and it deserves a large price: especially as you've no chance at all of growing a cactus plant to a large size (we mean something *large:* a globe 1' across or a spire 3' tall) in your apartment.

And cacti are tough. The really big ones can go for months or even years without water. But they cannot go on living in adverse conditions. With a really sunny window or balcony, you might be able to give a big cactus enough sun to keep it in growth (if you can keep the plant dormant and cool during the winter), provided you don't injure it or rot it, and provided the city's air pollution doesn't poison it, or insects attack it before you can stop them.

But in dim conditions, you can only expect that cactus to have a long and lingering demise—perhaps over years.

However, perhaps it's worth it to you to have an impressive plant for a year or so; and certainly, more large cacti last longer than large araucarias (Norfolk Island pine) in city apartments.

WHAT TO DO IF YOU DO BUY BIG

To get back to the jungle plants, if you insist on buying that big expensive specimen, you'll run up against some particular problems.

HUMIDITY (See the next two chapters.)

The biggest difference between your apartment and the greenhouse in which your sturdy plant was turned into a delicate exotic is the humidity. Your plant will require high humidity until it adapts (or dies). For small-leaved plants, the trauma that occurs because of the transportation and the changes in environment (greenhouse to distributor to florist or air-chilled supermarket) will express itself often by the loss of leaves, or of flowers and fruit if any (remember our orange tree?). Big-leaved plants will often turn brown at the leaf tips, dying back until you have one limp brown or yellow rag after another, stirring forlornly in the breeze.

Emergency Ward. Many of the problems you can bring home with large plants—or small—can be helped with emergency humidity.

If you have one of those yard-square, clear-plastic garbage bags, put it over the leaves of the plant (the whole plant if it will fit) for several hours a day. If you can't find one of these, tie off one end of a dry-cleaner's bag, or rig a plastic dropcloth into a tent. Misting several times a day will help. If you have a humidifier, move it nearer the plant.

Anything you can do to temporarily turn your apartment into a jungle is to the good. But these are emergency measures; the plant has got to learn to live with you in the real world, so, after a couple of weeks, start to harden it off by allowing it into the dryness of your apartment for progressively longer periods. If it shows signs of resentment, put it back into the jungle for a while.

All this may sound like a great deal of bother, but that's what you get when you buy a large plant.

LIGHT

Have you ever been in a greenhouse? Even on a cloudy day it seems bright. And it is. The amount and intensity of light that a greenhouse plant gets—even a plant grown under the whitewash that greenhousemen use to shade some plants that object to full sun—is much greater than what you can give it in your apartment.

What's that you say? You have very large windows with good exposure? Great! (We wish we did.) But how much of your light comes from *overhead?* If you're in a greenhouse, a great deal; if you're in an apartment, none.

And the problem is worsened by the fact that if you move a plant that has been grown under whitewash in a greenhouse into that bright, sunny window, you can sunburn it at the same time that it may not be getting enough hours of light!

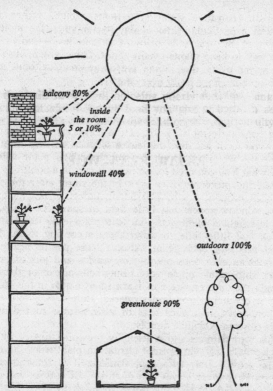

Available light (less if your window is dirty).

For southern plant-lovers the problem is not so severe: their conditions are milder, and the intensity of the light closer to that of the greenhouse. When you have a choice, buy plants from growers to the *north* of you.

The best you can do for a new large plant in your apartment is to move it not into direct sun (unless it's a tree or shrub *requiring* direct sun), but into the brightest location you have with *little* sun. An east window, for example.

For supplementary lighting for big plants, see Chapter 12.

WATERING

Greenhouse plants are watered a lot. They are often on

automatic constant watering systems which, rather than water at a particular time of day, water when the moisture content of the soil falls below a certain level—which is a great way to keep plants evenly moist. Other greenhouse systems water every day. Some greenhousemen, without automatic systems, hose-water every day.

All of which tells you that the plant you get, though it might, if raised in your home, require a thorough drying between waterings, may very well have become accustomed to being constantly moist. Look at the leaves of your plant. If, when you let it get dry, the leaves seem to go very limp, increase the watering. Don't be stubborn. The plant will require what it's been used to, not what it says in a book.

Watering problems often start in the store, after the plant has been brought north. The florist, unless he has an awful lot of window space, has little light to spare for big plants (the less light a plant gets—up to a point—the less water it needs), and little time to water them according to the individual needs of each plant. Also, a large pot of heavy soil can hold an enormous amount of water—and lots of greenhouses ship plants up in very heavy soil instead of the light soil mix they prefer. So, you'll often find plants in the florist's to be overwatered—or underwatered. Either way, root damage can begin, and once a plant suffers some root damage, things can run downhill rapidly.

This root damage shows itself by browning tips or by loss of the whole leaf (in normal attrition a plant loses the older bottom leaves first; with root damage, it is sometimes the newer and younger leaves that die first). Of course, you don't see those dead leaves: the florist removes them or he trims the brown parts with scissors (gotta be neat, right?). So, to repeat a warning we've made before, be very hesitant about buying a plant with trimmed tips.

If you buy a plant and the tips start to turn brown, and then you improve conditions to the point where the browning stops, *you* should trim off the brown tips, but they'll never grow back green.

FEEDING

In general, don't feed a plant as soon as you bring it into the house, unless you know for a fact that it is growing in a "soil-less" mix. (See Chapter 7, SOIL AND SOIL MIXES, for what that means.) The plant has been getting plenty of food in the greenhouse, to make it grow as big as it has, and coming into your apartment it is going to go into some degree of shock no matter what you do. Feeding it while in shock may burn the roots, and at the least is a waste. In fact, a sure way to kill is to fertilize a plant that is already in trouble. Your plant has enough problems just trying to adjust to the real world.

TAKE GOOD CARE OF YOURSELF, YOU BELONG TO ME

There are a lot of minor problems in bringing any plant home that you can sidestep with a little care.

Temperature. If you take a plant from a warm greenhouse into a cold, air-conditioned apartment, the plant may drop some leaves. If you take a cool-greenhouse plant into a hot apartment, you can sit around and watch it collapse. If you take any plant from a very cool supermarket into a hot apartment, it will experience some shock. If you take a plant out of a warm shop into winter weather, make sure it's wrapped in several layers of paper, or you may have a terminal case on your hands by the time you get it home.

Draughts. A draught is a current of contrasting air (for example, a cold blast into a warm room). A breeze is an air current that doesn't contrast enough to cause damage. Plants need air circulation, but they will go into shock if they sit in a draught. The difference may seem semantic, but it's real.

A word about air conditioners: they really are very useful and desirable, because most plants are unhappy in temperatures over 85°, and prefer it below 80, with a 10–15° drop at night. But don't set your plant in the blast from an air conditioner or you're likely to kill it. Also, make sure your air conditioner doesn't dry your air out—*plants need the humidity.*

Many plants also resent sitting in winds. They lose moisture through their leaves and a strong wind causes that moisture to be lost at a greater rate. This calls for more watering. If you're watering at a pre-set time, rather than as the plant needs it, you may let your plant go too dry. (Do you know that wrapping of shrubs in winter isn't to keep them warm; it's to keep the breeze off them so that they don't lose excess moisture through their leaves.)

Radiators. In an apartment environment, radiators are **a** plant's worse enemy, generating heat and drying out the air. They also tend to be placed right in front of windows, which are the best places for plants to get light. There are various solutions to this problem, from shutting off your radiators, through building special trays to cover the radiators (see RAISING HUMIDITY, Chapter 5), to growing under lights (although those lights can be hot in the summer, too). However you solve the problem, it is not one you can ignore.

About that large plant: we haven't given you all the answers, but plants are wonderfully adaptive. If you can just keep your big plant going for a while (how long depends on your conditions and the plant), it may well adjust to your apartment. It will then be a marvelously tough plant—unless, God forbid, you should have to move it again.

PART II

CULTURE

4. Humidity

There comes a time when you have to stop kidding yourself.

You've been growing some nice foliage plants on your windowsills and you decide you'd like to have something that flowers. So you bring home a gloxinia tuber and you pot it up (you're already too smart to go out and buy a big plant in flower), and put it on your windowsill, and the thing comes up. Now, the growth isn't bad (not as compact as you'd like, but you know your light is nothing to write home about), and, lo and behold, you get a couple of buds. And those flower stalks start to lengthen and the buds start to swell . . .

And then the buds turn brown and shrivel. *That's* the time you have to quit kidding yourself and ask, do you really want to grow exotic plants or do you want to be happy with a palm, a little bit of philodendron, a nice syngonium, and a *Dracaena marginata?*

Because now you *know* what you've only suspected before: which is that you have got lousy humidity in your "typical" city apartment.

(Sometimes we'd like to shake country-dwelling experts when they say a plant should do well in "house humidity." *Our* house humidity, before we did something to raise it, went as low as 12% in midwinter. What, besides cacti, will do well in that!)

WHAT IS IT?

Humidity is moisture held in the air. Not rain (though the humidity approaches 100% during rain), and not the water you pour on the roots of the plant, but the invisible water content of the air.

"Relative humidity" is the ratio between the amount of moisture the air actually holds and the amount it *could* hold, without forming dew, fog, or some other kind of precipitation.

Warm air holds more moisture than cold air. There is

more moisture in the air at 70° temperature and 50% humidity than there is at 40° temperature and 50% humidity. In the summer, the humidity is usually high enough to grow exotic plants without much help. In fact, sometimes the humidity is uncomfortably high in summer. And this is what the drippy humidity of the jungle is like. But in the winter, the air is drier to begin with, and when that air is brought inside and heated, the humidity nosedives.

The truth is that, on a winter's day when your steam-heat is going full blast, your apartment is likely to be drier than a desert. And most houseplants are jungle plants.

You can figure out for yourself why plants don't do well for you.

A HYGROMETER

A hygrometer is an instrument used to measure the moisture content (relative humidity) of the air. Accurate ones can be quite expensive; less accurate ones can cost as little as $4—little enough to pay for the truth.

We bought a hygrometer and checked our humidity. It was nothing less than shocking. But at least we couldn't kid ourselves anymore, and we were on our way to improving our conditions (see the next chapter).

PEOPLE AND PLANTS

People perspire and plants transpire. The two processes are analogous.

In people, water evaporates off the skin to help keep the body temperature stable. Plants do much the same thing when they transpire. The warmer it is, the more they transpire: the stronger the breeze blowing over the leaf surfaces, the more water they bring up from the soil and transpire; the less humidity in the air, the more they transpire.

No matter how much water you put at a leafy plant's roots, if there is insufficient humidity in the air, the leaf will burn and die.

If people have too little humidity in *their* environment, their delicate membranes (such as nose, throat, eyes) can suffer. (Inlaid floors and furniture also warp from loss of moisture.) And your skin can dry out, too, without sufficient humidity. The English are famous for their complexions and their gardens. They have much less steam heating than we do—and higher humidity indoors and out than most U.S. city dwellers.

When we lived without plants, we used to wake up mornings with raw throats. When plants drop their leaves and flowers and their buds blast, they may be showing comparable symptoms.

WHAT DO YOU WANT?

You have options.

1. You can raise just those plants that don't require much humidity, in which case you can turn to Chapters 24 and 25, and read about CACTI and EASIER SUCCULENTS. So long as you have good bright light and sun. Or, if you have a dry apartment and not much light, you can grow philodendron and a couple of dracaenas. Lots of people do. Although even tough houseplants like these don't do their best in low humidity.

2. You can grow high-humidity container gardens, in which case, turn to Chapter 18, GROWING PLANTS IN A PROTECTED ENVIRONMENT. This can be a very rewarding approach to plants in a dry apartment.

3. Or, you can take the route that will not only allow you to grow healthy plants, but that will help you to have healthier eyes, skin, nose, throat, etc., and turn to the next chapter, RAISING HUMIDITY.

5. Raising Humidity

HOUSES AREN'T APARTMENTS

If you own your own home, low humidity can be simply, though expensively, solved; a contractor can hook a humidifier to your home heating system, so that when the heat goes on, the humidifier does too.

However, in an apartment, and on limited funds, solving the problem calls for more imagination.

BLASTED BEGONIA BUDS

At a plant society meeting, a lady asked a problems panel a question about bud blast: why did the buds on her begonias form and develop, but shrivel (blast) and drop before opening? The consensus was lack of humidity. Bud formation is largely a matter of light, but whether they open or blast is often a matter of humidity.

When this member was told that very likely she had too low a humidity in her growing area she indignantly protested that she always left an open pail of water in the room, as if that settled that. The panel hemmed a little, a few throats were cleared, and one panelist muttered something we translated as, "Well, the water doesn't evaporate fast enough."

An open pail of water is not sufficient to really raise the humidity in a growing area. It's barely a drop in the bucket, so to speak. Though one drop is better than none; vases of flowers are another drop; so are vases full of cuttings.

GROUPING

Water evaporates into the air from wet or damp surfaces. The plants in a room "exhale" (transpire) water from their leaves, returning the water they've sucked up from the soil.

So, one of the simplest ways of raising the humidity for your plants is to have a lot of plants, dozens and dozens of them, and to group them together. Plants grown together create a better environment for one another and for you.

However, when the dry steam heat goes on in your apartment it takes more than the plants themselves to keep the humidity up.

Here are a few more ways to beat the humidity problem.

PEBBLE TRAYS

These are waterproof trays of any rustproof material filled with a layer or two of medium gravel and set on your radiators. Water is poured into the tray to about three quarters of the way up the gravel. Plants can then be set right onto the gravel (not in the water) and will live comfortably, with the heat being absorbed by the water and the water evaporating around them.

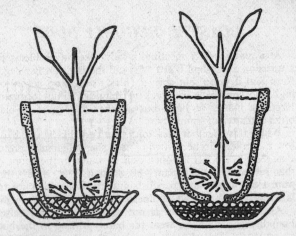

Pebbles lift the pot, allowing the excess water to drain away from the roots.

It is not enough just to fill a plant's saucer with gravel and pour the water in. Certainly that is better than nothing—but not much. The leaves get very little of that evaporating moisture because the saucer is usually very little wider than the top of the pot. If you want to use a saucer, it has to be at least as wide across as the plant is—in other words, the size of a small pebble tray.

Be sure that the water doesn't come up to the bottom of your pot, or the plant's roots will rot from being constantly wet and so getting no air. The plants are intended to sit *over* the water, not *in* it.

We have used many kinds of trays.

Our first were the trays from inside our old-fashioned radiator covers, which were intended to be kept filled with water for just this purpose—evaporation. But these were always smaller than the tops of our radiators, which meant that if a plant hung a branch over the edge of the tray, it was directly over the heat, and it got burned. (Really, the water does make it possible to grow your plants on a radiator top, while if you try it on the bare top, you'll kill your plants).

So, we went hunting for wider trays.

We tried baking sheets, but they are too shallow and they rust.

We inherited some really fine stainless steel trays which

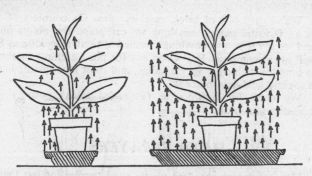

The pebble tray should be as wide as the leaf spread because water evaporates upward.

came originally from a kitchen supply house. Inches deep and quite durable, these are gems for the purpose, but very expensive.

Some friends have had trays made from aluminum by a metalworker, but, again, these can run into money, and to tell the truth, we don't find them things of beauty.

Other friends have gone to commercial lighting houses and bought those shaped plastic fluorescent-light covers. While these are not very sturdy, they will do the job. Available from the same suppliers is a plastic gridwork—called "eggcrating"—which is good for putting into the trays instead of pebbles. Pebbles have more surface for evaporation, but this grid is easier to clean.

Really great (and cheap as only something from the garbage can be) are the large enamel vegetable bins from discarded refrigerators. These bins last forever and never rust or discolor.

PEBBLE SUBSTITUTES

For about a year now we've been trying perlite, a volcanic rock, as a substitute for ordinary stone pebbles. Since the principle is that the more surface you have, the more evaporation you'll get (which is why a pebble tray is superior to an open pail of water), perlite may be superior in that it does have much more surface area than a tray of pebbles. Perlite does tend to get a bit dingy after a while, but if you keep it groomed, the white is quite cheering.

We've used bits of brick, marbles, glass Go counters (Go is an Oriental game), anything we can stand the plants on; and we say this: use anything you find attractive, as long as it will not decompose. But watch out for marble chips; marble is limestone which is very alkaline, and most houseplants like a slightly acid environment.

We don't use vermiculite (expanded mica) because it squashes into mush.

HAND SPRAYERS

You can get an excellent plastic hand sprayer for less than $2 and you can get a brass two-hand sprayer (it looks like a Buck Rogers flit-gun) for more than $15. (Don't use a real flit-gun—it rusts immediately.) Of course, the brass sprayer should last for years and the plastic will often conk out after a few months of very heavy use. Perhaps it depends on how you see yourself.

In our favorite wholesale florist-supply catalog there are backpack type sprayers designed for greenhouses; just pump up the pressure and you can spray your apartment garden (and your apartment) in seconds.

Then there is the one we tried first: an empty Windex bottle and sprayer, which is guaranteed to give you finger-cramp after 15 strokes and requires a minute per plant to give a good spraying.

For price and efficiency, we recommend the $2 number as quite satisfactory.

For maximum effect from a hand-held sprayer, spray early in the day, and then again as often as you can (without leaving water constantly on the leaves), then stop as twilight approaches. As the day dims, the plant's processes slow down, and water should not be left on the leaves in the dark.

(We have been asked, rather snidely, "Who stops spraying the plants in nature? When it rains at night in the forest or jungle, what happens then?" Well, what happens in the forest or jungle is that a lot of leaves are lost or damaged by rot. However, jungle leaves are expendable. Can you say the same about your apartment garden?)

But a hand sprayer cannot solve all your humidity problems. On a dry day the moisture it sprays into the air is gone within an hour or less. What a hand sprayer does do is provide a decent supplement for other methods of increasing your humidity, as well as being handy for washing off leaves.

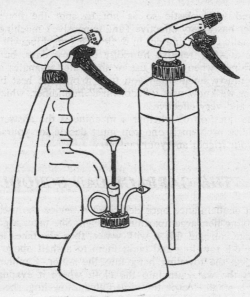

Plastic or brass, you need a sprayer for every plant area.

Hanging plants are too high to get much benefit of the evaporation from a pebble tray, and so are especially grateful for a hand-spraying.

HUMIDIFIERS

Room humidifiers can be very good things, although they vary in their effectiveness. Most small, mechanical room humidifiers will raise the general humidity about 10-15%. In the immediate vicinity of the humidifier, the humidity will be raised more, of course, so keep the humidifier close to the plants.

If the steam heat is on, wheel your humidifier into the bedroom and run it at night, too: it will do wonders for your membranes.

We have an old humidifier. A motor spins a gadget which sucks up water from a reservoir and forces it out through small holes, making a gentle fog—effective only in the immediate vicinity. A friend of ours has a much newer machine which sprays and spits—the area around it has to be kept covered with plastic so as not to spot the floor. Floss's mother has a very effective (and expensive) machine with an automatic cut-off and cut-in device; this machine will keep her house at 40% relative humidity on most days, but it must be drained when not in use or the water stagnates and gives off a musty smell when you turn it on. The best bromeliad grower we know uses a "cool mist" humidifier, which is very quiet and very effective.

The question of whether a machine is the answer to your humidity problem is one you must decide for yourself. Consult your friends and your budget.

THE GARBAGE-CAN SCHOOL

An acquaintance once described a device she uses for humidifying her large apartment garden. She takes a galvanized garbage can and fills it with water; then she takes lengths of terrycloth toweling and tacks them to a shelf above the pail, and lets the toweling hang into the water. Capillary action draws the water up into the cloth where it evaporates. By using a small electric fan aimed at the toweling, she increases the evaporation, and distributes the humidity.

This sounds quite interesting. though we fear that the toweling could grow musty and the device must be far from beautiful. We include it here to give you an idea of how you can use your imagination without spending a lot of money.

PLASTIC "GREENHOUSES"

In the chapter on BUYING LARGE PLANTS, we described using large plastic garbage bags or plastic dropcloths as an emergency measure for large plants. A small plastic bag works just as well on a small plant. And if you have the inclination, there is no reason why you can't make a window into a plastic "greenhouse," by hanging plastic dropcloths to close off an area. Plants are themselves great regulators of humidity and great purifiers of the air. Kept in a rather self-contained area of this sort, they will keep their own humidity high and their own air good (as long as the window is closed).

Do open the dropcloths for a while each day to allow air to circulate: stagnant air encourages fungous diseases. And you have to be sure your "greenhouse" isn't so well closed that the sun builds up too much heat.

6. Watering

The other day a gentleman called us about a large schefflera he had bought for his office. "How often do I water it?" he wanted to know.

Scheffleras are simple, we told him. You feel the soil in the pot, and when the soil is dry a little below the surface, you water.

"Yes," he answered, "but how *often* is that?"

The "often," we explained in our best houseplant-course manner, depends on many factors: the size of the pot, the heat of the location, the heaviness of the soil, the season of the year, the humidity, whether the roots have plenty of room or are potbound, whether the plant is in active growth or resting, how much light the plant is getting. . . .

"No, you don't understand." His temper was obviously beginning to fray, as he tried a further explanation. "I mean, how many times a *week?*"

There is no standard "magic" formula for watering plants. *You* as the grower may try to impose some sort of schedule on them (we all do it to some extent), but even the same plant varies in its watering needs.

We didn't satisfy that caller, and we may not be able to satisfy you, either. There are lots of things in this book that are simple: soil mixes are as simple as mudpies; potting is simple and easy; even bottle gardening is simple once you get the knack. But watering takes judgment.

("Judgment, yes, but how many times a week?")

THE PLANTS

CACTI

Of course, the first thing you have to consider is the plant. It's generally agreed that cacti have to go well-dry between

[87]

waterings, right? Well, not all the time! If cacti are in a good, well-drained soil mix, as they should be, then in the summer months you'll have to water them every few days.

But, if they are in a heavy soil, a soil that does not dry out quickly, then you must try to let them go dry between waterings. Cacti in heavy soil won't enjoy as vigorous growth as those in a light soil. If you must have your cacti in heavy soil, stick your finger into the medium and feel for damp. With cacti in large pots—larger than 4", say—don't water again until you can feel the soil dry down to ½–1". In small pots, cacti go dry so quickly *in the summer* that it's safe to assume that if the soil *looks* dry, it's time to water.

And when you water, water well and allow the excess to drain off. How it annoys us when people tell us proudly that they tickle their cacti with a teaspoon of water whenever it rains in Flagstaff, Arizona!

Yes, water well and allow the excess to drain off—that's good watering advice for every plant.

Dormancy. Your cacti will grow more slowly during the winter months. This is desirable. When a plant slows down or stops growth completely, you must slow down or stop watering. A plant uses water at a much slower rate when it is dormant or resting. To water it at the same old rate would leave a lot of water around the roots, choke the plant, and lead to rot and loss. (See Chapter 24, CACTI AND CACTUSLIKE PLANTS, for more on dormancy and cacti.)

GARDENIAS AND FERNS

Gardenias and ferns are at the other end of the watering range from cacti. They must have wet soil all the time they are in active growth. If not, gardenias will drop their buds and ferns will do poorly for you, no matter what your humidity. But even these demanding plants must have the watering reduced *slightly* for the darker months.

Feel the soil surface. If it's at all dry, water. In fact, with gardenias and ferns you hardly have to feel. In the summer months, if you think they may need water, they do. And, after you water, discard the water sitting in that saucer. Even these water-lovers must breathe a little.

(The roots of plants must have *air* as well as water: not big air pockets, but a certain porosity in the soil. We'll discuss this in Chapter 7, SOIL AND SOIL MIXES.)

Don't hang your ferns too high. If they are difficult to get at, you may neglect their watering.

PHILO AND FRIENDS

This whole group of foliage plants requiring similar culture (heart-leaf philodendron, pothos, syngonium, nephthytis, spathiphyllum, tradescantia, zebrina, schefflera, cissus, aglaonema) is great because they give you lots of leeway. They don't mind being watered heavily (as long as they are not kept soaking), but they don't mind drying out between waterings, either.

For the most part, though, they prefer going *slightly* dry between waterings: feel the soil. If it's dry to a depth of a quarter inch, water.

Dormancy. Most of these plants will not have an actual dormancy. They may slow down somewhat, but if you are feeling the soil rather than watering on a timetable, you should be able to continue watering according to the same clue: when the soil is dry down to a quarter inch.

MORE FINICKY EXOTICS (AND OTHERS)

This is a large group of heavy drinkers: chamaedorea palms, monstera, philodendrons (other than heart-leaf), dieffenbachias, dracaenas, aphelandra, citrus, camellias, peperomias, pileas, pellionias, etc. These plants, some woody, some herbaceous, don't want to dry out between waterings. If big drinkers do go dry, some of them wilt; some of them get root damage; some sacrifice leaves, flowers, or fruit; others will just repine. Feel the surface of the soil: when the surface is dry, water well and then throw away the excess. If the soil is dry farther down, you're late.

Dormancy. Most of these plants will drink heavily all winter in a hot apartment. Camellias are an exception. Reduce their watering to just enough to keep them evenly moist for the dim months (when they should be in a *cool* but bright location).

SUCCULENTS

Not all succulents take the same watering. The jungle cacti

and crown of thorns like to be treated like the more finicky exotics above; some of the other euphorbias like to be treated like cactus and go quite dry; hoyas fall into the middle ground. See Chapter 25, EASIER SUCCULENTS.

ORCHIDS AND BROMELIADS

These are special watering problems. See Chapters 23 and 26.

GESNERIADS

The large tuberous gesneriads go into complete dormancy and must be rested without water. Some of the smaller ones may be kept out of dormancy indefinitely, and so should be uniformly moist all the time.

Most of the fibrous-rooted gesneriads like to go barely surface-dry between waterings.

See Chapter 22, GESNERIADS.

AFRICAN VIOLETS

Though these are fibrous-rooted gesneriads they deserve a mention of their own. There is difference of opinion on watering these plants. Some good growers like to dry them very slightly between waterings (just surface-dry). Others like to keep them evenly moist. African violets do so well being "wick watered" that we have to go along with those who say keep them evenly moist, especially if you want to grow *big* violets. We'll discuss and describe wick watering shortly.

BEGONIAS

Begonias vary in their demands. The semperflorens types will do well if allowed to go rather dry between waterings, while the canes prefer to go only *somewhat* dry between waterings. The rhizome types like to go just *barely surface-dry* between waterings, but the rexes like to stay evenly moist. So, if you're a lazy waterer (with sun), grow the semps and canes; if you're willing to take a little care, try the rhizome types (we find them the greatest); but only if you can supply their rather strict requirements should you have a go at rexes. (See RHIZOMES, page 345–347).

TERRARIUMS

Terrariums have to be watered the way porcupines make love: very carefully. Since they have no holes, the only drainage they have is whatever gravel or other material you may have put at the bottom of the container and there is really no place for excess water to go.

These containers must be kept evenly moist, so keep them under observation. When the soil surface appears to be going dry, water sparingly. If, after a day or so the surface seems dry again, water some more. But never give a great douse of water to terrariums: even if you can drain the excess off afterward, you will have dirtied the sides and made the soil heavier.

ANNUALS AND VEGETABLES

Water these heavily, especially in summer. It's hard to imagine the amount of water a tomato plant will drink if given the opportunity. And flower and fruit will suffer if you don't water enough.

GENERAL WATERING PRINCIPLES

- In hot weather, you must water more than in cool;
- On bright days, you must water more than on dull;
- Large pots need less frequent watering than small (for the same plant);
- Water less on humid days than on dry;
- During winter, when the heat is on, those plants in active growth may have to be watered more than they were during the summer months;
- But, usually, spring and summer months mean more watering than in the fall and winter;
- Plants in bright, sunny locations need more water than the same kinds of plants in dull locations;
- Potbound plants need more frequent watering than those with sufficient root room;
- Plants in active growth need more water than dormant plants or plants in slow growth;
- Seedlings of *any* plant (cactus, orchid, bromel, anything) have to be kept evenly moist;

- Plants in clay pots usually need watering more often than plants in plastic pots;
- Plants in heavy soil need watering less often than plants in a light, airy soil.

WATERING—TOP OR BOTTOM

It doesn't matter all that much. If you have a few plants, bottom watering may be practical. If you have a large collection, it may be impossible to water your whole collection from the bottom more than twice a year (on rotation).

We prefer watering from the top (nature's way), because you then have less danger of fertilizer salts building up on the surface. These nutritional residues are in the soil, whether you feed or not. Watering from the bottom washes these salts to the surface; watering from the top washes them out of the pot. These salts can build up on the pot and on the soil surface and damage the plant.

TOP

If you water from the top, don't sprinkle a few drops and run. Give your plant a healthy drink, then come back later and give it another. Then pour the excess water out of the saucer.

You cannot overwater a plant in a well-drained soil mix, but you can damage it by leaving it soaking in water without a chance for its roots to breathe.

BOTTOM

If you water from the bottom, leave your plants in water *below* the soil line, and allow capillary action to draw the water up to the surface. That way you're certain, when you see the surface wet, that the plant is wet through.

Allow the plant to drain before returning it to its place.

If a plant has gone very dry, water it from the bottom, whatever your customary method. With dry plants, the soil has pulled away from the sides of the pot slightly, which means that when you water from the top, the water runs down the sides and out, very likely leaving a dry ball at the center.

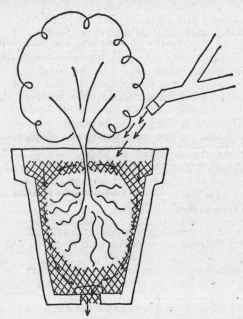

If the rootball is extremely dry, top watering may not penetrate it at all.

TICKLING

You tickle a plant when you water only enough so that the top of the soil gets wet: nothing gets to the center of the rootball.

Roots will grow toward water, and if you water only the surface, then the roots will grow toward the surface, taking the water that is available there. What happens then is that the deep roots die off and your plant becomes shallow-rooted and unstable. Should you ever let the top of the soil dry out, the plant dies: there are no deep roots to drink that last bit of water that might be hiding in the center of a normally-watered pot.

WICK WATERING

If you grow plants that need constant water at their roots,

you may want to wick water. But for plants that like to go dry between waterings, these devices are deadly.

There are a number of patented wick waterers on the market, or you can make your own. These devices depend on a reservoir of water and some material which conducts the water from the reservoir into the soil. Feed can be kept in the reservoir water for a constant feed program. For some plants they are great—though the patented ones can run into a small fortune if you've got a lot of plants.

But the best use for wick waterers is as vacation insurance: hooked up to some wick waterers, you can leave your plants for as long as 2 weeks and the reservoir will keep them watered and happy.

DO YOUR OWN

Here's one wick waterer you can make yourself.

A wick (a piece of something both absorbent and non-decaying, like the remains of a nylon stocking or Banlon shirt) is drawn *halfway* into an ordinary pot through the bottom hole. Now, crock up the pot and plant it, just as you would ordinarily (you'll have a tail of wick hanging out the bottom, but don't let it throw you). Once the pot is planted, water well and set it aside to drain.

Take a large, deep saucer and fill it with gravel, so that the gravel humps up higher than the saucer. (See the drawing below.) The gravel hump is to keep the pot out of the water.

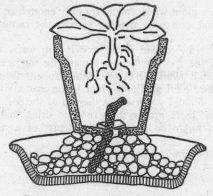

Cross section of a simple wick waterer.

Fill the saucer to the top with water.

Set the plant on the gravel hump and work the wick down into the gravel, all the way to the bottom of the saucer.

And there you've got it. The wick should keep a steady pull of water coming into the pot.

FINE TUNING

You want a constant moisture in the pot; you don't want the plant awash, and you don't want it to dry out.

The amount of water you pull into the pot depends on the thickness of the wick, and how deep it is into the pot. Remember, we told you to keep the wick halfway into the pot: it's easier to pull that wick *out* a little to reduce watering, than to push it *in* a little to increase it.

You may want to experiment with different thicknesses of wick and different substances, but we suggest you start with a strip of nylon stocking from ¼″ to ½″ thick.

And there you are: all your watering worries solved, right?

(Yes, but, how many times a *week* . . . ?)

7. Soil and Soil Mixes

"Why make a soil *mix* at all?" we've been asked. "Who mixes God's soil?"

Worms and various grubs and maggots, decaying vegetation, rainfall . . . shall we go on?

LET IT ALL STAY OUT

"I let nature take care of its own." That's fine for the outdoor gardener, especially if nature has provided that gardener with a rich, loamy soil in the first place. But that's an outdoor garden.

"I just go down to the park and dig up a shovelful of soil," some apartment gardeners tell us with happy smiles. And they *are* getting a bargain, because, in addition to free soil, they're getting free insect eggs, free weed seeds, free fungous diseases, free dog and pigeon droppings. Not to mention the historical value of soil that's been walked on, spat on, sun-baked and frostbit, used and reused for a hundred years.

And then, to take home this historical, hard-baked soil and pot into it a tender, delicate exotic (as most of our houseplants are), and to expect it to *live*—it's like feeding a starving man a charcoal briquet.

Believe us, we speak from experience, because we started out gardening just that way.

THE EGGS AND US

For a long time we, on the eighth floor, were bothered by ants on our windowsills. The ants themselves don't eat plants, but they farm and use the "honeydew" of aphids and scale—both of which can be real problems (see Chapter 13, PESTS AND PROBLEMS). How did the ants get into our garden? As eggs in soil *we* dug up from the park.

WHAT DO YOU WANT?

We understand that it's hard for some people to get passionate about soil and perhaps this chapter will tell more about soil than you want to know. If you're only growing a few plants and you don't really care about soil, skip to page 108 for the "One-Minute Course."

But when you find yourself growing a lot of plants, you'll want to put together your own soil mixes. Then come back here and read what you skipped.

PASTEURIZING AND STERILIZING

We could have gotten rid of those insect eggs by pasteurizing the soil. Anyone can do it who has an oven. You moisten the soil and stick a thermometer into the middle, then you bake it. You bake it until the temperature hits about 180° and then you hold it there for about 30 minutes. But even at this level, you've begun to *sterilize* the soil. "Sterile" means all the organisms are dead. Plants can't live in sterile soil:

neither beast nor plant can survive without the helpful bacteria destroyed by sterilization.

In fact, we tried pasteurizing soil once. We baked and had to leave the doors and windows open because it *stinks*. Afterward we stored some of this pasteurized soil and when we opened its box, the surface was covered with a blue fungus! You see, we'd killed off its competition. Now, maybe that fungus was harmless, but it was very scary, and so we threw it all out.

And why should you go through all this trouble? Aside from the stink, that stuff is just too heavy and inappropriate for potting houseplants. And the elements for making your own houseplant soil are dirt cheap.

(A friend of ours defines soil and dirt: soil is what you pot a plant into; dirt is what you dig out from under your fingernails afterward.)

Let the manufacturer pasteurize the soil, he has the equipment for it and you won't have to smell it and you won't have to worry about blue mold.

In our basic mix for houseplants, topsoil takes up less than 20% of the bulk. So there's no need for you to steal from the park.

WHAT IS SOIL?

Soil is various organic and mineral elements in various stages of decay and erosion. The soil has more or fewer nutrients, depending on the balance of these elements. Plants, like people, need many different elements of nutrition for a well-balanced diet. So, a good soil must contain a balance of these organic and mineral parts. (For a discussion of plant nutrients, see Chapter 8.)

However, soil does more than provide nutrition for a plant, it must also hold water for the plant's roots. The nutrients that a plant needs are available to the plant only when they are dissolved in water—your plant does not eat dry foods. So, you can see that the soil's ability to hold water is as important as its ability to provide nutrition—in fact, they are inseparable.

Also, roots need air: a free exchange of the gases in the roots with the outside world is vital, and soil must provide this aeration. So, a soil that is compacted too heavily for tiny air spaces to remain (as that dug-up soil watered in a pot tends to be) would choke off the roots. Good drainage is essential to prevent water from settling permanently around the roots of a plant and rotting them.

Finally, soil must provide a firm anchorage for the plant; a plant that is loose and wobbly in its soil will not grow vigorously. In situations where a soil does not or cannot provide this anchorage (as in hydroponic culture where no soil is used), supports in the form of stakes or other anchoring means must be rigged.

So this is what we want our soil to provide: food, water, air, and a place to put down roots—sounds almost like people.

BASIC SOIL MIX

We'll tell you more about soil theory as we go along, but now let's get into what we use for a basic houseplant soil mix.

What follows isn't our "dream soil." If *we* lived in a house in the country instead of on the eighth floor in a city, we would "compost" all our vegetable garbage—lawn clippings, dead leaves, etc.—and pot directly into this light and airy compost. This soil mix is our apartment compromise. Please don't think we're saying that ours is the only possible successful soil mix—far from it.

1 quart pasteurized topsoil
1 quart Canadian sphagnum peat moss
1 quart humus
1 quart coarse perlite
1 quart horticultural grade vermiculite
1 tablespoon bone meal
1 tablespoon dry cow manure
1 teaspoon superphosphate
1 teaspoon ground limestone
1 tablespoon wood ashes
2 tablespoons ground eggshells

If this seems a little like grandma's home brew, it is. As we have grown along with our plants we have added or removed elements (mostly added) to meet the needs and probable deficiencies of our plants. And we still add a bit more of this and that while potting up particular plants.

Let's take the ingredients one by one, and see how they fulfill your plant's requirements.

TOPSOIL

If you hold a chunk of topsoil in your hand, you can see bits of shiny minerals in it. If we were top-dressing a lawn instead of making a potting mix, perhaps we could stop here. But we're not planting a lawn, we are planting houseplants.

Topsoil anchors a plant and is nutritive and holds water all too well. But used alone as a potting medium it is too heavy to allow for the fourth element—aeration. And without this fourth, the other three hardly matter.

A 50-pound bag of topsoil will cost from $1 to $4, depending on whether you buy wholesale or from a florist. (All these soil ingredients are proportionately more expensive in smaller sizes.)

PEAT MOSS

This is "Canadian" or "sphagnum" peat moss, a light brown in color, not the "Michigan" or "sedge" peat moss, which is dark brown, heavy, and poor for houseplants.

Peat moss is "pre-soil." Give it a few more millennia and it will become soil. But at this stage of its decay the nutrient potential it holds is still locked up. In your potting mix, the peat does slowly decay and provide *some* nutrient, but what it mostly does is provide aeration, water-holding, and acidity to the soil (most houseplants can absorb food only in an acid environment).

Then, you might ask, why not make a mix of primarily topsoil and peat moss? Many growers do, and achieve success with it. But we who grow most of our plants on the dry side have found that peat moss has a tendency to dry out, and once dried it is murder to re-wet—you have to soak it and soak it. Some of our most notable failures have been with plants that came to us from growers who use a mix that is heavy on peat. (It is interesting that people who grow a lot of plants often have trouble growing a plant in someone else's soil mix.)

A 4-cubic-foot bale of peat will vary in price from, say, $2.50 to $10, depending on where you buy it.

HUMUS

The humus we use is further decomposed peat moss. It is

acid and holds moisture well, but is very heavy. It has a good deal of nutrition in it, though, which makes it desirable as a soil-mix ingredient.

One problem with humus is that it looks about the same color when wet or dry. If you are using a mix with extra humus in it (say, for a terrarium), you may find that your soil has dried out without getting the characteristically paler "dry" look. Do keep an eye on high-humus mixes.

A 50-pound sack of humus will cost about the same as topsoil.

PERLITE

This is volcanic rock, expanded by high temperatures, and slightly alkaline.

We use perlite where those who have access to sand use sand. (If you have access to *coarse builder's sand*, try it, but don't bother with fine beach sand.) Perlite is primarily for aeration, having no absorptive powers. To our minds, the coarseness of the perlite makes it more desirable than sand. Then, too, perlite is much lighter than sand, which makes a difference in carrying around buckets of mix or large potted plants.

Perlite is white and tends to pick up the colors of algae and mineral salts that are in the soil. It also has this somewhat annoying property: when you water from the top, the heavier parts of your soil mix will tend to wash down, while the perlite will tend to float up. So, after a while you can have a layer of perlite sitting on the surface of your soil. Actually, if you don't mind the appearance, this isn't too bad because the perlite acts as a bit of a mulch, and helps to keep the moisture in.

Perlite costs, wholesale, about $2.50 for 4 cubic feet.

VERMICULITE

Vermiculite is the mineral mica expanded by high heat. Like perlite, it provides drainage; unlike perlite it does hold moisture—along with whatever nutrients the moisture contains.

Remember that a plant takes nutrients from its soil only when those nutrients have been dissolved in water. The nutrients exist in the mix in the form of mineral salts. These salts dissolve in the water, and if other circumstances are favorable (see "Acidity—Alkalinity" below), the plant absorbs them from the water—but only from the water. Not directly from the soil.

Vermiculite costs about the same as perlite.

BONE MEAL

Bone meal is ground animal bones.

The best cactus growers we know use bone meal as their only plant food, and anyone who grows bulbs swears by it, too. It is slow to dissolve and so not readily available to the plant until enough time has passed for it to break down. We often add an extra spoonful of it when potting up slow-growing or bulbous plants.

The effective part of bone meal is almost entirely phosphorus—which is needed by the plant to help it mature.

For less than $2 you can buy, retail, enough to last you for a couple of years at a tablespoon or so each time you prepare some mix. But since we frequently throw some extra in when repotting, it doesn't last us that long.

DRY COW MANURE

You'll note that the recipe calls for *dry* cow manure, not fresh. Fresh manure will burn the roots of your plant.

At one poverty-stricken point in our horticultural career we would go down to Riverside Park, here in New York City, and follow the mounted police as they ambled along the paths, looking for fresh horse manure (with a plastic container and a plastic bag the operation was almost painless), which we would soak into a manure tea. But we have since given that up for the more practical, if more expensive, processed stuff.

Manure is an inefficient food, in terms of the major nutrients: very little of its bulk—only about 5%, even dried—is actually counted in the three major mineral foods (nitrogen, phosphorus, and potash). But it contains a wealth of trace elements, present in minute amounts but terribly important for the well-being of your plants.

A 5-pound bag of dry cow manure costs about 89¢.

SUPERPHOSPHATE

Superphosphate is a good food for your flowering plants, supplying phosphorus. It comes in both powder and granular form. The powder is more quickly available to the plant, but the granules stay in the soil longer.

A 5-pound box will cost about $1.25, but you may have trouble finding it.

LIMESTONE

Limestone is used primarily to neutralize some of the acidity in other components of the soil mix (see below "Acidity—Alkalinity"). For example, both peat and humus are quite acid.

A 1-pound bag should cost about 39¢ in the five-and-dime.

WOOD ASHES

Wood ashes come free—if you know someone with a fireplace; otherwise just forget them. They provide potash, which is a stem-builder, but potash is also somewhat available in the soil and in chemical fertilizers.

EGGSHELLS

Eggshells provide some calcium to the plants. By a recent soil test we've made, eggshells do neutralize acidity, duplicating the action of limestone. So, if you don't have limestone, use more eggshell.

After all the egg has been scooped out, we allow our eggshells to dry completely, then store them until we have a lot. We grind them to a powder in the blender and store the ground powder in plastic boxes until they are needed for the mix.

We enjoy the satisfaction of recycling the eggshells so directly.

SPECIAL NEEDS

These are the ingredients of our basic soil mix. But we aren't rigid about them or about their proportions: sometimes we mix up a soil for a plant with special needs.

ACID-LOVERS

There are plants that will do their best only in a soil with a high acid content (one that would be rather too high for most houseplants): amaryllis, mums, camellias, podocarpus, ferns, gardenias, pittosporum, hydrangea, all the citrus fruits, and azaleas, for example.

For these plants, we take our basic mix and add an extra helping of *peat moss*. This does the double duty of providing acid and additional drainage. (See FEEDING, Chapter 8.)

TERRARIUMS

Since fertilizing terrariums and bottle gardens can be a problem (you can only feed when you water, which should be very seldom), we like to start out with a richer soil mix for them. An extra helping of *humus* gives the soil what we want, and, as it's not watered much, this humus-rich soil doesn't get compacted.

FERNS

Ferns require good, good drainage and a soil mix that will keep them evenly moist. Some (such as staghorn ferns) want the same kind of rooting material that orchids like, but those require such high humidity that they make poor houseplants. For apartment ferns, outside of terrariums, we combine equal parts of our acid-lovers' soil mix (see above) and chopped sphagnum moss (measure wet).

Sphagnum moss. As humus is further decomposed peat moss, so the peat moss we use is further decomposed sphagnum moss. Sphagnum moss is available both in sheets and loose (called "long-haired" sphagnum to distinguish it from the finely-cut "milled" sphagnum moss).

For ferns, cut the sheet moss into ½" squares or cut the long-hair into ½" to 1" pieces and combine it with the acid mix.

ACIDITY—ALKALINITY

From time to time, in our function as consultants, people will call us and ask if such and such a plant wants an acid or an alkaline soil.

The temptation is to sound very sage and ponder a while and then say, "Setcreasea? Oh, yes, a slightly acid soil."

Well, the truth of the matter is that virtually *all* houseplants prefer an acid soil. The exceptions are the grasses and vegetables, which largely prefer an alkaline soil. So, if you treat all your houseplants as acid-likers, you won't go far wrong.

Now, for those of you who've been wondering just what the hell we mean by acid and alkaline—here goes.

Everything that is wet or soluble can be defined along the pH scale—which describes a substance's potential for Hydrogen, the amount of the element hydrogen it can hold in its structure.

The scale centers at 7.0 (which describes a *neutral* condition, neither acid nor alkaline), and rises into higher numbers for more and more alkaline substances and descends into lower and lower numbers for substances of increasing acidity.

Cornell University sells a soil-test kit for under $5 that will measure your soil's acidity-alkalinity.

Most of the components of our potting soil are acid—from slightly acid to quite acid—and so, we add some lime or eggshells to the mix to bring the acidity closer to neutral. But if we brought the pH to 7.0 (neutral), most of our houseplants would do poorly.

Don't think, though, that a plant's acid requirements are strict: any plant will permit you a *range* of pH for best growth. In fact, any plant will permit you a range of soil mixes for best growth, too.

The whole question of pH, of acidity and alkalinity, is a complicated one, and one you need not fully grasp to grow healthy, happy houseplants. But you must know that most of your plants *prefer* slightly acid soil, and you should know that unless the pH is within the right range, a plant will not absorb the food it needs.

As we said above, food is absorbed into the roots in liquid form. The fertilizer salts are dissolved in water and taken in through the roots. But they are taken in through the roots only when the *ion balance* (the relationship between acidity and alkalinity) is within the right range.

In general, you need to know which potting materials are acid (topsoil, humus, peat moss) and which are alkaline (perlite, limestone, eggshells). If your soil mix tests too much one way or the other, or if you are feeding your plants correctly and they still show signs of being poorly fed (meaning that they are not *absorbing* the food you give them), an adjustment of the soil's pH may be the solution to your difficulty.

SOIL-LESS MIXES

There is a great deal of controversy today about whether soil mixes or soil-*less* mixes are best for houseplants. A soil-less mix is one without soil or humus, manure or eggshells, or other organic elements, except for peat moss.

We can't settle the controversy for you. It depends on your situation. We've known many successful growers on both sides.

For ourselves, the soil-less mixes are often too much trouble. Plants in soil-less mixes demand constant feeding—and with our style of life we can't guarantee that. Also, the soil-less mixes are intended to hold water less well: that provides greater aeration at the roots, but also requires more frequent watering.

But the soil-less mixes have some definite advantages.

Many of the bugs that live in the soil mixes are discouraged in the soil-less mixes.

Fungous problems are rarer in the soil-less mixes.

The ingredients are uniform from month to month—which may not be the case when buying topsoil and humus.

But soil-less growers must introduce trace elements into their mix chemically or organically. These trace elements—required by the plants in tiny amounts, but nonetheless very important—are already in topsoil and humus. They are mostly missing in mixes without topsoil and humus.

The most famous of the soil-less mixes, the Cornell Epiphytic* Mix, calls for the addition of a commercial pack-

---

*Epiphytes are "air plants." They take their nutrition and water mostly from the moist jungle air. They may live upon other plants, but they are not parasites. They may also live on rocks or telephone wires. In nature, many gesneriads, ferns, orchids, and bromeliads are epiphytes. When epiphytes are potted for houseplants, their soil mix must be extremely porous.

age of trace elements when mixing up a large amount (bushels) of the mix, but the recipe excludes the trace elements when mixing up a small amount. It's just as desirable in the small amounts of mix, but you can't add an amount small enough.

If you wish to try a soil-less mix, use our basic soil mix (on page 88) and leave out the topsoil, humus, manure, and eggshells—but you'll have to feed with a food containing trace elements.

A LAST WORD ON SOIL-LESS MIXES

The best growers we know agree on this: if you do use a soil-less mix, use it only for small plants. When they grow to large specimens, they should be transferred into a soil mix. Don't ask us why: it just works better that way.

SPECIAL INGREDIENTS FOR CERTAIN EPIPHYTES

Not all plants will be happy in our basic soil mix, even with amendments.

ORCHIDS

Except for terrestrial orchids, like bletilla, most orchids will rot if potted up into a mix with more than a tiny bit of soil in it, so we give orchids any of the following ingredients, either straight or mixed.

Fir Bark (also called orchid bark). As its name states, this is the coarsely-chopped bark of the fir tree. It is available in coarse to fine grades, with the medium and fine grades for orchid potting, and the coarse grade for mulches or garden paths.

Be sure your hands are wet when you handle this stuff: it is full of tiny splinters that are difficult to remove. Wetting seems to prevent the splinters from stabbing you.

Fir bark eventually breaks down, but it certainly endures long enough for all practical purposes.

When you pot into plastic or any of the lightweight materials with fir bark, crock the pot with real crock, or gravel or bricks, not screening: the bark is very light, and a plastic pot will tip over unless it is weighted.

Fir bark is a difficult medium for orchids. The chunks of bark must be tight around the roots of the plant, but they are not easy to keep in place. Also, watering from the bottom becomes a real problem because the bark floats to the top and away. With fir bark, water from the top, but water well.

Osmunda Fiber. Osmunda is a genus of fern. The roots are chopped up and dried and this fiber is then used to pot up orchids and other epiphytic plants. It has perfect drainage, some nutrition, and is long-lasting.

Osmunda can be jammed tight around the roots of your orchid without damaging them, and it will then stay in the pot when you water it from the bottom. The fiber takes a while to absorb water, so leave it soaking.

One warning about osmunda—something no one told us until it was too late: some time after you've potted your orchids into this medium, you will likely see mold develop on the surface and throughout. Don't let it upset you the way it did us. We thought the plants were ruined and threw out a whole batch of orchid offsets. This mold is harmless and natural. It will disappear in time.

Tree Fern. This is the dried remains of another kind of fern, slabs of which are used as "rafts" for epiphytic orchids, and the broken-up bits as a potting material.

The orchid is attached to a slab of the fern and it is hung. To water, you must dip the roots and the slab or raft into a bucket.

This medium also provides perfect drainage and absorbs no water in its stems—though some may remain in the interstices of the slab.

A plant on tree fern requires frequent watering and a high-humidity atmosphere.

Sphagnum Moss. See "Ferns," page 103. This moss behaves much like osmunda fiber (without developing the mold), but it does tend to dry out, and then must be soaked.

Bromeliads

In nature, bromeliads live mostly on trees, their roots worked into the pockets of detritus that collects in the trees' joints. This detritus has some amount of organic matter (like leaves), but mostly it just provides excellent drainage.

Bromeliads take little nourishment through their roots, and little water, for that matter. The roots are primarily an anchor for the plant.

There is little in this soil-less mix to hold water at the roots of the bromeliad and promote rot.

1 part pea gravel
1 part peat moss
1 part perlite
1 part tree fern bits
1 part medium fir bark
1 part sterile coarse sand

For terrestrial bromels, like cryptanthus, we use our basic soil mix, adding a measure of pea gravel.

THE ONE-MINUTE COURSE— PREPACKAGED MIXES

There are several brands of prepackaged soil mixes on the market. They are identified variously as potting mix, soil mix, African violet mix, philodendron mix, soil mix with peat, soil mix with humus, houseplant mix, and so on.

Yes, you can buy them, but, no, you should not use them straight from the package.

These prepackaged soils are lovely dark browns in color because they are high in humus, which gives them good nutritional value, but, because of the humus, they compact more and more as they are watered, until your plant's roots can't breathe at all.

To make a prepackaged mix workable is very simple. Buy a bag of perlite (that's that white stuff, very lightweight, that looks like tiny pebbles), and mix it with the soil in the proportion of 1 part perlite to 2 parts soil mix. You can use that for any of your exotic houseplants that can be potted in soil at all. (You can't pot epiphytes in one minute.)

This package-plus-perlite mix is okay if you have only a few plants to pot, but with a lot of plants it can cost a lot of money to buy small amounts of bagged soil.

8. Feeding

When Stan was an actor he was involved in the production of a modern Greek play. As the opening neared, the director was giving out notes on the performances, but none to Stan. After the session, young and eager, he went up to the director.

"Any suggestions for me?" he asked.

The director eyed him tiredly. "Act less," he said.

In feeding your plants, you, too, will be better repaid for restraint.

Feed less than it tells you on the box, less food and less often. The manufacturer's recommendations are for *maximum* dosages—and maximum profits. Your plants can really suffer if you follow his suggestions. And the worst of it is, you'll rarely recognize that what's bothering your plant is overfeeding.

WHEN DO YOU FEED?

You cannot fertilize a plant out of poor conditions. If the light is too low, or the humidity too low, or the soil too heavy, or the watering too little, feeding can only hurt, not help. **Feed only healthy plants living in decent conditions.**

Plants suffering from insect infestations or from diseases have enough to worry about without being hassled with fertilizer. Only a healthy plant can use the food. (An exception is a chlorotic plant. Chlorosis is a deficiency disease correctible with acid food. See page 152.)

Don't feed just before or just after transplanting. For 2 weeks after, the plant can't absorb the food anyway, and you take a chance on damaging it.

Don't feed young seedlings (see SEEDS, Chapter 16), you'll just burn their tender roots.

Don't feed plants in dormancy or going dormant.

WHY FEED AT ALL?

That's a good question. If you're mixing a soil like the one we recommend, chock full of nutrients to begin with, why feed until the soil is depleted—perhaps after a year or so?

The truth is that, what with water washing out the minerals, and with the demands of the plant, the soil in a pot gets depleted after only a couple of months. There is *some* nutritive value left, but much of it has been just washed away. And that's why we feed.

THE NUMBERS RACKET

Probably the most confusing part of plant foods is the numbers on their labels.

These numbers refer to the percentages of the three major plant-food elements: nitrogen, phosphorus, potassium. These are the macro-nutrients that a plant requires.

A plant that says on its label 15-30-15 is 15% nitrogen, 30% phosphorus and 15% potassium: this means that 60% of what you're buying goes into these major elements. (The rest would be inert materials and, perhaps, a small percentage of trace elements.)

Plant foods that show 5-10-5, 10-20-10, or 15-30-15 on their labels all have the same proportions (that is 1-2-1), but only 20% of the first product is available as food compared to 60% of the third. Certainly you would have to use much less of the stronger food, but the weaker may be easier for you to control.

Trace elements are not always listed by percentages on the package, if they are listed at all. The plant requires only minute amounts of them—but it does require them. These micro-nutrients already exist in some of the "organic" fertilizers, but must be manufactured into chemical foods.

Calcium, vital to healthy plants, is also not listed by percentage. Plants need more calcium than they do of the trace elements, but less than they do of the macro-elements.

THE MACRO-NUTRIENTS

Let's look in more detail at the major plant-food elements and see how they contribute to the growth of a plant.

NITROGEN

Nitrogen is always listed first on the label. If there is *no* nitrogen, there will be a zero: 0-12-1, as in bone meal.

This element is necessary for the vigorous growth of shoots and leaves, and it is an essential part of the chemical structure of chlorophyll. Without enough nitrogen, leaf growth will be puny and your plant won't photosynthesize properly (that is, it won't be able to make its food).

Too much nitrogen in proportion to the other food elements may inhibit flower formation and result in weak stems. For example, an African-violet grower feeding just on fish emulsion (5-1-1) can find his plants becoming shy to flower.

PHOSPHORUS

Phosphorus is always the second number on the label, though sometimes it is shown as phosphoric acid, which is a form in which plants can absorb this element.

Phosphorus helps build strong roots and sturdy stems; it also contributes to good bud formation and flower color, and then to good seed and fruit production.

POTASSIUM

Potassium is the third figure on the label, and also known as potash. If you're growing in a decent soil, there should be a good deal of potash in it to begin with.

This element also helps promote good flowering and sturdy stems, and aids in resistance to disease.

CALCIUM

This element is often not listed on the label at all and isn't present in many foods, but it is essential to your plants' well-being. It is present in bone meal, lime, and eggshells, which we include in our basic soil mix. Even soil-less-mix growers include limestone as a source of calcium in their mixes.

THE MICRO-NUTRIENTS
(TRACE ELEMENTS)

Plants need these micro-nutrients in only trace amounts, but, as with people, their absence can lead to very striking deficiency diseases.

Among the trace elements your plants need are: iron, zinc, magnesium, manganese, boron, copper, molybdenum. Some makers list them on the label, some don't. (If they are not on the plant-food label, you can't be sure that they've been included in the food. We haven't listed them all, and it's fairly certain that science hasn't yet determined them all.

The "organic" (animal, vegetable, mineral) foods contain various trace elements.

ORGANICS—CHEMICALS

There is, for us, no conflict between the organic and the chemical fertilizers in the apartment garden—we use both, in their places.

We like to include organics in the soil mix itself: bone meal, wood ashes, superphosphate, manure, eggshells.

But when it comes to regular feeding we alternate the very convenient, water-soluble chemical foods with fish emulsion; this way, we never have to worry about our trace elements.

WHAT IS AVAILABLE?

If you go to a garden center or nursery, you'll see a vast array of plant foods; and the advertising copy on every one says it's the best.

Fish Emulsion. This food is literally ocean fish. A very good source of nitrogen, its formula is generally 5-1-1, which shows it to be an inefficient food, with only 7% in the major nutrient elements. However, it is packed with trace elements. You may find some seaweed emulsions, too. By all means, try them.

Manure. There is horse manure, cow manure, sheep manure, bird manure (both land birds and sea birds). They are variously strong sources of nitrogen, mostly, and are variously efficient: cow manure can be as low as 2% nitrogen. We like to include dried cow manure in the soil for slow-release nitrogen and trace elements.

Bone meal. Here is a very slow source of natural phosphorus and calcium. It is ground and steamed animal bones. Its analysis will run about 0-12-1.

People eat bone meal, too, but prepared more sterilely.

Superphosphate. This is phosphoric rock which has been treated with an acid to release the phosphoric acid. If all the acid hasn't been converted, it can eat right through the box—as ours did. It should analyze at about 0-20-0—which is singlemindedness for you.

Wood ashes. A source of slowly released potash and calcium, in low concentration. About 6% potash.

Eggshells. Eggshells certainly contain calcium; it's hard to say how much is available to the plant, but it is worth using.

Limestone. Here is the most commonly used source of calcium. Often recommended is "dolomitic limestone," which contains magnesium in addition to calcium.

You can make an eggshell or a limestone "tea" to water your alkaline lovers. A couple of tablespoons left for a few days in a quart of water, shaken periodically and then allowed to settle before pouring off the water, will sweeten quite well. (Try this on your nasturtiums.)

CHEMICAL FERTILIZERS

These are easy and convenient to use. We use the soluble ones, but *at no more than half the recommended strength.*

They can be dangerous if you overfeed and detrimental if you use a food that's inappropriate to a particular plant—say, too much nitrogen for a flowering plant.

Here's an important thought: DON'T BE LOYAL. Rotate your foods; switch from one chemical to another, or from chemical to organic, or from organic to chemical, but vary your feeding. It's the only sure way your plant has of getting a balanced diet.

[113]

Soluble Powders. These are the most commonly used and for us the most convenient: they dissolve readily in your watering can for easy application. They come in any formula you could possibly want; for example: 20-20-20, 18-18-18, 30-10-10, 10-30-20, 25-5-20, 9-45-15, 21-7-7—this last for acid-loving azaleas. Examine the literature and the label before deciding. When a maker puts out several different formulas, he will tell you the best use of each.

Liquids. Aside from the various organic emulsions, there are many concentrated chemical liquids on the market. We prefer the soluble powders, generally. The liquids don't measure as easily, they don't come in as wide a choice of formulas—and they tend to spill. But they are nutritionally as sound as the powders.

Tablets and Sticks. We don't use these any more. We tried them, and they started to form mold pockets. Also, they tend to leave lots of residue in the soil.

Slow-Release. This is an interesting idea. (The first time we saw one brand's plastic balls in the soil, we thought they were insect eggs!) You put them right into the soil with your potting mix and only a bit is released with each watering. As far as we know, they are made by only two companies, Mag-Amp and Osmocote, and are not widely available. They are sold in a very limited number of formulas.

WHAT GETS WHAT?

The truth of the matter is that in summer, when everything is running away from us, we're just as likely to give everything an *extremely* dilute shot of 15-30-15 *almost* every time we water (plants in soil must have just plain water occasionally). This method isn't preferred, but it is a way of keeping up with a large apartment garden while trying to deal with a hectic world. (For our vacation we hire a plant-sitter and *nothing* gets fertilized.)

When things slow down, the following is our regimen.

FOLIAGE PLANTS

Understand that all houseplants flower except the ferns. But there are plants that are grown primarily for foliage.

When that 10-year-old snake plant suddenly blooms with white flowers, that's an unexpected bonus.

Foliage plants generally like a high-nitrogen food (say, fish emulsion). But you cannot ignore completely the other elements of nutrition if you want strong stems and roots. Vary with a dilute 15-30-15 once every few months.

FLOWERING PLANTS

Give your flowerers a food with a high middle number (phosphorus). It doesn't have to be always a balanced 10-20-10, it can be something like 2-10-10 (Hi-Bloom) or 12-36-14 (Peters' African Violet Special), but do vary it with an occasional organic fertilizer.

ACID-LOVERS

Acid-lovers are quick to go chlorotic. These symptoms—pale leaves with dark stems, and general debility in the plant—indicate that the acid level of your soil is too low and your plant is not absorbing iron or any of several other trace elements. (See page 163.) Miracid, Spoonit, and Green Gard all contain acid and chelated iron which will bring the acid-lovers into line, and dramatically cure their chlorosis.

But even these plants (such as azalea, camellias, citrus fruits, and gardenias) don't want a totally acid diet: you may want to give them one acid feeding in four.

FOLIAR FEEDING

In foliar feeding you spray the leaves of a plant with liquid plant food (in dilution, of course), instead of feeding them at their roots. Except for orchids and bromeliads (see Chapters 23 and 26), it's not worth it. Recent investigations show that most houseplants are poor foliar feeders, and the food just stains the leaves.

HOW OFTEN?

That's a tough question. Frequency of feeding should depend on the season, the growth activity, the size of the plant, the amount you're watering (if you're watering a lot, you wash out more nutrients and they have to be replaced), and whether or not the plant is potbound.

Generally speaking, foliage and flowering plants in active growth in spring and summer, and in good cultural condition, should be fed about every 2 or 3 weeks with a half-strength food of one kind or another.

In winter most plants in natural light want no food at all.

If you have a plant in flower for you in winter, feed it a bit less than you would in the spring.

Plants in soil-less mixes must be on a constant-feed program, fed at every watering at about ⅛ strength.

Plants kept in wick waterers in soil-less mix should get the same ⅛ strength feeding: those in soil mix should be in constant feed of an even weaker dilution, and flushed out from the top with plain water every couple of months.

Under fluorescent lights, as long as your plants are in active growth, feed as if it were summer.

Slow-growing plants will want feeding only once a month, and that with a dilute food.

If you want to keep your plants on the smaller side, feed them a bit less and tend to keep them underpotted.

REMINDERS

Feed less than the manufacturer's suggestions, and vary your feeding during the year.

Bon appétit!

9. Grooming and Pruning

TAKE A SHOWER WITH A FRIEND

The least you can do for your city-dwelling plants is to take them in for an occasional shower. Country growers can't imagine how much sooty dirt there is in city air, and even indoors a lot of it settles on a plant's leaves. If dirt is allowed to remain on the leaves, you can have a reduction in photosynthesis, leaf damage, and dull leaves.

We've read what we should do is take a soft, damp sponge or rag and gently wipe down each leaf. Well, aside from the soot being gritty and possibly scratching the leaves, we haven't the time to do that for plants with a lot of leaves. Besides, we can, between us, carry even very large plants into our shower.

You can do some washing by misting heavily, but it's not the same as sloshing water over the tops and undersides of your plants' leaves. They love it, and will reward you with cleaner air for yourself and a shinier, healthier look.

Small plants don't have to be put under the shower itself if you have a showerhead attachment you can slip over a faucet; the big ones, however, get brought inside the curtains just like people.

Cover the soil with some plastic so you don't wash your mix away, and allow the plant to drain somewhat before carrying it, dripping, through the apartment. And do your showering early in the day; an evening shower might lead to fungous problems.

However you manage it, for looks and health, take a shower with a plant friend.

SHINING IS NOT GROOMING

Applying a leaf shine is not grooming. Not only does it not help your plant but it can hurt it by clogging the pores and holding the dust. Fortunately, most pores are on the undersides of leaves, so many shined plants do survive—but why do anything so potentially harmful?

THE QUICK AND THE DYING

Every plant suffers from attrition: it has to happen. Leaves age, flowers fade, the dog knocks over a pot and a stem gets broken. Dead and dying material should be removed from a plant because, left on, they can hurt the plant.

Deadheads (dead flowers) and flowers past their prime should always be removed routinely. Some plants will continue to flower well only if you remove the deadheads, and all plants may suffer from rot if rotting flowers are left on. Pinch them off as near to the stem as you can.

Dead or dying leaves should also be taken off. Nothing leads to fungous diseases so quickly as dead African violet leaves left on the plant. Besides being a home for rot and insects, a dying leaf takes some nutrition from the parent plant which could better go to the healthy leaves.

All leaves have a limited life span, and must be expected to die off eventually. The larger, older leaves of a healthy plant die first. In the case of rhizomatous begonias like *B. erythrophylla* (beefsteak begonia), these older dying leaves shade the healthy growth, and you can help your plant along by removing these as soon as they fade or discolor. (If it's your younger leaves that are fading, you've got troubles. See Chapter 14.)

With your fingers, snap the bad leaves off as close to the main stem as you can, without hurting the main stem.

But not all *damaged* leaves need be removed. Some can be badly injured and survive. We brought home a *Dracaena fragrans* (corn plant) that had been raised in a greenhouse, next to some thorny cacti. Moving the larger plant in and out, several scratches and gouges were taken out of the large leaf blades. Fortunately, most of the injury was done along the length of the leaves—that is, not cutting across the vein system, which probably would have killed a large portion of those leaves.

The plant has been in our apartment for 3 years now, it has trebled its size, and all of those injured leaves are still there, functioning as leaves should, photosynthesizing like crazy—but only from those areas that are not injured.

This was owner's choice. We prefer a *D. fragrans* holding on to even damaged leaves to one with a partly bare stem. We could have removed the slit leaves; many growers do. We don't require perfection of our friends.

We have a number of chlorophytum (spider plants). Allowed to go too long in their pots one season, the leaf tips began to go brown. We repotted them and trimmed off the brown tips; the plants are now healthy and those trimmed leaves are fine.

However, leaves do not become whole again; those dracaena scratches will never close up—the chlorophytum leaves will never grow new tips—though, of course, both plants have grown new leaves.

STEMS

You always want to cut back injured, dead, or dying stems.

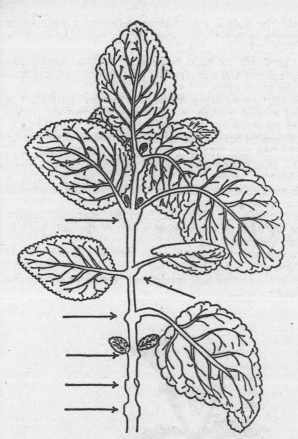

Nodes and internodes. The arrows point to the nodes. The distance between two nodes is called the "internode."

You might cut back stems to stimulate growth on your plant. The growing tip of your plant contains hormones called auxins. These auxins *inhibit new growth elsewhere*. That's right: a healthily growing plant inhibts itself. That's why you can have a healthy cane begonia with long, bare stems and a sprouting of leaves at the tip. Cut off the tip, and new growth will start farther down because the inhibitions have been removed (we all need to lose a few of our inhibitions).

On page 119 you'll see a diagram of a stem, showing

"nodes." The node is that thickened place on a stem where new growth or leaves come from. When you make a cut (a sharp knife dipped in alcohol is best), do it just *above* a node or the plant will die back to the node anyhow, leaving you with a dead stub and a chance that the "dieback" will continue down the whole stem.

You might want to cut stems back because your plant is old and in weak growth. A *Philodendron rubra* (the undersides of the leaves are deep red) we'd had for years had gotten into trouble because some silly fools had let it go without water for too long. The long stem was mostly bare and what was left wasn't handsome. So, the silly fools cut the whole thing back to within a few inches of the soil, and after a month we had a new sprout, and today we have a strongly growing "new" plant.

We mentioned cane begonias. Even the longest and leggiest can be cut back to within about a foot of the soil, and will resprout like crazy.

Semperflorens begonias respond well to pruning too. If they have gone a bit straggly, cut them back to within 6–8″ of the pot, and they will spring back with new growth and increased flowering.

Pinching out the growing tip stimulates branching (Nematanthus 'Black Magic').

Many of the wandering Jews should have "haircuts," frequent cuttings back to within a foot of the pot, to keep them from getting too shaggy.

A coleus must be "pinched back" (you just reach into the growing tip and literally *pinch* it off). If you let it alone it will grow like a tall weed. Pinch out the tip while the plant is

Pinching out the top pair of leaves (Sinningia *'Tinkerbells'*).

young and it will make two branches. Pinch out those two and each will make two more. And so on, until you have a lovely and bushy plant. Basil works the same way, and you have a double incentive there, because the bushier the plant the more leaves for you to pick later on.

We grow lots of lovely scented geraniums. We keep them on our brightest windowsill for the winter, but that isn't enough to keep them from getting spindly reaching for more light. Come spring, we hack them back, and get new, much more compact growth. In general, earliest spring is a great time to do your heaviest pruning.

Columneas, hypocyrtas, aeschynanthus, all the trailing or upright (not rosettes, like African violets or ˉgloxinias) gesneriads are bushier and flower better for early and frequent pinching out.

How early do you start? We have a blue-ribbon-grower friend who pinches out her cuttings as soon as they're rooted! And she grows the greatest gesneriads and begonias you could want to see.

Is your dracaena leggy? You can air-layer it (see VEGETATIVE PROPAGATION, Chapter 17), or you can just lop the top off. The main stem will branch—usually.

However, you must know what plant you're lopping the top off of: we've never heard of anyone successfully topping a palm. So don't be an indiscriminate headhunter.

CROWNS

Plants that grow in rosette shape (such as African violets and gloxinias) have to be groomed to get rid of *suckers*.

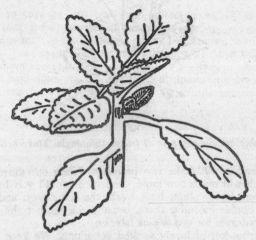

Sucker in a gloxinia leaf axil.

Suckers are small plants, growing elsewhere than in the center (the growing tip). On a glox they come from a leaf axil, growing off to the side. In an African violet, look down the center of the plant: do you see something growing like an-

Spread the rosette to see the African violet sucker.

other "center" off to one side? That's a sucker. Get them out and they root easily (see VEGETATIVE PROPAGATION), but if they're left on the plant, they inhibit flowering.

SYMMETRY

Whether you're grooming for size, for growth, or for health, try to groom symmetrically. Bonsai plants may be shaped for *a*symmetry, but the normal run of houseplants look much better in a generally symmetrical shape.

So, remember this: if you're cutting off only one branch or stem to even up a plant, that cutting will stimulate that stem into branching and new growth—leaving the other stems behind. To keep everything even, when you cut one branch sharply, give the others a little pinch, just to keep everything branching at the same rate.

10. Pots

So you go to that downtown garden center and you stare at the profusion of pots: clay pots, soft plastic pots, hard plastic pots, ceramic pots, thick plastic pots, thin plastic pots, peat pots, rubber pots, composition pots, metal pots, pottery pots on macramé ropes, and on the way down you looked into an antique store and saw a pair of nineteenth-century cloisonné pots. And then there are the shapes: round, square, standard, azalea, bulb pans, geranium pots, and ornamental shapes that beggar description.

Let's make a few quick definitions: In a "standard" pot, the depth and the width across the top are equal, though it looks deeper than that. In an azalea pot, the depth is about ¾ of the width. In a bulb pan, the depth is about ½ the width. In a geranium pot, the depth is slightly *more* than the width.

Pot sizes refer to their measurements across the top: a 4″ standard pot, a 4″ bulb pan, a 4″ azalea pot, all measure the same 4″ across the top. Square pots are measured *diagonally*.

CHOOSING A POT

Let's say you went to a meeting of your local American Gloxinia and Gesneriad Society and in the raffle you won a lovely *Nautilocalyx bullatus* in a 4″ azalea pot. The plant is about 1½′ high, very dark green with small white flowers already at the axils. The grower comes over to you and confides that the plant really needs repotting. You had already suspected this because the plant refused to stand by itself and had to be propped between two others on the raffle table.

So, you take the plant home and run out to buy a pot in the five-and-dime. You've got your first clue in the original pot. Probably, the original grower knew what he was doing, and the plant is healthy and well grown and in flower, so you assume that the azalea pot is the right shape. (Actually, since you've gone to a few meetings already this year, you know that most gesneriads like to be in azalea pots because their rooting systems are shallow.)

An azalea pot, then—but what size? Well, the plant is now in a 4″ pot, so, though you hope eventually to grow it up to a 4′ beauty, you cannot throw it right into a 12″ pot. That would leave too much wet soil outside the roots which would stay wet too long and lead to rot.

But a 5″ pot would mean repotting again in a few months, right? And what's wrong with that? Nothing. The most desirable way to pot up most houseplants—avocados are a notable exception—is to put them in pots about 1″ larger than what they're in now (that is, 4″ to 5″, then 5″ to 6″, etc.), and then repot when you have to.

So, a 5″ azalea pot, but of what material? That decorative container looks very pretty—it's expensive, but pretty. While you're turning it over to look at the price, look at the bottom for drainage holes. Do you see any? No? Then put it down and keep looking, because a good pot must have drainage.

Drainage means that when you water the plant, any excess water can run out of the bottom. Roots in soil must have air as well as water, for growth.

On to those piles of clay and plastic pots over there—they all have drainage holes. And here we run into the clay-versus-plastic controversy. Are you already on one side or the other? Then think again, because there is no real controversy. For some plants in some situations clay is superior, and for other plants in other situations plastic is superior, and most often it doesn't matter one little bit.

Clay is heavy and plastic is light; clay is expensive and plastic is cheap; clay shows those white stains which indicate salt accumulations and plastic does not (though the salts are there); but clay is porous (it breathes) and most plastics are not; and clay allows a plant to dry out more quickly than does plastic—a decided advantage for plants that want to dry out well between waterings (like cacti and succulents), and a decided disadvantage when you have plants that want to maintain a constant moisture around the roots (like anthuriums and rex begonias and gloxinias in bud and so on), and for most growers, clay is just better-looking than plastic.

You did your homework after winning the raffle and found that the original grower kept his nautilocalyx on the damp side, never allowing it to become very dry between waterings, so you choose a plastic pot because it's better than clay at retaining moisture. (The store offers you a choice, in 5″ azalea pots—white, green, gray, rust, and a few mottled designs—but you've made enough decisions for one day, so now you just close your eyes and grab.)

And so you have a pot that will do the job for you quite well—though, if you had chosen clay, you wouldn't have gone wrong, either, and if there had been only 6″ pots available, the plant would still have done well. Does this sound contradictory? It's not—not really. You've gone through a lot of decisions to get "the right" pot for your plant, and the truth of the matter is that your plant is a living creature, not a computer read-out. With computers, things are either yes or no; with life and plants, there are maybe's.

WHAT GOES WHERE

- Rhizomatous begonias want azalea pots.
- Most spring bulbs want bulb pans.
- Bromeliads are happy in azalea pots.
- Geraniums want standard pots (or geranium pots, if you can find them).
- Cane and semperflorens begonias want standard pots.
- Most large foliage plants want standard pots.
- Avocados want standard pots—very large for the plant's size.
- Cacti want azalea pots—usually clay.

- Azaleas want azalea pots (as you may have guessed).
- Most windowsill vegetables want deepish pots.
- African violets want azalea pots (as do most other gesneriads).
- Plants with trailing habits like to be hung.
- Plants with spreading habits like a lot of soil surface (try a large bulb pan, for example, for an episcia or a maranta).
- Give tall-growing treelike plants clay pots so they are less likely to fall over.
- Don't use transparent pots except under fluorescent lights: sunlight will burn roots. You have perhaps noticed that, in nature, most roots are kept in the dark.
- Look at the roots of a plant after you turn it out of its original pot (see the next chapter, POTTING), and be sensible: what size and shape pot will *that* root system be happy in. Don't be stubborn; if it looks as if it needs it, use a larger pot.
- And as a final thought, pot *nothing* in soft plastic or rubbery pots: for our plants they are deadly.

DECORATIVE CONTAINERS

Yes, you can use glazed decorative containers. First of all, you drill a hole into the bottom with a high-speed drill, after which you can pot it up as if it were plastic.

Or you may do what many growers do and use a decorative container to hide a clay or plastic one. Just put some gravel in the bottom of the container to raise the inner pot so

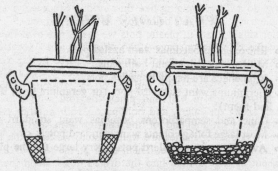

A pot within a pot can be dangerous.

that it doesn't sit in water. It would be wise every now and then to lift the inner pot out and pour off any water that has collected in the bottom.

As for the hand-crafted clay pots, if they have holes, use them as is; if they don't, use them as you would the glazed pots.

SQUARE POTS

These are available only in azalea depth, in plastic, peat, and various composition stuff, but not clay. They have an advantage for the apartment grower over round pots. Square pots fit against one another for a slightly more efficient use of space.

HANGING BASKETS

These are called "baskets" because they are often wire frames, like baskets, which then must have a sheet moss or composition liner to keep the soil from falling out. These wire things aren't very practical for an apartment, where you have to worry about the water dripping down to a wooden floor or a rug.

Plastic hanging pots are more practical: they have their own saucers to catch the water, but they aren't very beautiful.

You can buy "orchid hangers," made of thick wire, which will clip onto clay pots and hang them. The water does come out the bottom, though.

We do a lot of hanging like that by our windows, over our pebble trays. The plants below *love* to be dripped on.

For small plants in plastic pots we make our own hangers. (See the drawing on page 129.) We take a 4″ (or larger) plastic pot and with a pointy knife drill three holes, equidistant, near the rim. We then take two pieces of twistable but strong wire, one 12″ long and the other 24″ long. We bend the longer piece in half and pinch the fold with a pair of pliers. Using the pliers, and holding on with another pair of pliers, we twist the end of the shorter wire into the fold. When a couple of inches are well twisted, we bend the twisted end into a hook shape. Then, each of the three free ends are bent up and hooked into the drilled holes. Bend the ends farther so that they are secure, and you've done it.

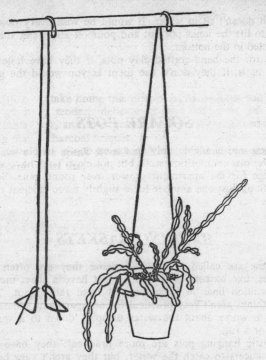

"Orchid hangers" are either 18" or 2' long.

REUSING OLD POTS

You can, of course, reuse old pots, but you cannot put plants into *dirty* old pots and expect them to survive. Unwashed pots can have bugs, bug eggs, fertilizer-salts deposits, fungi, and all kinds of other diseases.

To clean pots, it's not enough to wash out the old soil. You've got to soak them and scrub them. Leave your used pots soaking overnight (or longer) in a solution of 9 parts hot water to 1 part chlorine bleach. This will kill off pretty much everything, and the next day, scrubbing in hot water will get rid of the rest.

If you find some salt deposits stubborn, use a dull knife to scrape them off.

And now that you have a plant and a pot, let's pot up.

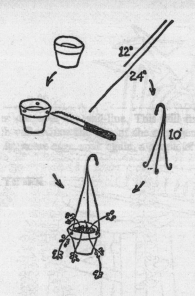

Making your own hanging basket is easy.

11. And Potting

There is a school of thought that holds that you should repot everything as soon as it comes into your house—kind of like throwing a child in water to learn to swim.

Another school of thought holds that you should wait until a plant has accustomed itself to your conditions before potting, to reduce trauma.

Whichever school is your alma mater, we want to remind you that every plant that comes into your house—whatever its source—should be *isolated* before it goes into your garden, to make sure that no new insect pests or diseases are introduced.

NOT FOR CACTI

If you want to transplant or repot cacti, see Chapter 24,

Each plant in its own pot, all surrounded with peat moss.

CACTI AND CACTUSLIKE PLANTS. Cacti need different repotting techniques from those described in this chapter.

IT'S EASY

Potting is a simple procedure and quick to do, once you have your materials gathered.

To start with, let's get back to that nautilocalyx you won at the raffle—the one for which you bought a 5″ plastic azalea pot.

If you had bought, instead, a clay pot, you'd now set it in some warm water to soak. It's poor policy to pot into a dry clay pot: the clay absorbs water from the soil, making your plant dry out *too* fast. Also, roots can get damaged by coming into contact with dry clay.

But your pot is plastic, so rinse it to get rid of any dust or dirt picked up in the store. Lay out some newspapers or a plastic sheet over a good-sized surface (potting can be messy work, and it's best to have a little elbow room and a surface that doesn't mind getting wet), a table, say, or even the floor if you have no other place. We like to repot around our bathroom sink, where it's easy to wipe up the slosh.

Now, let's put together the materials you'll need for repotting: the soil mix; some crocking material; a watering can or jar; a spoon; and, of course, the pot and the plant.

Plants shouldn't sit around out of their pots, so you'll want to have the soil mixed and the crock ready and in the pot before you unpot the plant.

If the plant is dry, water it well (leave cacti dry—see Chapter 24) while we discuss crock and crocking.

CROCK

Crock is material put into the bottom of a pot, before the soil or plant goes in. Its purpose is to keep the roots from coming through the hole or holes in the bottom of the pot, and to prevent the soil from caking up in the hole or holes, and to provide free drainage. (Crock is also referred to as "drainage material.") Originally, crock was pieces of broken crockery, clay flowerpots—something greenhouse gardeners always seemed to have plenty of. In city apartments, however, unless you're willing to buy clay pots just to break them for crock, you've got to look elsewhere for drainage material.

For example, we have used chunks of brick, broken up with a hammer. That's fine, if you can steal enough bricks from construction sites and don't break your thumb.

So, for all our small and medium-sized pots, the bulk of our potting, we use *pea gravel* or *screening* as materials that are sufficiently cheap and always at hand.

Pea gravel is available at building-supply places or large garden-supply stores. The screening we use is aluminum or plastic window-screening and is available at hardware stores. It is sold by the yard, and $1 will buy enough for hundreds of small pots.

We cut the screening, with ordinary scissors, into the shape and size of our pot bottoms, and press it into the inside of the pot.

For those of you who don't mind getting fingers hit by a hammer, here's how to crock large pots with shards or brick bits: take pieces small enough to form a layer; make certain the holes are all covered (if you're using a clay pot and clay pot shards, turn a piece of crock so that the curve rises over the hole, rather than going into it); then build a layer of crock about ⅕ the height of the pot. With gravel, just pour in a layer about that height.

TURNING OUT

Once the screening or crock is in place and the soil mix at hand, turn the plant out of its pot.

To turn a single-stemmed plant out of its pot, put your hand over the soil, with the stem between two fingers, and upright. Turn the pot upside down and, with your free hand on the bottom, gently try to lift the pot off. If the pot refuses to come off, rap the edges of the pot against a hard surface (your hand should still be holding the plant and soil in place). Try not to break the pot—though if it's clay, you'll at least get some crock out of it. If the pot still refuses to come free after a few knocks, take a dull, thin knife and run it carefully around the inside of the pot. That never fails.

If you don't want to resort to a knife, stick a pencil through the bottom hole and push gently. If you've used screening, the plant will be pushed out immediately and easily.

THE PLANT

With the plant out of the pot, look at the roots. It's important to get rid of as much of the old soil as you can, so separate the rootball with your fingers, and work out the used soil. This will stimulate the roots to grow into the fresh soil. We killed a camellia once by not loosening its rootball at all. (The exceptions are cacti and avocados which have easily-damaged roots that should *not* be disturbed.)

But be careful: you do not want to damage the roots by rough handling which might introduce the possibility of root rot. The line between rough handling and loosening is one you'll have to learn with practice.

SOIL

Lay the plant on a clean surface to wait, and spoon some soil mix into the crocked pot. Pick up the plant and place the roots onto the soil. Hold the plant erect so that you can see what it will look like when the soil is all in.

In general, you'll want to repot plants so that the soil comes up to the original level on the plant. There are some plants that don't care about neckline: if your nautilocalyx were leggy, you'd want to set it a little deeper—gesneriads don't care, that's one thing that makes them such fine houseplants. But let's assume your plant isn't leggy, and you want the same soil level. With the plant upright, judge by eye whether or not the level of the neckline comes about ½–¾" from the top. That should give you adequate watering room in a 5" pot.

If not, take out the plant and either spoon in more soil or spoon some out. Remember, you're allowed to scrunch the roots up—they don't grow stretched out anyway.

If the level looks right, spoon in more soil over the roots, and around the sides. Then press down with your thumbs until the soil is somewhat compacted. You don't want to press as hard as you can: the soil will get too heavy and you'll crush your roots. You also don't want the soil to be too loose, or the plant will not find anchorage in it and large airholes will be left around the roots.

With medium-large plants (plants one person can lift), try "tapping" instead of pressing the new soil around the roots. Just add soil and the plant, then lift the pot a fraction of an inch up and tap it down hard on the table. Add more soil and tap again. This will settle the soil and get rid of air pockets. You may want to use your thumbs also. Make sure the plant is firm in the pot.

(Be certain your soil mix is only *damp,* not soaking: wet soil compacts too heavily.)

STAKING

If your plant shows a tendency to keel over, it may need a stake—a stick to which it can be gently tied for support. The best time for staking is now as you pot your plant up—you

Twist around the stake first—*in order not to choke your plant.*

can put a stake into the soil, then without damaging the roots. The stake should be thick enough to support the plant, but not so thick as to be obtrusive. You want to see the plant, not the stake. Also, your stake should not show *above* the plant.

TROUBLE

Once the plant is set, water well and allow the excess to drain off. Fill in any holes in the soil that have developed as a result of the watering. Now spray the plant, and put it somewhere to grow beautifully.

You don't have to coddle it—not if you've done a good job of potting. Most repotted plants will be fine if you just keep them out of the sun for a day or so.

Occasionally, though, a plant will go into potting trauma: a general wilting of the leaves. Soft-stemmed plants especially resent having their roots handled and exposed to the air, and they sometimes show their resentment by drooping.

If your plant does this, spray the leaves with warm water and put the whole thing into a large, clear plastic bag, twisted closed. This emergency greenhouse is almost guaranteed to bring back traumatized plants.

The emergency room.

WHEN TO REPOT

A plant may need repotting when the roots are showing through the hole in the bottom; or when roots become visible at the top of the soil; or when the plant begins to demand water twice as often as it did; or when the soil gets hard from age and water is slow draining through.

But the one sure way to tell whether or not a plant wants repotting is to turn it out of its pot and look at the roots (see "Turning Out," page 132). If the roots are filling the pot, the plant wants repotting, whether it's showing symptoms or not. If the roots look all right, just slip the plant back into the pot, and no harm done.

POTTING LARGE PLANTS

Potting the big ones is more a problem of logistics than of

special techniques. Perhaps the answer is a friend or a Big-Plant-Pool of growers to help each other out.

A big plant with a woody stem is most easily handled by the stem (something you'd never do with a soft-stemmed plant). Water the plant well and lift it by the stem, while a friend pulls down on the pot (like taking a child out of his knickers), then set it on plastic sheeting or newspapers. As with other potting, you should have your crocked pot prepared—if the plant is going into a larger pot.

With some large plants you won't want to move up to a larger container—you reach a point where you just can't give it any more room. If you wish to return the plant to the same container, just take off as much soil as you handily can, put some fresh soil into the container and pot as usual. With large plants it's especially important that the stem be set quite upright.

If you're going into a new pot, scrape off *some* of the old soil, and continue as with any plant.

Be especially careful of the leaves when repotting large plants: they can get cut or torn quite easily.

If you're potting up a large avocado, disturb the roots as little as possible—damaged avocado roots can lead to rot (see Chapter 19, AVOCADOS).

If you come across a rootball too tough to loosen, then you might take a very sharp and very clean knife, and make a few easy slashes into the sides. This will stimulate new root growth, but it can also lead to rot. We consider it an emergency measure for when the rootball is too tough and full for ordinary breaking up.

POTTING SEEDLINGS

Seedlings are delicate things with tiny stems and small root systems, and quite easy to damage. When you have some seedlings to pot up, make sure everything is prepared before you start "pricking out" (see below) your baby plants.

Seedlings usually go into small pots—say 2-inchers—but aside from the size, the procedure is similar. Crock your clean pots as usual. But, instead of putting in only a bit of the soil you'll ultimately use, fill the pot right to the top with potting soil, and poke (dibble) a little hole in the center with a pencil. Now, with a spoon, or a straight pen with the tips separated (see drawing, page 183), lift your seedling out of its growing medium (this is called "pricking out"), and place it in the center of the hole you made. Press the seedling gently gently into place and then press down the soil around it. All of this time your hands have never touched the roots or stem of the plant. If you must touch something, lift by a leaf, which is expendable—the stem is not. Water, and put into a good light (though not direct sun—seedlings can't stand direct sun). You may want to mist or put into a plastic box for a while to keep the humidity high.

A leaf is expendable.

SPECIAL PLANTS

Not all pottings or repottings are the same. There are plants that go into special mediums that require different techniques. See Chapter 22, GESNERIADS; Chapter 23, BROMELIADS; Chapter 24, CACTI AND CACTUSLIKE PLANTS; and Chapter 26, ORCHIDS.

12. Growing Under Lights

We regard light gardening very positively. It turned our apartment from a place where we could flower only a few things on our brightest windowsills in the long days of late spring and summer, into a place where we can flower many things, all year round, in our darkest corners.

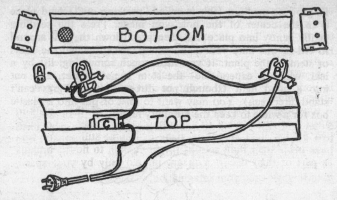

A single-tube 24" fixture: A—starter; B—terminals; C—ballast (transformer).

FLUORESCENT LIGHTS

What you can do for yourself and your apartment is limited only by your space and your budget.

If you've already got the shelving, for around $12 you can put up a pair of tubes that will flower gesneriads. Or you can spend $1,000 for a group of ready-made set-ups.

WHERE?

One of the nicest things about indoor lights is that they can go pretty much anywhere.

We have a front hallway that was as dark as a closet, but is bright and colorful now. Under a 3', 4-tube lighting fixture African violets and *Sinningia* 'Tinkerbells' are in flower, and episcias and *Begonia dregei* are thriving.

Our living room is on a narrow court, and quite dark. We have two sets of shelving in it: one (2 shelves) holds flowering gloxinias, miniature gesneriads, and a begonia; the other (4 shelves) we use for propagation boxes, seedlings, a few bottle gardens, and a couple of plastic flying saucers (see Chapter 18, GROWING IN A PROTECTIVE ENVIRONMENT).

The brightest room in the apartment is our office. We grow many plants in and around its two windows, and in the shadowed corners we have large light trays where bromeliads are flourishing and begonias and gloxinias and setcreaseas flower, and small foliage plants thrive. On the dark walls of this room we have put up, screwed right into the wall, 4 single-tube fixtures that are bright enough for propagation boxes and to flower some of the miniature sinningias we love so.

How's your bathroom? It should be the most humid room in your apartment and might be just the place to try ferns under lights.

We have friends who took the bottom of their walk-in closet and sacrificed it to a lighting set-up; others who have two 5'-high light stands in their bedroom; still others who have made their light set-ups bright enough to flower orchids as part of their decor. You are limited only by your space, your budget—and your imagination.

WHAT KIND OF LIGHT?

When we talk about gardening under lights we're talking about fluorescent lights.

Fluorescent tubes come in various colors, trade names, and spectrums. For practical purposes, at one end of the fluorescent spectrum is blue light, at the other end is red light. A combination of both is desirable for flowering; alone, blue light will give you great vegetative growth, and some flowering.

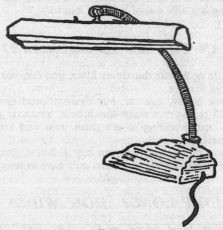

This "gooseneck" lamp holds two 18" fluorescent tubes.

The tubes most commonly available from every hardware store are the "cool white." These are tubes with a lot of blue light and a lot of intensity—which is why they give you such good vegetative growth. Leaves don't care all that much about spectrum, they just care about the light intensity. And "cool white" are the most intense tubes.

Also available, though not quite as widely, are the "warm white" and "daylight" tubes. These tubes have more red in their makeup and aren't as intense as the "cool white."

Now, we have flowered African violets, and various miniature gesneriads under our 2-tube desk lamp, which has only "cool white," so we can say from experience that you can flower under "cool white" alone.

But, we also know from experience that under the mixed spectrum of "cool white" and "warm white" (or "cool white" and "daylight"), gloxinias and begonias do better for us and the violets just as well.

HOW MANY TUBES?

For a shelf or a tray about 12″ to 14″ deep, 2 tubes are plenty. If you're looking to cover a larger area, you'll need 4 tubes. (Fixtures come in 1, 2, or 4 tubes. If you want 3 tubes, you're going to have to put it together yourself from 3 single-line fixtures of 1 tube each, or a double and a single, or by taking one tube out of a 4-tube fixture.)

CAN YOU DO IT YOURSELF?

Yes. Male or female, handy or klutz, you can put up your own lighting fixtures.

If you are handy, you can buy them stripped down or as parts for $5 or so for a single-line fixture. You can get a real bargain if you're willing to get them used and recondition them yourself.

If you are not handy, you can buy a 2-tube fixture from Macy's for less than $15, which you only have to assemble.

HOW LONG? HOW WIDE?

Fluorescent tubes come in 12″, 18″, 24″, 36″, 48″, 72″, and 96″ lengths, at 10 watts per *foot* (so that a 24″

tube is 20 watts, a 48″ tube is 40 watts, etc.). The 48-inchers are generally accepted to be the most efficient length. (If you're not interested in details about tubes and starters, skip to page 141.)

It works like this: as soon as you turn them on, fluorescent tubes start to die; they die from the ends in. (You've seen that darkness at the ends of a tube that has been used for a while.) But they die about the same amount whether you have 12″ or 8′ tubes. So, a 12-incher will lose about 4″ at each end and an 8-footer will lose about 4″ at each end: you can see which would be more practical. But the 8′ tubes are not available at all hardware stores, and, besides, they get hard to store and hard to handle, and the fixtures are available only in commercial, not home, fixtures—so what turns out to be the most available and most practical are the 4′ tubes.

You have less choice in tube width. Fluorescent tubes come in two widths: 1″ (T8) and 1½″ (T12). The thinner tubes are called "slimline." They give off the same amount of light, but it seems to us that the slimline gives off a little more heat. But we've been able to get 3′ tubes in *only* slimline.

WHAT ABOUT SINGLE PIN?

Some commercial fixtures come with a single thick pin at each end of the tube instead of the more common 2 thin pins. There is nothing functionally superior about them in a plant light set-up and they are more expensive.

TUBE LIFE

Fluorescent tubes have much longer lives than incandescent bulbs. One will last for two years. But you should change them after a year. Longer than that, and the efficiency falls too low for good flowering.

WHAT ABOUT STARTERS?

Starters are small devices that get most fluorescent tubes going by means of a little jolt of electricity. They wear out.

Rapid-start fixtures have their starters permanently built in, and they don't wear out. There are tubes sold specially for rapid-start fixtures, but the ordinary tubes will also work in those fixtures.

It is annoying when a starter is dying or dead, because you may have to test to find out if it's the tube or the starter that you've lost. But rapid-start fixtures are generally more expensive to begin with. The choice depends on whether you have more money or more time.

Starters are rather inexpensive and easy to change. But they are more trouble.

SPECIAL "PLANT" LIGHTS

In general, forget them. They are an expense that is unjustified by any evidence we've had shown to us.

We have friends who swear by one special tube or another, and other friends who laugh at them. We've found that the combination of "cool white" and "warm white" (half and half) works just fine. If you want to try the special tubes, go ahead, but they are usually much more expensive, without a commensurate return.*

INCANDESCENT LIGHTS

Incandescent lights are ordinary light bulbs and these have a minor place in growing; we have a nonplant friend with a mirrored wall and a chandelier with many incandescent bulbs in it. She stands a planter with some philo, snake plants, and a bit of nephthytis in front of the mirror, and these low-light plants do quite well.

We know a lighting engineer who insists that it is necessary to add some incandescent to the fluorescent light in order to flower plants. (We don't use it and we flower plants—he feels we're lying or exaggerating.)

But as far as using incandescent bulbs as plant lights, they are too hot to bring close to a plant, and when you put them far enough away, they do little good. A notable exception is

*We have recently gotten the word from excellent growers in the Bromeliad Society that they are flowering bromeliads under 4 to 6 Naturescent or Optima tubes (a Dura-lite product).

the use of spotlights as a *supplement* to window light for large foliage plants.

If you have large foliage plants, you may want to install one or more PAR 30, 150-watt spotlights as supplementary lighting for them.† Attached to the top of a door, or hung from the ceiling, or from tracks, you may find this kind of supplementary light the solution to insufficient light in a dim corner.

MERCURY VAPOR LAMPS

These are very expensive and very hot. For the most part, you have to have special equipment to handle one large enough to do a plant any good. They may make them more efficient or cooler or cheaper in the future, but, for now, these seem to be a rich man's toy.

HEAT

This is a real problem under lights. Many plants won't set buds if the temperature is too high. You can also scorch foliage and increase the watering demands of plants if the heat is too high. (At the moment of writing, it is summer and the temperature under our lights is approaching 90°. It makes us very nervous, so we spray and pour water into the trays under the plants, and direct the fan onto one set-up.)

BALLASTS

Ballasts are transformers; they take the electricity from the wires and distribute it to the tubes. The ballasts are the parts that get hot in fluorescent fixtures.

If overheating is a problem, you can cut into your ballast wires (ask an electrician or your hardware-store man how to do it) and place them on angle irons screwed into a wall, at a distance from the fixtures—keeping the ballasts horizontal, as they were originally.

Remember, though: fluorescent lighting is much, much

†A "PAR 30" is a Parabolic Arc Reflector spotlight whose beam covers an arc of 30°.

cooler than any equivalent amount of light from an incandescent bulb.

HUMIDITY

This is where your plant lives or dies under lights. The heat that a light set-up generates reduces the humidity within the growing area. You must arrange for humidity under your lights, or else when the buds form, they will blast.

Pebble trays, or their equivalents, are a necessity in light set-ups. Misting helps a bit, but less than in the open air. (Don't be afraid to spray into your tubes. They don't run hot enough to crack, and the electrical parts are well-enough protected not to be bothered.)

To help the humidity, you can enclose your set-up in plastic, but then the heat can build up, which, as we said above, can be a problem.

HOW MANY HOURS?

Except for the long-night plants which need about 12 hours of uninterrupted darkness (rhizomatous begonias, Christmas cacti, poinsettias), we would recommend about 16 hours a day of fluorescent light. This may seem like a lot, but the addition of a couple of hours may be just the thing to stimulate that shy bloomer into blossom. Some growers cut their lights back to 14 hours in the summer.

HOW MUCH TO MAINTAIN?

It is expensive to keep a large light set-up going. Starters cost, tubes cost, and, most of all, electricity costs. When we installed ours, we were shocked to see our electric bill more than double, then go up even further; but at the same time Con Ed got rate raises here in New York, so it's hard to tell.

If you're calculating the cost of a set-up, don't look at just the cost of the fixture or of the fixture and some replacement tubes. Power in the cities costs more than it does in the country, and nowhere will you see it more dramatically than in the increases each additional tube costs you at the end of the month.

If you want to make an estimate of how much extra money a light set-up is likely to cost you (we'll use one of our shelf set-ups as an example), do this: first, add the wattage of the tubes you wish to install—say, two 30-watt (that is, 3') tubes. Take this figure (60) and add 20% for the running of the ballast (12), which gives you 72. Multiply this by the number of hours you plan to run the set-up in a month. Sixteen hours a day by 30 days of the month equals 480 hours; 480 times 72 equals 34,560 watt hours, or about 35 kilowatt hours. Look at your bill and you can figure how much the light will cost you per month in your area.*

These figures don't include the cost of running a timer—an electric clock that turns the lights on and off—which is quite desirable.

In our area, not counting the timer, the cost of running this 2-tube set-up is about $1.50 a month. For that monthly $1.50, we get space for about 22 plants, with several always in flower.

CIRCLINE FIXTURES

These are circular fixtures, from 8" to 16" in diameter, at 22, 32, or 40 watts. You can use them in combination, too. They are great for giving a very intense light over a limited area—one of our friends has one over a large spherical plastic terrarium. But they seem to generate a lot of heat. Also, you can only put a plant or two (or a terrarium) under such a fixture.

HOW CLOSE TO THE TUBES?

Because fluorescent tubes are relatively cool, you can grow plants closer to them than you would think. In fact, the closer you grow to your tubes, the more compact your growth is likely to be. However, if you have one of the special so-called "plant lights," watch out; they give off a good deal of heat. Feel the tube when it's on.

Some plants, with very tender leaves, will scorch if they touch the tubes; others will not. But there's no need for the foliage to actually touch the tubes: grow mature plants

*Thanks to Al Katzenberger for the formula. Al teaches courses in indoor lighting.

within 4″ of the tubes and they should be fine; grow seedlings even closer—say, within 2–3″. But keep an eye on the seedlings: if they start to get pale, pull them farther away. The same with a mature plant: if you find it reacting adversely to being close to the tubes, lower the plant, or raise the tubes, or move it to a different light set-up where there's more room.

SPACE

Speaking of space, our light set-up starts out with enough room in winter but gets very crowded by summer. Plants grow moderately under lights in the winter when the world is dark outside, and they grow at an enormous rate under lights in the summer when the world is bright. (Some plants seem to "know" day length, even when they get only the faintest rays of natural light.) Be prepared. Plants will have to be moved out to make room.

Try to keep plants of about the same height under the same fixture: that way you won't have taller friends shading smaller friends.

WITH A LITTLE HELP

If you can, have some fixtures in a room that gets a little daylight, also. The combination of fluorescent light with even a little bit of daylight can make shy bloomers into real winners.

THE PLANTS

All right. What plants do well under lights?

Any moderate-size plant with moderate light demands should do very well under lights. The tall-growers are clumsy to grow in a light set-up because you'll find them going leggy unless you can provide light from the sides as well—not really practical in an apartment.

The sun lovers just hang on under lights: they do not thrive. There is, after all, an enormous difference between sunlight and fluorescent light.

So, stick to the many, many plants that are moderate in their light demands and you'll do fine. Here's a partial list.

- Most gesneriads will flourish under lights: columneas, aeschynanthus, hypocyrtas, sinningias (especially the many miniatures), gloxinias, streptocarpus, smithianthas, nautilocalyx, kohlerias, episcias, rechsteinerias, x-gloxineras, diastemas, koellikerias, alloplectus, chiritas, chrysothemis (though it grows too tall eventually and must be topped), codonanthes, gesnerias (a great terrarium mini), nematanthus, seemannias, phinea—and the list could go on and on. African violets? Of course.
- Begonias are also excellent under lights: many will flower, and virtually all will thrive.
- *Oxalis regnali* and *O. deppei* flower quite freely under lights.
- Bromeliads will produce excellent foliage under lights, and we know some growers who have flowered and reflowered them under lights.
- Some orchids will flower under lights.
- Hoyas have produced fine foliage for us under lights.
- Tomatoes have flowered lightly for us under lights.
- Herbs, such as basil, produce better under lights than in the sun: in the sun they go quickly to flower, but under lights, while you will get some flowers, you get excellent leaf growth.
- Most of the annuals that will flower on your windowsill will flower—though more sparingly—under lights.
- Miniature roses will flower under lights, though we prefer them on a windowsill.
- Geraniums won't flower for us in a light set-up, but the scented kinds do quite well vegetatively, making excellent foliage growth.
- The jungle cacti (epiphylum, rhipsalis, zygocactus) and wetter-growing succulents (like some euphorbias) do quite well under lights.
- Grow the wandering Jews close to the tubes and they thrive.
- All terrarium plants do well under lights (but do watch out for the heat): pilea, peperomia, pellionia, fittonia, and their friends.
- The small dracaenas and *Ficus diversifolia* seem quite happy in our light set-ups.

PROPAGATION

But if there is one area where fluorescent lighting is worthwhile above all others, it's in propagation. Apartment growers do with fluorescent lights what outdoor growers do with cold frames, and much more.

We started our tomato seeds on March 8 this year, under lights. We propagate literally thousands of various plants a year, all year long, under lights. See the Chapter on VEGETATIVE PROPAGATION: fluorescent light makes so many of these techniques possible.

13. Pests and Problems—
Insects Pests

There is a book entitled *Are You Your Garden's Worst Pest?* You may be. The apartment gardener spreads diseases and pests from plant to plant simply by handling them. But so does the breeze spread disease. Grouping plants close together can spread bugs. Even pets can spread them. Well, you *must* touch your plants, because one of the best ways of keeping your garden's insect population low is to inspect your plants often. Examine the undersides of leaves, leaf axils, growing tips, early and often, and you'll be able to see the colonies forming and deal with them before they get to be a major infestation.

You see, it is not necessary to keep your garden absolutely insect-free. Insect *control*, not insect *elimination*, should be your goal. After all, a healthy plant—even just a normally strong plant—can hold up under an insect attack.

KEEPING NORMAL INSECT
POPULATIONS LOW

Speaking now of insects, not diseases remember, there is

hardly a pest you will come across in the home that can't be controlled in a small population by very simple means.

For example, a washing of the plant in a solution of warm soapy water (and then a rinsing in clean water) will effectively reduce many sucking insects.

APHIDS (plant lice)

Aphids are small, soft-bodied, usually pale-green bugs, sometimes winged. They move slowly enough that you can catch a lot of them by hand.

The first sign of aphids can often be the white corpses on the leaves. These corpses look quite different from the live bugs, so don't think you have two problems.

Rinse the plant a few times in that warm soapy water, then wash the backs of the leaves well, and the growing tips especially, by rubbing gently between your fingers.

Repeat the examination and bathing every week or so if you continue to see them. Annuals are especially attractive to aphids.

SCALE

It's sometimes difficult to tell the difference between scale and the natural protuberances of some plants, especially as scale can take many forms and colors that seem to blend with the plant. We love to grow *Albizzia julibrisson* (powderpuff tree) as a pot plant, from seeds we get from the grounds of Columbia University. A student once brought us a seedling, asking if those bumps on the stem were scale or the tree. They were both!

If it scrapes off easily, or if it seems squishy under that hard shell, it's scale. We've seen an apparently healthy plant with stems literally covered with scale, the whole looking so "natural" it was hard to believe there was a problem.

Often, the first sign of scale is a sticky "honeydew" on the plant. This excrescence of the scale is not harmful in itself, but it makes a great medium for certain fungous diseases.

To get rid of the scale, or most of it, swish the plant through the warm soapy water several times, then rub your fingers gently over the scaly parts. The scale should come off easily. Then rinse and reexamine. Inspect again, until controlled. Citrus are very subject to scale. Watch for it on avocados, too.

SPIDER MITES (called "red spider")

This really is a dangerous pest, much more likely to kill a plant quickly than other insects.

It is especially insidious because it is all but invisible to the naked eye. It's quite visible under a low-power magnifying lens (a lens is a very handy garden tool), though you'll need a high-power lens to get a really good look at this little bugger.

Spider mites make finer webs than garden spiders. (You can see the mites with a hand lens.)

Learn to know, rather, its signs. Look for webs on the backs of leaves and in leaf axils—much smaller and more cobwebby than those made by a garden spider. (Yes, it is perfectly normal to have some garden spiders in your apartment, even desirable, because they will eat many small insects. But most of all, look for the graininess that comes into a leaf that is being sucked by red spider. The leaf loses its sheen and some of its green—looking very close up like a pointillist's impression of a leaf, with its spots of green and spots of gray. Once the leaves have lost their color, they will not come back—though they may not fall off. If you get rid of the spider mites and the plant is basically healthy, you can expect new foliage to grow.

Hold the infested plant under a stream of vigorously running tepid water. Most of them are knocked off. But you'll have to repeat the treatment every few days for a while.

If you have spider mite, it may well be that your general humidity level is too low—they thrive in low humidity—though once you have an infestation, raising the humidity level alone won't get rid of it.

Ivy is very susceptible to this, as are mini roses.

With a plant very far gone with red spider, we'll just throw it out, soil and all.

MITES

Other mites (and there are several varieties) are invisible to the naked eye, and all but the strongest hand lenses. If you think you may have them, take the plant or an infected leaf to a plant clinic or a plant pathologist and let someone examine it with a microscope designed for plant inspection.

Symptoms of mite infestation vary from plant to plant. With cyclamen mite, an infested cyclamen plant's leaves have the strange look of rubber or plastic that has melted and solidified again in a coarse, grainy condition. With other plants, the new growth may come in twisted, or leaves may fall off for no apparent reason, or buds may blast in good humidity. (There are many reasons for leaves falling and buds blasting, and we'll discuss them in the next chapter.)

Swish the plant through the soapy water several times, rinsing it in clear water a few times. If you cannot control this insect with water, you'll have to use something more potent, which we'll discuss soon.

African violets are susceptible to mites; we've never had them on ours, but the best violeteer we know says he throws out his mite-infested plants, because they spread too easily.

WHITE FLY

This is a real problem in the apartment, in the greenhouse, in the garden, and in the fields. This insect looks like a tiny white moth rather than a fly and it flies away from a plant in clouds when disturbed. It has a life cycle of 5 days. That's right, 5 days from laid egg to egg-laying adult. Which means two things. First, it mutates so rapidly that it often becomes resistant to once-effective insecticides. And, second, if you want to kill it, you've got to attack it every 3 days for a couple of weeks. Which is a pain. If you're washing off your plants, there aren't many plants that can take a washing every 3 days for weeks: the leaves get too bruised, especially as this insect attacks mostly soft-leafed plants.

At any rate, do wash the plant well in soapy water, and rub gently at the backs of the leaves, to kill as many eggs and nonflying young as possible. If you wash the plants in your bathroom, the adults that aren't drowned will be attracted to your mirror, where they can be killed.

One way to keep white fly at a minimum is to avoid the plants they especially like, such as lantana and fuchsia (most attractive to this insect) and basil and tomatoes. (Ouch!)

MEALY BUG

You see those cottony masses in the leaf axils? No, Virginia, that is not the way the plant grows, that is mealy bug, which is a difficult insect to get rid of completely. It can be especially troublesome on cacti because some cacti naturally have structures which look like "cottony masses."

Washing won't eliminate mealy bug because the cottony stuff keeps water off. With this pest we go another route.

Take a cotton swab (Q-tip) and dip it into rubbing alcohol, then touch the mealy bug wherever you can see it. (By the way, those stationary white things are adults and egg masses. The young nymphs are pinkish, tiny, and quite active. Get them, too.) Then rinse the plant off in clear water.

This is a process you'll have to repeat on a regular basis, because there is no way alcohol can get all the mealy bug young, but if you keep it up you'll hold the pest under control and never have to spray with an insecticide.

FUNGUS GNATS

See those tiny black flies circling around your plants and walking over the soil? They are not fruit flies (which are usually lighter in color) but fungus gnats. These are more a cosmetic problem than a threat to your plant. It is just not beautiful to have these black flies swarming around (and sometimes getting in your food).

Here's their life cycle: the flying adults lay eggs in the soil which hatch into maggots (very thin transparent worms from ⅛ to ½" long). These maggots eventually develop into the flies. The flies do nothing directly, but the maggots feed off decomposing matter in your soil—which means that if there is a root problem, they might start eating your roots.

To get rid of them, leave your plant soaking overnight in clear water just over the soil-line. This will drown the maggots, which will reduce the size of the next generation. When the adults lay more eggs, soak again, a couple of weeks later.

NEMATODES

There is more written and less known about nematodes than any other insect. They are also called wireworms, but the harmful ones are not visible to the naked eye. They cause new growth to come in gnarled, and buds and roots to be distorted also. We have been told by an excellent amateur grower (a botanist) and a trustworthy commercial grower both, that if you soak a plant for 2 hours in a solution containing 1 teaspoon of chlorine bleach to 1 quart of water, you will get rid of them without harm to the plant.

But the only way to know for sure if you have nematodes is to send your soil to a county agent or some such place to be tested.

ROOT (or SOIL) MEALY BUG

This is a different species of mealy bug visible only at the roots of the plant. Take a cutting for propagation and throw the plant out immediately.

SPRINGTAILS

These are not real insects but "proto-insects," or pre-insects. They come to the surface and jump around when you water. They don't eat adult plant roots, but they *may* be harmful to the roots of seedlings. They are, again, more of an appearance problem than a pest.

Soak overnight as with FUNGUS GNATS.

SLUGS

Slugs are snails without shells, and while a minor problem in apartments, they *will* bite chunks out of your leaves. Aside from the holes in your leaves, look for their slimy trails.

For a homey cure, sink jar tops into the soil, level with the soil, and fill the tops with *beer*. That should do it.

If you are a teetotaler, try sneaking up on them. Leave your plants in the dark until near midnight, then turn on the lights and you'll find them on the plants.

Look, you always miss some. But persevere and you will beat the bugs by hand.

WHERE DO THE BUGS COME FROM, DADDY?

People call us with their pest problems and demand how such or such a bug could have come into their apartment on the twentieth floor. Well, they may have brought the bug in on some other plant, or in some bit of soil, or the person in the apartment above had the bug and it was washed down in a heavy watering. Or they visited a friend and touched a buggy plant. We went walking through Central Park one day and came home with aphids in our hair—a very outré happening, you must admit. (As far as we know, people and plants have no bugs in common—so don't worry.)

You see those clever little ants marching around your windowsill? *They* may be the source of infection for aphids and scale. The little monsters farm aphids and scale, collecting juices from them as a farmer milks cows. Ants will plant these insect pests where they don't exist and carry them from plant to plant. So, you see those ants? Kill, Igor, kill!

WHAT MORE CAN YOU DO?

Against some of these problems, there's not much you can do. Don't handle other people's buggy plants. And keep your plants healthy: bugs will attack weak plants first.

ISOLATION

But above all, when you bring a new plant into your apartment, don't thrust it immediately into your garden. Even plants from friends can be buggy. And plants from florists or greenhouses *will very likely* be buggy. Put the plant in isolation. If you have no space in which to set it apart, wrap it up in a plastic bag. Better that than to give your plants a new bug to deal with.

SPRAYS

Chemical sprays are poisons, to one degree or another, and should be handled carefully. A spray that will kill a bug, can bother you—not *will* but *can*. Individuals vary in their sensitivity to various sprays.

We have a friend, a professional estate gardener, who told us of his experience using a "bomb" (insecticide under pressure) to get rid of aphids.

He was wearing protective mask and clothing and was spraying the plants in the greenhouse when he noticed the pressure had fallen way down and he felt a coldness in the lower part of his body. He looked down and saw that the hose was disconnected and spraying *him*. He threw everything on the greenhouse floor and ran to an outside trough, shedding his protective clothing as he went. He washed himself off and showered and washed again at home.

"What happened?"

"Nothing much," he answered.

"Nothing?"

"Well, I had double vision for a while, and shortness of breath for a couple of weeks, and weakness in my legs and pains in my joints, and headaches—nothing much. And you know, when I went back into the greenhouse next day, those damn bloody aphids were still *jumping!*"

That was the part that bothered him most.

Headaches, double vision, etc. . . .

Be careful with sprays. Use them only as directed and in a ventilated room. Avoid breathing them, and if you can use a respirator while spraying, do.

We use very few sprays in our home.

By law, some insecticides must be marked "POISON," and those we don't even think about.

Some are marked "WARNING," and those we don't use.
Some are marked "CAUTION," and these we *might* use.

Ced-o Flora

Ced-o Flora is a commercial spray made from petroleum distillates, cedar and hemlock oils, and soap; it is very good against scale insects and mealy bugs that can't be controlled by hand picking and washing. It is also supposed to be good for aphids and spider mites, but we've always found washing adequate to control those.

This insecticide comes in a liquid to be diluted, 3 teaspoons to a pint of water.

Malathion

Malathion is a more widely available chemical brew which is effective against the same stuff (scale, mealy bug, aphids) but we've found it usually doesn't do much against mites, though the label says it should. It is also a rather good household spray for roaches in a more concentrated dilution. Instructions are on the label. Also on the label are the various warnings, and you'd better follow them.

This insecticide will also work as a drench for fungus gnats and springtails in the soil. Prepare it according to directions for a spray, but pour it through the soil or sit the pot in a bowl of the mixture. We much prefer, if we're using malathion, to use it as a drench or as a dip—there are fewer fumes to cope with. (The smell of this stuff is fierce, and some people are really bothered by it.) To use as a dip, prepare as for a spray and just dip the whole top of the plant into it.

To fight white fly, use malathion as a spray or dip every 3 days—and good luck.

There are a whole group of plants that will be defoliated by this insecticide, so read that part of the label, too.

All things considered, wouldn't you really rather use soapy water?

Kelthane

We have always controlled mites by washing, or by discarding the far-gone cases. However, if washing hasn't worked and you are reluctant to throw out the plant, you may want to try two spaced sprayings of this miticide, a week apart.

It comes in an emulsion and a wettable powder; choose the emulsion—it's easier to handle.

Prepared Aerosol Sprays

More plants are probably killed by aerosol sprays than are cured by them. The propellant in the can will seriously harm the plant if it isn't held quite a distance away—and at that distance you are spraying a good bit of the rest of the world, too. (A question under investigation today is whether the breathing of all propellants doesn't constitute a health hazard for people.)

Also, many prepared sprays make claims that are only marginally true—promising to cure everything but bubonic plague when the active ingredients are actually present in very small amounts.

When you must spray an insecticide, mix your own. Keep a separate plastic sprayer for the purpose, and mix no more than you need for the current spraying, throwing out the excess and washing out the sprayer.

Keep all plant poisons away from pets and children, and from civilians who don't know how to use them.

Before you start, real *all* the label, not just the highlights.

Ventilate. Spraying in a closed room is a good way to get sick.

Avoid breathing the spray and wash it off your skin.

And, most of all, don't spray unless you're certain you have a serious problem, a problem not controllable by gentler means. For a while, we were getting call after call from people who were spraying prophylactically, and wondering why their plants were showing signs of leaf burn. From the sprays, of course.

No-Pest Strips

One sees these advertised a great deal. They are supposed to hang while they release Vapona into the air. Don't, please, don't use them. They can be harmful to your plants and, more important, harmful to you and your family.

Systemic Poisons

Categorically, don't use systemics (such as Isotox or Metasystox-R) in the home or garden.

A systemic poison is one which, after being poured on the soil or sprayed onto the plant, stays within the tissues of the plant. So, when the bug bites a leaf, or sucks a bit of sap, it dies. Good, no? God, no! Not in your apartment it's not. Because when you handle that plant, or your dog or child chews on a leaf, you or they are handling or eating some of the poison. The same is true of your outdoor vegetable garden. Those vegetables will contain the poison.

Think on that.

14. Pests and Problems— Diseases and Environment

Most of what apartment and home growers take to be diseases aren't actual diseases at all, but environmental problems.

A rubber tree which has stood in a window all winter, suddenly, in the spring, shows browning on the leaves. Well, that's probably not a disease but sunburn. The sun's angle changes with the lengthening days, and a window that had little or no direct sun in winter may have quite a bit in spring or summer.

Spots appear on the leaves of an African violet. Is it fungus? Examination and questioning reveals that the owner has been watering with cold water and the spots are waterspots.

Holes appear in the leaves of a classroom avocado overnight without any sign of an insect pest. The teacher discovers a student nervously tapping a pencil against a leaf.

A fiddle-leaf fig shows holes the size of a dime. Some caterpillar? No, a dog. The pet's tail and the growing-leaf buds were on the same level. The wagging tail brushed against the leaf buds and tiny injuries made tiny holes which grew as the leaf grew.

Young and old leaves on an episcia are browning. Some fungus? No, heat. The plant is in a closed casement window, and the heat that builds up inside those windows is fierce, going well over 100% during the warm months.

Growth is weak and yellowish on an asparagus fern. Nematodes, the owner suggests. Lack of plant food turns out to be the answer.

Rot at the soil-line with a cactus? Overwatering in soil that isn't well-enough drained.

A *Dracaena marginata* whose leaves are droopy all the time? Not some exotic disease, but watering too seldom and too little.

A gardenia which dropped many leaves on one side of the plant. Red spider? Gardenias are prone to that pest, but a cold draft was the villain in this case.

Large brown areas showing up on a dieffenbachia leaf? Not sunburn this time, but fertilizer burn.

YOUR ENVIRONMENT

The list could go on and on. As consultants, we've answered literally hundreds of questions of just this sort, and sometimes it's not easy to sort them out. Certainly you, the grower, have to know the environment the plant requires before you can even begin to know whether it's a disease or an environmental problem—but there are things you can look for.

If your plants are showing brown edges or brown tips to their leaves, it may well be that either your humidity is too low, or the plant needs repotting. See "ROOT DAMAGE," page 162.

If you are feeding your plants at the strength recommended on the plant-food label, you are probably feeding too much.

If you find a lot of spotting on your leaves, your watering may be careless. Switch your watering routine and water from the bottom for a while. (But, if the spots show themselves as rings, or spread, consider that you may have a fungous disease.) It is possible, too, from careless watering, to promote fungous diseases on your leaves.

If growth is thin and spindly, consider whether the plant is getting enough sun. Or, it may be that your plant food is providing too much of a particular nutrient for the particular plant. Or, your temperature may be too high. Weak growth is sometimes a matter of heat, especially under fluorescent lights, and it is often a matter of light, especially on not-very-bright windowsills.

If you get lush vegetative growth but no, or few, flowers on a plant that is supposed to flower freely, you're probably feeding the plant too much nitrogen.

If your plant is dropping leaves, first of all check for bugs, then for sudden changes in the environment. If you find neither, knock the plant out of the pot and check for root damage (see "ROOT DAMAGE," page 162).

If your gloxinia leaves curl, it may be heat, it may be lack of humidity, but then it may be a virus—in which case you can throw that plant out.

If your African violet leaves reach upward for the light, move the plant closer to the light.

If your ferns make weaker and weaker growth, with the old growth dying off faster than the new comes in, consider the possibility that your environment just isn't suited to ferns. There are thousands of exotic plants sold daily around this country that will not survive because a proper environment cannot be maintained for them in houses and apartments.

If that bromeliad you bought in spike has finished flowering and now is beginning to die, don't rush to the doctor— bromeliads usually do die after flowering, though some may take a couple of years to pop off. (See Chapter 23.)

If you're growing green peppers on your windowsill and the growth is poor and the leaves yellowish and spotted, the chances are that you do not have a fungus; if your achimenes are in a good bright window but refuse to flower no matter what you do, it's probably not your feeding or your watering. For both it's probably air pollution. Many plants are pollution-sensitive and just won't do well in dirty city air.

The painters came in and you moved your beautiful healthy monstera from a bright north window to about the same light in an obstructed east window—and it's going downhill. No disease; the plant just resents being moved.

Or, that beaucarnea, whose tops were browning when you had it alone in the living room, thrives when you put it among those cane begonias. No miracle; it's just happy to have that extra bit of humidity.

So you've bought this plant, and you've had it for a week, right? And the buds and leaves are dropping and the thing looks a sorry mess. Is it some rare tropical disease? No, it's *trauma!* See Chapter 3, BUYING LARGE PLANTS, for what trauma is and what you can do.

WHAT TO DO

To solve environmental problems, you must first know a plant's environmental needs. Then, you can buy plants more suited to your environment; or you can upgrade your environment in terms of lights, fresh air, temperature, and humidity; or you can create your own micro-environment inside a terrarium.

But then we've also found that a plant, put into a completely wrong environment and treated in the completely wrong manner *may* survive. Some small fraction do. If you've "trained" a plant to, say, get along on only half as much water as it should have and then you read this book and say, "My God, I'm supposed to be watering that twice as much!" and then start watering like crazy, you are very likely to kill that plant with kindness.

What does it mean?

If you have a plant that's doing well with the kind of care you've been giving it, don't change. If the plant is not doing well, then by all means, do change. If you bring a new plant into the house, treat it as we suggest, but don't change successful care on anyone's say-so. If it works, do it. That's how we learned.

FERTILIZER SALTS

Here's an environmental problem that every grower faces whether they fertilize heavily or not, because there are fertilizer salts right in the soil. Though, it is more of a problem with plants that are heavily fed.

Salts build up a little with every watering, washing out of the soil and depositing on its surface and on the pot. A heavy build-up at the neckline of the plant (the place where the stem meets the soil) can be a killer because the salts will eat right through the stem of a plant.

On the pot, the salts will damage any leaf that rests on the rim of the pot: African violet leaves are quite prone to be killed this way.

To get rid of heavily concentrated deposits, scrape what you can off the soil surface, and then flush the pot out with several waterings of clear water. If your mix is light, you will not be overwatering, just housecleaning. On the pot, scrape what you can off the rim.

If you're using plastic pots, the likelihood of lost leaves is reduced. If you're using clay, you might try this: before potting a violet or gloxinia into a clay pot, melt some candle wax, and, with a thin paintbrush, brush some wax around the rim. The wax will keep the salts out of contact with the leaves.

BUD DROP

Gardenia buds drop, gloxinia buds blast: it's the same thing, really. The plant is resenting its environment. Most often, bud blast and drop can be traced to insufficient watering or insufficient humidity—though drastic temperature changes can cause it, too.

Plants bought in bud from the florist will *most often* blast or drop. They may then go on and give you new buds next flowering, but those greenhouse buds will often just not open for you, unless you can simulate greenhouse conditions.

Your own plants, in bud, must be treated with the consideration a swelling bud deserves, and be watered well (except for cacti and bromels which can fend for themselves), and kept in good humidity. Even some plants which might ordinarily not resent going dry, like geraniums, will blast if allowed to go dry while in bud.

ROOT DAMAGE

Root rot can sometimes be caused by a fungous disease, but mostly it's an environmental problem: underwatering kills the small roots and then overwatering rots them; or too heavy a soil holds water around the roots constantly, and rots them; or careless repotting damages roots, which rots them. It all comes down to the same thing.

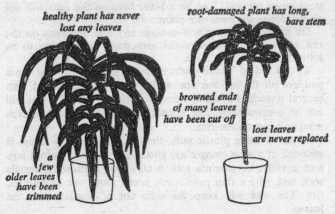

healthy plant has never lost any leaves

root-damaged plant has long, bare stem

browned ends of many leaves have been cut off

lost leaves are never replaced

a few older leaves have been trimmed

First of all, keep any plant suspected of root damage a little on the dry side.

Turn the plant out of its pot, and sniff for rotten roots. Then, look at the visible roots: are they plump and healthy-looking, or are they blackish and shriveled? If the roots look unhealthy, cut away everything that looks rotten or damaged, right back to the good tissue. Then, dust the living ends with mineral sulfur or with a fungicide, such as *zineb* or *captan*. (We don't use fungicides; if *you* must, follow all the cautions, and we suggest you use a respirator.)

Repot the plant into a *smaller,* clean, pot and new soil; prune the top-growth back as much as you pruned the roots; water sparingly for a while; and lots of luck.

DISEASES

In nature (even in outdoor gardens, sometimes) there is a balance which keeps many insect infestations and diseases in check. In the "unnatural" environment of an apartment, these checks rarely exist, and a disease or infestation can run a terribly quick course. An indoor gardener must be prepared to throw out plants that cannot be cured by home means.

CHLOROSIS

This is a deficiency disease and, as such, noncontagious; it is caused by a lack of available iron or other minerals in the plant's food or soil. The operative word here is "available." It's no use burying an iron nail in the soil: the plant can't absorb iron in that form.

There are special acid-rich or iron-rich foods which provide the iron in "chelated" form—a form in which the plant can absorb it—or you can buy chelated iron itself. We prefer a food with iron chelates in it. The straight stuff can be quite dangerous for the plant—a little going a very long way. Unless you plan to have a garden that specializes in plants like gardenias, camellias, and citrus plants, you won't ever use up a box of chelated iron. But it may not be an iron deficiency. Feeding with an acid food permits the plant's roots to absorb many trace elements it may be having trouble absorbing.

For commercial names, look for Green Gard, Spoonit, or Miracid.

Chlorosis is readily identified. The disease shows itself by a paling of the leaves, with the veins standing out darker than the rest of the leaves.

If your plants show signs of chlorosis, check your soil's acidity level—that is, its pH—with a *good* test kit or by sending soil to your county agent for testing. An alkaline soil will lead to mineral deficiencies.

BOTRYTIS

This fungous disease (promoted by poor air circulation and overcrowding) can be a real problem to the home African violet grower. It appears as a grayish mold, usually on the upper leaves. It is extremely contagious, spread by insects as well as by your touching plants. There is no sure control. Your best bet is to throw out the plant and isolate its neighbors. If you wish to try and keep it, remove all the visibly affected leaves and destroy them. Isolate the plant and do not water from the top at all. Don't spray the leaves and do try to improve the air circulation.

LEAF SPOT

Get this one diagnosed in a clinic before you attack it yourself. It appears as dark soggy spots, which may fall away, leaving holes. It's a bacterial disease, but controllable by frequent dippings in *zineb* (1 tablespoon of the wettable powder to a gallon of water). Be sure you heed the warnings on the label.

MILDEWS

This shouldn't be much of a problem in most apartments, but you may find it in a high-humidity special situation. We have often controlled mildew by cutting the affected parts away with a scissors and then increasing air circulation. If that won't help, we understand the fungicide *karathane* as a dip or spray (2 teaspoons to a gallon of water) works well. Remember to read the label cautions.

OTHER FUNGOUS DISEASES

Most fungous diseases can be *controlled* by good sanitation: remove all deadheads and dead or dying foliage; don't reuse soil; make sure your tools are cleaned from use to use (especially if you suspect fungous diseases). You may also want to reduce your insect population, even though the bugs themselves don't constitute a major problem. If they are present, they are the heavies spreading the fungi around.

It is very difficult to *cure* fungous diseases, and that's a sad fact. You can prevent them by good sanitation, and these fungicides will often keep them from spreading, but won't really cure.

Good sanitation (see GROOMING AND PRUNING, Chapter 9), good air circulation, and some care in watering are your best guards against fungous diseases.

If you do decide to spray with a fungicide, please follow all the precautions we gave you in the previous chapter, and wear a protective respirator. Remember, poisons are your *last* line of defense, not your first.

PART III

—◆—

PROPAGATION

15. Propagation Boxes

Propagation boxes work. We had 50 students in our house-plant propagation course, and 51 successful prop boxes (*ours* was successful, too).

A propagation box is a true friend—where else will you find someone willing to give you so many plants over so long a time for so small an investment?

A propagation box is a transparent container, usually closed, with some sterile medium in it. Into the sterile medium you put cuttings which usually root and which may subsequently become beautiful plants.

This closed box becomes a miniature greenhouse, with 100% relative humidity—very favorable for most vegetative propagation (that is, cuttings from leaves, stems, and rhizomes).

PLASTIC

One of our favorite kinds of prop boxes is a cheap, clear-plastic shoe box, available in the five-and-dime for about 50¢. The cover fits securely and it measures not quite 12"x7"x4". This 4" depth is about the shallowest you can use for cuttings from large plants.

Then, there are wide clear-plastic refrigerator boxes, about 12"x11"x4". They are marvelous for the number of cuttings they'll hold.

And the clear-topped plastic bread boxes, 12"x5"x5", are great for those extra-height cuttings and for fitting onto narrow light shelves.

You might get the idea from reading this that we are kinky for plastic. Well, we lead the least "plastic" lives of anyone we know, but for the apartment gardener, plastic boxes and bags make so many things possible cheaply—which were im-

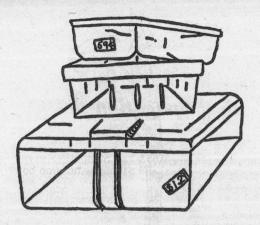

As long as it's transparent it can be a propagation box.

possible before, or possible only with considerable expense—like these inexpensive "greenhouses."

MEDIA

There is a lot of talk among growers about the best medium for cuttings: sterile sand, straight perlite, straight peat moss, straight vermiculite, home-mixed combinations of two or three, even commercially prepared mixtures.

You can have success with any or all of them—certainly, no grower would continue with a medium with which he failed. The important requisites for any rooting medium are that it provides some resistance for the roots and that it holds moisture.

WATERNIKS AND SOILNIKS

Rooting in water, certainly the simplest and most available and commonest rooting medium, is seldom used by anyone who knows better, because the roots that grow in water are *adapted to water* and not to soil. These cuttings, when they are taken out of the water and potted into soil, must then grow land roots. Very often, the rooted cuttings just don't make the adjustment, and they die, or grow weakly. At the very least, you get severe setbacks.

Some cuttings rooted in water are never potted up. This syngonium has been in the vase for 2 years.

Now, we can hear those mutters rising—"But I always root my cuttings in water, and 110% are successful." (Don't you just love people who *never* fail?) For those of you lucky enough to be able to grow marvelous plants from cuttings started in water, we can only say, more power to you.

And to those of you who just stick the cutting into the ground and watch it grow, let us say that we just stick a cutting into the ground—and it rots. There are many fungi in the soil, just waiting to grab hold of your cuttings.

STERILITY

The special mediums mentioned above are all fairly sterile when you get them.

Sterility is impossible to maintain completely, outside of a laboratory. As soon as any medium is exposed to air, it is exposed to the spores of fungi and mold and wilt and all the other air-borne problems lurking everywhere. But these sterile mediums do not provide as welcoming an environment for the problems as soil does.

VERMICULITE

For our money, the best of the rooting mediums is vermiculite. It holds moisture, but not too much, and it's easy to handle, being less dusty than perlite (though the dust of either is an irritant).

We also find vermiculite aesthetically more desirable—it's brownish and less prone to show algae. (However, if we're out of vermiculite, we don't hesitate to make a prop box with perlite.)

One drawback to vermiculite is that it will go squishy if handled much. But you don't want to handle it, anyhow; the more you handle it the less sterile it becomes, and the more your chance of failure.

For descriptions and cost of media, see SOIL AND SOIL MIXES, Chapter 7.

RE-USE?

Don't use your medium more than once for propagation—again, you reduce your chances for success. But you can include this used propagation medium in your next batch of soil mix.

BUILDING THE BOX

Let's make a prop box.

Buy a clear-plastic box and wash it. If it's not new, wash it in 9 parts hot water to 1 part chlorine bleach.

Pour in about 1½" of dry, new vermiculite. With a small pitcher or cup, water over all the surface quite well—until all the vermiculite looks well dampened. Tilt the box, causing the water to run partway up the sides—all the sides (you're doing this to wet the vermiculite you missed). Then tilt the box so that the water gathers in one corner. (If there is no excess water, add some—you haven't used enough to begin with.) Using the lid to hold in the medium, gently and carefully pour off the water. The wet surface of the medium has a good deal of cohesion at this point and you can tilt the box much farther than you'd think—but do not dump the whole thing in your sink. When all the unabsorbed water is poured off, your box is ready to use. You needn't punch holes in it or anything like that: this level of watering will maintain a good water balance for weeks.

Stick your cuttings into the medium so that they stand upright, not quite touching the bottom, close your box, and set it under fluorescent light or in a bright but not sunny window.

In the spring, some speed-demon cuttings will begin to show signs of roots within 3 days—but most will take much longer. You can check for rooting by pulling a cutting from the vermiculite, without worrying that you'll damage any young roots—the vermiculite is that light.

Once you've examined the cutting for roots, you can then gently reinsert it into the medium, it if isn't ready to pot up.

Try to keep your hands out of the vermiculite.

AN OPEN BOX

An open box (one without a cover) is for cuttings that tend to rot in the 100% humidity of the closed boxes—such as succulents, geraniums, some cane-type begonias, and some begonia rhizome cuttings.

The open box we use is a large enamel refrigerator tray, about 22"x18"x6" which holds many cuttings. As of this writing it has: 3 kinds of succulents, 6 kinds of begonias, 3 kinds of wandering Jew, peperomia, *Philodendron rubrum*, 2 kinds of geraniums, 2 cryptanthus pups, and many small bits of plants too varied to be identified from the typewriter, about 50 cuttings in all—and it's still not full.

We put this box together in the same way as the closed box, except that we were less concerned with getting all the excess water poured off: since the box is open, the water evaporates relatively quickly, thereby adding to the general humidity of the room. This means that we have to water it every couple of days, as if it were a single plant—not allowing it to go dry even for one day. If most rootless or barely rooted cuttings are allowed to go dry even for one day they will succumb—though you can cut off a bit from the end of the stem, soak the cutting in water overnight, and sometimes get enough recovery to try them again.

This open box has two very definite advantages: as we indicated before, it enables us to root cuttings that rot in high humidity; and the cuttings that do root are strong as the very devil because they are already adjusted to our room humidity.

HARDENING OFF

Cuttings made in a very-high-humidity propagation atmosphere require a period of "hardening off." That is, they must be slowly accustomed to the lower humidity of the world outside the prop box. A cutting rooted in 100% humidity, potted up, and set out on your windowsill without some protection will likely be dead in a few hours. We use a plastic bag as a temporary tent, keeping it closed for a day or so, then opening it a tiny bit for a day or so, and so on until the plant is hardened enough to come out.

MORTALITY

The major disadvantage of the open box is the high mortality rate. In the closed boxes about 80% of our cuttings survive to become plants—in the open box, it's closer to 60% survival. But, as we said, those are *strong*.

FLUORESCENT VS. NATURAL LIGHT

We root cuttings under both natural and fluorescent light.

Under natural light (good bright light without much or any direct sun), rooting depends on the season: it is faster while the days are lengthening and slower when they get short, in the fall.

Under fluorescent lights, there are no seasons, and everything roots more quickly. Part of the reason may be that we set our lights in banks, and a small amount of heat is generated: the light below heats the box above.

Whatever the reason, we must say that while you can root under natural light, we hope that you'll get at least one fluorescent fixture for propagation. Even a single-tube fixture will do for rooting.

PINCHING CUTTINGS

You might not think so, but the time to start pinching back (that is, either pinching or cutting out a bit at the growing tip of the cutting) is as soon as the plant starts showing signs of rooting—this makes for a much "thriftier" plant, with more branching and stockier growth.

HOW MUCH ROOTING?

Once it is out of the prop box, the plant depends entirely on its root system for nourishment. If the roots are too small, they will not be able to support the plant—both in terms of anchoring it and in terms of providing food.

Now, it is not necessary to wait for a fully developed root system before potting up your cuttings. For a small cutting, roots about 1″ long should be able to do the job; for larger cuttings, 1½″.

IF NOT A PROP BOX, WHAT?

Aside from the open and closed propagation boxes, there are other, more or less expensive means for propagating cuttings: peat pots, Jiffy-7's, and individual pots—to name three.

PEAT POTS

These are small pots made of peat moss pressed into the shape of a square or round pot. The grower fills it with medium—usually a prepared commercial rooting mix.

The mix and pot are kept wet all the time, of course, and when the cutting is rooted it is planted, pot and all.

We don't like them: it's been our experience that the roots *do* have some difficulty in piercing the pot. Also, we have sometimes found the pot to be a source of mold. But there *is* little transplant trauma.

Put your Jiffy-7 in water about 10 minutes before you need it. Seedbed cross-section.

JIFFY-7's

These round peat pellets are imported from Scandinavia. When put in water they expand to 7 times their dry height—hence the name. Wrapped in a plastic net, the expanding peat is kept from crumbling. They contain some extra nutrients, so a cutting can actually get a start in a Jiffy-7.

A hole is poked into the open top of the swelled Jiffy with a pencil, a cutting is inserted, and the excess water is squeezed out as you press the peat around the cutting.

In a greenhouse these are merely set somewhere to be watered and get light. In our apartment, we stand them in little plastic pots and put them 1, 2, or 3 to a plastic bag, blown up and sealed off with a wire Twist'em. The bag is then hung near the end of a fluorescent tube. Cuttings don't need your best fluorescent light.

The roots grow through the plastic netting very easily, and the whole device is planted when roots are seen coming through the side of the netting. Again, there is little transplant trauma—though the new plant must be hardened off.

Jiffy-7's can also be used without a plastic bag; just put them in small pots and stand in a plant tray. This works especially well for geraniums and some of the fussier upright begonias.

For us, these pellets are a very good idea. They are readily available (though in small amounts they are rather expensive—as much as 10¢ each), they work, they are easy to handle, and they are consistent. We buy them from a wholesaler for about $22 per thousand, or less than 2½¢ each. What we can't use, our favorite plant societies will sell at their supply tables.

INDIVIDUAL POTS

If you don't have a prop box (or what you have is full) but you do have some rooting medium and plastic flowerpots, you might want to try this method: screen the bottom of a 4″ plastic pot; fill the pot with vermiculite or perlite; wet it well and allow the excess water to drain off; take your 3 or 4 cuttings and stand them in the pot, pressing the medium very gently around each cutting to make it stand; put the whole thing into a plastic bag large enough to hold everything without touching the sides of the bag (that can lead to rot); blow up the bag; seal it off with a Twist'em; and stand it in the light. In no more time than with a prop box, you should have rooted cuttings.

16. Growing Plants from Seed

If you want the most plants and the greatest variety at the least cost, you grow them from seed.

We grow almost all of our seedlings by the following method.

THE METHOD

Take a 4″ plastic azalea pot, and fill it to the neck with your standard potting mix (no crock or screening is necessary).

Water.

Cover the damp soil with milled sphagnum moss (we'll describe this marvelous stuff in a bit), to a depth of only 1/8–3/16″, but well enough to cover the soil completely.

Mist the surface gently but *repeatedly* with water, until the moss is quite wet.

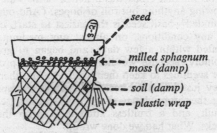

seed
milled sphagnum moss (damp)
soil (damp)
plastic wrap

Sprinkle your seed over the surface of the milled moss.

Again, mist gently.

Cover with a piece of clear plastic, rubber-banded into place.

Fill in a label with date and name and slip under the rubber band.

Put under fluorescent lights, 2″ or so from the tubes.

That's all there is to our "secret" method, and you're welcome to it. We have terrific success with it with herbs, vegetables, annuals, houseplants, exotics—everything you can imagine except for very large seeds or the very slowest seeds, which we do with Jiffy-7's or long-hair sphagnum moss.

Now, let's take the steps in more detail.

THE POT

We like to use azalea pots for seedbeds because they take less soil to fill than do standard pots. If you have only standard pots, of course you can use them, just as you can use pots both larger and smaller. But we would suggest you don't use a clay pot—they get fungi on them, while plastic doesn't.

Don't crock: you won't be watering enough for soil to wash out.

If you want to plant a *lot* of seed (hundreds and thousands), use a small propagation box instead of a pot, and put your medium in damp.

MILLED SPAGNUM MOSS

When we began using this stuff, it seemed almost magic to us.

You see, one of the main enemies of seed propagators is "damp-off" or "damping-off." This is caused by various fungi in the soil which attack only the very youngest seedlings.

One of our first crops was a flat of basil, which we started not knowing anything but full of hopes. (And our hopes were well founded—basil seed is the easiest to start, coming up in almost any conditions, on almost any medium.) The basil germinated within a few days, and began to grow (albeit a little spindly, because we didn't know about providing extra light for seedlings to keep them thrifty). And then, one morning, they just began to keel over, whole clumps at a time, bending their tops down to the soil—agony, self-recrimination, guilt, and a fruitless attempt to prop them up with toothpicks. What had we done wrong!

We hadn't done anything but plant the seeds in soil. It was "damp-off" attacking our babies—and there was nothing we knew to do. Finally, with only 1 or 2 left out of our hundred or so seedlings, we transplanted into another medium, and actually saved 1 plant. (Fortunately, we had planted only half our seed, and could have another go.)

This doesn't happen to us any more because we use milled sphagnum moss on the soil. Sphagnum moss (both milled and the long-hair) has a fungicidal action. While there are several mediums (perlite, vermiculite, etc.) that are not favorable to the damp-off fungi, only sphagnum has this natural antibiotic action.

The layer of moss protects the seedlings while they are most vulnerable; and by the time they put their roots down into the soil, they seem immune. Regardless of the whys of it (perhaps the moss extends its action to the soil beneath; perhaps it is the neckline of the plant that is most vulnerable), it works phenomenally well.

Milled sphagnum moss is very lightweight, so be careful when you spray or you'll send it flying all over the table.

SOIL

We use our standard soil mix underneath the moss (see Chapter 7).

There are no nutrients in the moss itself, and if seedlings are grown in moss alone, they must be fed with very dilute fertilizer (those roots are tender) as soon as the seed's own food is gone, or the seedlings must be transplanted almost immediately. Now, our life is such that we are never ready for transplanting on the same day that the seedlings are. So for us, the moss-on-soil method is more practical. We can leave the seedlings in place until we're ready to transplant, knowing that while they're waiting, those roots are living in soil, getting used to soil, where they will eventually go permanently.

Seedlings will stay alive in plain moss for months, though, getting more and more stunted as they stay without food or transplant.

SOWING THE SEED

We find this technique satisfactory for everything except large seeds. Crease a piece of paper about 3"x5". Pour your seed into the center of the crease. Hold the V over the soil and tap-tap-tap the paper, tilting it, until the seeds come rolling down onto the damp moss. Move the paper around so as to distribute the seed over the surface. This always gives us a nice even distribution of seed.

If you mist again when the seed is on the moss, do so *gently* so as not to blow the seed around.

MOSS AGAIN?

Do not cover fine seed with additional moss. Whatever your seeding medium, covering the seed can be a cause of low germination. Under the conditions we create with our seeding technique, hardly any houseplant seed needs covering—and certainly none should be covered more than to its own depth.

In addition to moisture, many houseplant seeds need light to trigger germination. So, with fine seed, skip that final layer of moss. Even with medium seed, consider it optional.

COVERING

We cover the pot with clear plastic to keep the moisture in, and we don't take that cover off until it's time to transplant.

If we see the *surface* of the seedbed getting the least bit dry, we set our pot in water to moisten it from the bottom. In this way neither seed nor seedling is disturbed by top watering.

LIGHTS

Seeds germinate quickly under fluorescent lights.

Seedlings grown within a couple of inches of a fluorescent tube grow compactly and sturdily. In natural light, they grow leggy in our windows or get burned by the sun—seedlings cannot take direct sun. (In nature, even cactus seedlings get shaded by the parent plant.)

WHAT ABOUT LARGE SEEDS?

Many houseplants have large seeds: philodendrons, monstera, nasturtiums, and our darling albizzia (powderpuff tree), for example.

For large seed, we use either long-haired sphagnum moss or Jiffy-7's.

To use the long-haired moss, wet a handful thoroughly and squeeze it out well, and stuff it into a 3″ plastic pot. Insert a few seeds down into the fibers of the moss; cover the pot with plastic, label it, and set under lights.

We swell the Jiffy-7 in water and make a hole in the top with a pencil. We put a large seed in the hole, press the peat over the seed, put the pellet into a plastic bag, and set under lights. Be careful not to let them dry out.

DIFFICULT SUBJECTS

We don't propagate everything from seed.

Ferns don't make seeds at all; they have a sexual cycle like something from a science fiction film.

Orchids set seed, but have no built-in food supply, as do all the other seeds we deal with, so they require special techniques approaching laboratory conditions.

Some seeds (like palms, camellias, anthuriums, and lilies) may take months to germinate, and that's not really practical for the hobbyist; though you can try if you're able to keep your medium moist for that length of time.

GERMINATION

Not all seeds come up. It's a sad fact of life. Only a percentage make it to become seedlings, even under the optimum conditions we try to create.

Recently, we planted the seeds from pods of two gesneriads: *Gesneria christii* and *Phinea multiflora*. Perhaps 5% of the gesneria seed came up, while it seemed that 200% of the phinea seed made it (an exaggeration, but we hope you get the point).

The proportion of seed that comes up is described as its "viability."

VIABILITY

What determines it? There may be genetic factors at work, but of the conditions we can control, let's say that viability is most often affected by age and keeping conditions.

If you're going to keep your seed a long time, you'll most often lose a high percentage of them. *Sinningia pusilla* seed is finer than grains of pepper, and after as little as *2 weeks* it starts to lose its viability.

Of course, most seed will hold better than that, but, if you are going to keep it for more than a few weeks, keep it in the fridge. That will lengthen its life.

Fresh seed come up more promptly than stale seed. But if you've sown a bed with stale seed, don't give up too quickly; you'll find seed coming up weeks and perhaps months after you've given up. That's one reason labels are so important.

HOW LONG?

Some seeds seem almost to spring back at you after you plant them. Mustard-greens seed are up in 2 days, basil in 4. Some seeds, as we said before, may take months.

Lots of houseplants are slow, taking a month or more to germinate; but many gesneriads come up after a week or so. Annuals tend to germinate fast, as do vegetables. Parsley is supposed to be slow, but if you leave the seeds soaking *overnight* in warm water before planting, they will come up within a week.

What's most important is that you don't allow your seed to dry out while waiting for them to come up.

TRANSPLANTING

We wait until the seedling shows "true" leaves before transplanting.

MONOCOTS AND DICOTS

Some seeds are monocotyledinous and some are dicotyledinous. Most houseplants are dicots: that is, there are *two* "seed" leaves which provide nutrition for the emerging plant. (Peanuts, peas, beans are examples of dicotyledinous seeds.) The monocots look like grass coming up: a single spear of green like a blade of grass. Corn and freesias, lilies, chives, and other true bulbs come up this way.

Sometimes you see a seedling sending up only one cotyledon. Streptocarpus grows that way: one cotyledon, then one true leaf. There *were* two of each, but only one developed—so you see only the one. But they are still dicots.

We wait for a pair of true leaves, or for a single true leaf on a plant like a strep, and then we transplant.

Once you watch your first batch of seedlings come up, the whole thing becomes quite clear.

THAT YOUNG? REALLY?

Yes, we really transplant babies that young. You don't do a seedling any good waiting for it to mature: quite the contrary. We transplant promptly because it's somehow the *youngest* seedlings that take the move with the least setback.

COMMUNITY POT OR THUMB POT?

You can pot the seedlings into a community pot (a 4″ azalea pot will hold, perhaps, a dozen seedlings) or you can pot them into very small individual pots. We like those 1-ounce plastic medicine cups, with holes burned into their bottoms with a hot icepick.

COMMUNITY POT

This is a way-station. Setting a dozen seedlings into one

pot saves room, work (community pots needn't be watered as often as individual pots), and medium. But the seedlings must be transplanted again when they begin to outgrow the community.

The second move can be into a larger community pot, or fewer seedlings into the same size pot, or into individual small pots. Wherever, you must provide some extra humidity for newly-potted seedlings, perhaps by setting the pot in a plastic bag.

THUMB POTS

Plants that go into thumb pots have so little medium at their roots that they are apt to dry out quickly, so we keep them in plastic shoe boxes, under lights. This gives them a humid atmosphere, and they require only occasional watering. Some of the miniatures we grow never move out of those tiny pots until they go into their final home. A vigorous basil seedling, though, will go directly into a 2″ pot.

Without the use of plastic or glass it would be murder to raise seedlings, because of their need for constant moisture without being drowned.

HOW TO TRANSPLANT

See below for a diagram of the tool we use to prick seedlings. (Though a knifepoint or the end of a plant label will serve.)

We dig into the soil and take a seedling out with a bit of

Press the penpoint against the gas ring; the metal will quickly soften enough to spread and bend up.

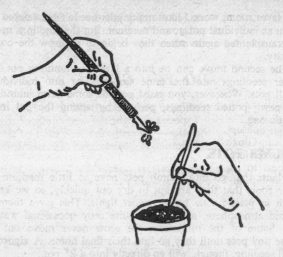

"Untouched by human hands."

soil around its roots. We don't touch the roots, we don't touch the stems, and we try not to touch the leaves. (Sometimes you can't help it—as when you dump a seedling into your lap—but then you lift only by a leaf.)

Dibble (poke) a hole into your medium, large enough to take the soil and roots you've dug up.

Drop the seedling's rootball into the hole, and gently firm the soil into place. That's all there is to it, aside from misting, providing for future humidity, watering gently, and giving a place under your fluorescent lights to keep the seedlings thrifty.

SELF-SEEDING IN A TERRARIUM

One of the dividends one can have with miniature gesneriads is that they may self-seed very easily. *Sinningia pusilla* and *S.* 'White Sprite' are almost sure to do so. If you are growing some in a terrarium, you may find, one day, a little carpet of green surrounding the parent plant—dozens of seedlings.

If you keep your terrarium moist, you can leave them there for a while, but we would suggest you prick some of the seedlings out to give the remaining ones a little more room. Treat them, then, like any miniature gesneriad seedlings: high humidity and good fluorescent light, going to live, finally, in a protected environment.

WHERE DO YOU GET SEED?

We'll list some seedsmen in the back of the book, but we wanted here to put in a special plug for the seed funds of the national houseplant societies—especially the seed fund of the American Gloxinia and Gesneriad Society, and the American Begonia Society.

Access to these seed funds is one of the advantages of membership, and if you're interested in growing these plants, you can't find a better source of interesting seed.

For example, the AGGS fund is constantly getting in seed for new hybrid miniatures.

Growing from seed is easy, but slow. You can get hundreds of plants for a little investment—perhaps pennies, but they are tiny plants and must grow up before you get anything in the way of flowers or the mature foliage.

But, coleus are lovely to look at a few weeks after planting; you can get your first basil snippings within a month after your seed goes in; you can get your first yellow tomato flowers 3 months after seeding; a miniature sinningia will go from germination to flowers in 2–3 months; and a gloxinia will take about 5 months from seed to flower. That's fast enough for us.

17. Vegetative Propagation

Vegetative propagation describes any multiplication without sex. People can't do it. Even artificial insemination requires sex. If vegetative propagation were possible among people, Van Gogh could have grown another Vincent by planting that ear.

Although as one of our students said in our houseplat propagation course, we know more ways to do it than th Kama Sutra, we don't have that kind of space here, so we'l including only those methods we have found *widely* successfu for us, our friends, and our students.

Not all plants propagate the same way, vegetatively. Yo cannot cut off a bromeliad leaf and expect to get a new plant. You can *root* a coleus leaf, but you won't get a new plant from it. When you root an African violet leaf, you ge perhaps 5 new plants from the one leaf.

In the same vein, there is often more than one way to prop agate the same plant: spider plants (chlorophytum) wil propagate by division, but they also propagate by means o runners or stolons (the little spiders they make on their flow ering stems, which give them their name).

DIVISION

Division is a means of propagating plants that grow in clumps, such as cymbidium orchids, semperflorens begonias, spathiphyllum, chlorophytum (spider plant), anthurium, some ferns, maranta (prayer plant), calathea, and the like.

Plants that can be divided grow with several stems coming out of the soil.

Florists or greenhousemen sometimes pot up several plants into a single container, to give a bushier appearance. This kind of planting can be divided in the same way we describe below.

Say you have a plant that has really spread, a maranta, in a large pot, with quite a few stems. You don't want to separate out each stem, though a nurseryman might. You want to wind up with 2 or 3 plants, with enough room around the roots of each for growth, and with enough stems in each to make a reasonably attractive plant.

HERE'S HOW

First, spread a few layers of newspaper or a tarp on a working surface.

Prepare the number of pots that you're likely to need—in this case 3—all crocked, and with potting soil standing by.

Turn the plant out of its pot, as we described in Chapter 11, and look at the root mass. Loosen it a bit and let some of

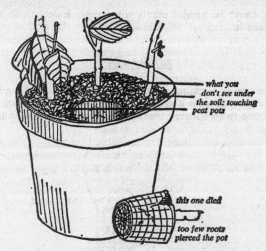

what you
don't see under
the soil: touching
peat pots

this one died

too few roots
pierced the pot

How a "bushy plant" is made by a commercial grower. Four rooted poinsettia cuttings in a 6" pot.

the soil fall away. You want to be able to see some of what you're doing, but you don't want to traumatize the plant by bare-rooting it.

Visualizing the plant in 3 parts, put your hands in the soil between two clumps of stems and tug apart. If the clumps come apart easily, with roots on both, fine. If not, work at them, remove a bit more soil, perhaps, and tug a little harder. Don't break any stems—that is not the idea.

When a clump comes away (it will have *less* than a third of the roots with it), lay it on the paper and divide the remaining rootball and stems in half. Work in exactly the same way.

Pot each clump into an appropriate size pot as described in Chapter 11, firm the clumps into place, water, label, and keep in modest light for a day or two. It's quicker to do than describe.

Most plants take division quite well, any trauma depending on how roughly you've handled the roots. If a plant shows trauma, give it a few mistings and speak soothingly to it (or yourself).

Some plants don't divide so easily: the underground stems by which they spread may be quite tough. Separating out cymbidium orchids, for example, may require a sharp, *sterile*

knife. Don't be afraid; plants with tough underground stem
can take it.

STOLONS

A stolon is a runner. Spider plants, episcias, and saxifrag
(strawberry begonia) are the most common houseplants t
propagate from stolons, a simpler and safer method than d
vision.

*This episcia stolon is well rooted and ready to pot up. It has its
own stolon which has also formed roots in the propagation box*

A stolon forms at the end of a stem, at some distance
from the parent plant. With episcias, the stems are rather
short and fleshy like the parent plant. With saxifrage, the
stems hang down like threads. With chlorophytum, the stems
are hard and stiff, bending only because of the weight of the
plantlets at their tips.

The surest way to get these saxifrage and episcia stolons
rooted and independent is to take a small pot of soil (kept
moist) and rest the bottom of the plantlet on it, while still attached to the mother plant, using a hairpin to hold it in
place. The plantlet will make roots which will grow into this

little pot, and then the stolon can be cut off near the new plant. (Cut the bare stem off near the mother.)

With spider plants it is even simpler. As the plantlets mature, they grow roots of their own, even in midair. When you can see that the roots are well developed, just cut the stolons off and pot them up on the spot. They almost always take.

With the saxifrage and/or episcia, however, if you don't find it convenient to leave little pots of soil all over the place (we never remember to water them), you might want to cut the stolons off near the plantlet, and root them in a closed propagation box. (See PROPAGATION BOXES, Chapter 15.)

Episcias will root readily in a closed prop box, from all but the tiniest plantlets, to pot out after a couple of weeks (or less). You don't want to keep them in the box any longer than necessary because they tend to make aerial roots all along their stems. These roots take water from the damp air of the box, and look rather unsightly. They will die quickly when the plant comes into a more normal environment, but why give the plant this additional problem?

Episcias are high-humidity plants, happiest at a relative humidity near 60%. When they come out of your prop box, unless you are putting them immediately into a protected environment, put the potted-up plantlets into a plastic bag for a few days, gradually opening the bag more and more to accustom them to the reality of your apartment.

Saxifrage plantlets will be ready to pot out in a few weeks, and will require little hardening off.

Both the episcia and the saxifrage will be happy in our all-purpose soil mix (see Chapter 7), and the chlorophytum will be happy in almost anything.

CUTTINGS (TIP AND STEM)

Aside from cacti and succulents, which we'll deal with later, what will propagate from a tip cutting or stem cutting? Many many houseplants.

achimenes	aphelandra
aeschynanthus	aralia
allophytum	azalea
alloplectus	basil (ocimum)
aloe	begonias
alternanthera	canes

upright
hairy-leaved
semps
hiemalis
tuberous
beloperone (shrimp plant)
camellia
capsicum (peppers)
chrysanthemums
cissus
citrus
clerodendron
codiaeum (croton)
coleus
columnea
cordyline
crassula
crossandra
diastema
dieffenbachia
dizygotheca
dracaena
euonymus
euphorbia
fatshedera
fatsia
ficus
fittonia
fuchsia
gardenia
gesneria
gloxinia
gynura
hoffmania
hoya
hedera (ivy)
helxine
hibiscus
hypoestes
impatiens
iresine
ixora
jacobinia
kalanchoe
koellekeria

kohleria
lampranthus (ice plant)
lavendula
malphigia
mentha (mint)
monstera
nautilocalyx
nematanthus
nephthytis
orchid
   epidendrum
   dendrobium
passiflora
pelargonium (geraniums)
pellionia
peperomia
philodendron
pilea
pittosporum
plectranthus (Swedish ivy)
podocarpus
polyscias
portulaca
rechsteineria
rhoeo
rosemary
saintpaulia (African violets)
salvia
schefflera
scindapsus
sedum
senecio
setcreasea
siderasis
sinningia
smithiantha
streptocarpus
   saxorum
   holstii
syngonium
thyme
tolmiea
tradescantia
vinca
zebrina

And that's really only a partial list.

Perhaps it would be well to name a few families that *won't* propagate from tip or stem cuttings: orchids (except for cane types), bromeliads, ferns, true bulbs (though many tuberous plants will), and palms.

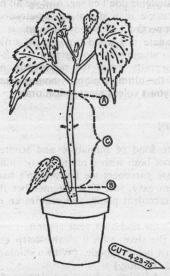

Cutting a cane-type begonia. (A) Cut is made just below a node; root the top. (B) Second cut is made just above a node; new growth will develop. (C) Discard the middle piece.

TAKING A CUTTING

Let's take a coleus, cut it, box it, and root it.

Pick a stem in good growth—not too young and thin, not too old and "woody"—and cut it off, about 4″ from the tip, with a sterile razor or knife (one that's been cleaned in alcohol) just below a node (see Chapter 9, GROOMING AND PRUNING, for a picture of nodes). Except for miniatures, 4″ is a good approximate length for cuttings.

Cut off that leftover bit of stem (internode) on the plant, and throw it away.

Cut away (or pinch away) the lowest pair of leaves to bare the node and make for good insertion into the medium. Stick this bare node and about ¾″ of stem into your medium, cover the prop box, and put it under your lights. You should see signs of root within 3 days, and your cutting may well be ready for potting within a week.

Rooting Hormone? We do not use rooting hormone, ever, for anything. Our students don't either. And we all have success.

Rooting hormone may stimulate some woody cuttings to strike roots, but we don't do woody cuttings.

It *may* stimulate soft-wood cuttings to strike roots more quickly, but the amount of rooting you get after a couple of weeks or so is pretty much the same, with or without the hormone—and the ultimate plant is no stronger. So, why use it? It won't get you a coleus plant in less time.

GERANIUMS

We are quite fond of miniature and scented-leaf geraniums, and we root both with a minimum of difficulty (though some greenhouse gardeners we know don't find it so easy). You'll find them easy, too, if you remember that geraniums are somewhat succulent plants and require an *open* propagation situation.

First, identify the nodes on your geranium and make a cut, *straight across* the stem, with a clean, sharp razor, about 4" from the tip, just below a node. (With a miniature, your cutting should be 2–3" long.)

Once cut, lay the cutting down on a dry surface and allow the cut end to callus (dry out) for an hour or so. Go back to the parent plant and cut off that extra bit of stem back to the next node.

Trim off the bottom pair of leaves—again, to allow a bit of stem to be below the surface of your medium, to hold the cutting upright.

Now, instead of vermiculite, we're going to root this cutting in a *Jiffy-7.* We've described these peat pellets in the previous chapters. Set as many pellets as you have cuttings in about an inch of water to soak.

When the peat pellet is swelled all through and the cutting has formed a callus, remove the pellet from the water. Take a pencil and punch a hole in the top (that's the side without netting) to a depth of about ¾–1". Insert the cutting into the hole and *squeeze* the jiff closed around the base of the cutting, squeezing out the extra water in the process.

Set the jiff into a 2¼" plastic pot, for support, and place the cutting among your plants, where you can keep an eye on it, keep it from going dry, and where it will get some light. If that pellet goes dry, you will lose your cutting.

You don't have to use the Jiffy-7 for geraniums: we've also had success putting them into *open* propagation boxes. You can fit quite a few geranium cuttings in an open plastic shoe box, with an inch of vermiculite in the bottom, set at the margin of your fluorescent lights.

When rooted (sometimes as long as several weeks), pot up into a pot not much bigger than the Jiffy-7: we've found geraniums happiest in smallish pots.

Cane-type begonias propagate from cuttings in these same ways, but more quickly.

TED'S SEMP

You can sometimes get a surprising number of tip cuttings from a single plant. One of the estate-gardeners we know brought a large semperflorens begonia into a flower show. The plant was 18″ across, but since he had 8 more in the greenhouse just like it, he left that one for our propagation course students.

We took *150* tip cuttings from that one plant—and then broke it into 20 clumps for division!

PREFERENCE

Dieffenbachia, *Ficus elastica* (rubber tree), dracaenas, coffea, schefflera, and other large, thick-stemmed plants, which *can* be propagated by tip cuttings, are often better off being *air-layered*. We'll get to that later.

WHAT PART OF THE PLANT?

When you take your cuttings, it's best to choose the most upright tip or stem you can find. These will usually grow into upright plants. A few plants (like Norfolk Island pine) will only make *sideward* growth if propagated from a side shoot.

PETIOLE CUTTINGS

The petiole is the little stem that holds the leaf. There are

After the peperomia petiole is rooted, plantlets form at the base of the leaf.

some plants that will frequently make a plant (or several plants) from this petiole with its leaf stuck into rooting medium. African violets, gloxinias, episcias, streptocarpus, peperomia, hoya, rex and rhizomatous begonias (like the beefsteak begonia), Chinese evergreen (aglaonema), and syngonium can readily be propagated this way, provided that the leaf blade and petiole were in good shape to begin with.

Gloxinias are rather slow to propagate this way because they must first form a tuber at the base of the petiole, and then form some small plantlet growth. Between the forming of the tuber and the new plantlet growth, the tuber may decide to go dormant (that is, go into a rest period), showing no growth on top at all.

African violets are very commonly propagated this way, so let's do one together.

First, cut off an African violet leaf, neither too young nor too old, of a good green color (not pale), without scars or breaks, if you can; these are the leaves that strike roots most quickly.

Once you've selected your leaf (or leaves), cut it so that no more than ¾–1″ of petiole remains (more petiole and your leaf will take longer to root). Remove the remaining petiole from the parent plant. Set the leaf upright in a propagation box, inserting it so that the leaf blade barely misses touching the medium.

Unlike many other forms of propagation, you do not transplant or pot up the leaf when root growth shows itself—it is not roots you are after, but plantlets, and they can take 2 months or more before they show themselves.

If you've had a leaf in medium for a long time and it has rooted but shows no sign of making plantlets, remove the petiole from the medium and gently reset it. Or you can just wait. As long as the leaf is mostly green and firm, there's hope. Or you can throw the leaf out and try another: some leaves never work.

Wait until the plantlets are 1–1½″ above the medium before removing them from the parent leaf (sometimes the parent leaf rots off, sometimes it stays firm and can be used again).

When the plantlets are the proper height, remove leaf and all from the prop box (including the medium sticking to the roots), and lay it on a piece of paper. You should be able to see how many plantlets you have and how they are joined. Separate them and plant them in individual pots. Don't allow them to go dry, and move them up to larger pots as soon as the roots begin to fill the little pots.

REX BEGONIAS (and other rhizomatous begonias)

Apartment growers often have trouble with rex begonias because of their humidity requirements. If you're having trouble with one, you might want to try to propagate it before the parent plant collapses entirely: sometimes the plant you've grown from a propagated plantlet is more tolerant of your conditions.

Begonias shoot plantlets faster than do African violets, but the technique is similar. You'll want a bit more petiole, though, for rex and other rhizomatous begonia leaves, and you can try them in an open prop box, where you can provide an 80% relative humidity for them. They often rot in 100% humidity boxes. If you have two leaves, try one in an open, and one in a closed box.

When you get plantlets, pot them up the same way.

Aglaonema and syngonium are the easiest of the lot to propagate by leaf: just cut off a healthy leaf with 2″ or 3″ of petiole, and stick it in an open prop box; then pot it up when it roots.

There are several things you can do with the leaf (or parts of the leaf) aside from sticking the whole thing in rooting medium.

WEDGING

You can get many plants from leaf *wedges* of gloxinia, streptocarpus, and rhizomatous begonias.

Cut the leaf into wedges (see drawing, page 197), then insert the wedges, pointy side down, into the medium, and cover the box until they either shrivel and die or shoot plantlets.

Jim Wyrtzen, an excellent amateur-turned-commercial grower in this area, tells this story of wedging streptocarpus leaves. Taking leaves from the same plant, he cut them up and put them in prop boxes of straight vermiculite, in four categories: with some of the midrib (the thick vein going up the leaf as an extension of the petiole) and with rooting hormone; without midrib but with hormone; with midrib but without hormone; and without either midrib or hormone. The last category—*without* midrib or hormone—rooted fastest under identical conditions.

Jim spoke of getting many plants from one streptocarpus leaf: the most we've ever managed was 8 plants (that is, 8 tubers which then developed into plants) from one medium-sized gloxinia leaf (there were 12 wedges to begin with), but 8 plants from one leaf is enough for us.

Wedging does not seem to work for African violet leaves.

HUB AND CONE CUTTING

A hub cutting is a petiole cutting with most of the leaf removed (see the drawing on page 197). If the leaf was healthy to begin with, you can get a plant (or plants) from this little bit of gloxinia, begonia (rhizome type), or streptocarpus leaf, as well as from the whole leaf. Set it into the medium as if it were a petiole cutting.

The piece that's left over can be made into a cone cutting (See drawing on the right.) After removing the hub, roll the leaf blade that remains into a cone (the ends should over-

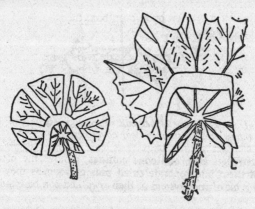

Begonia leaves. B. erythrophylla *shows hub and 5 wedges; B.* ricinifolia *shows hub and cone.*

lap). Stand this cone up on the medium, insert it a fraction of an inch into the medium, then pour a little of the medium down *into* the cone. Cover, and hope. (We've already taken 6 small plants from a cone cutting of *Begonia masoniana,* the Iron Cross begonia, but, we must say this: when this method is successful it is *very* successful, but we've seen more failures than successes with hubs. Still, it's quite an interesting procedure.)

If you don't want to make a cone of the leftover blade, wedge it.

Prop box with wedges, hubs, and a cone cutting.

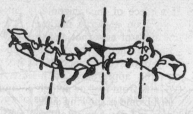

A recently broken piece of begonia rhizome, ready to cut. Those leaflike things are old stipules (leaf coverings).

With wedge, hub, and cone cuttings, remove the plantlets and pot them into separate small pots as soon as they have formed a bit of root system of their own and can be handled.

RHIZOMES—BEGONIAS

A rhizome is a thickened stem which runs along the ground or underground.

In rhizomatous begonias, the rhizome looks hairy; leaves grow out of its upper surface and roots grow out of its bot-

A rooted rhizome chunk, ready for potting.

tom surface. If a piece of this rhizome is cut off (or even broken off) and set on a sterile medium, it will, within a week or so, show signs of new root and top growth.

This is a desirable method of propagation because the plants you get from this rhizome cutting are usually quite strong and have the appearance of mature plants much sooner than do plants from leaf or petiole cuttings.

As soon as the rhizome is showing signs of rooting, remove it from the medium and pot it up in our standard soil mix.

A piece of rhizome even ½" long can give you a good-sized plant within a month.

RHIZOMES—FERNS

Ferns spread by means of rhizomes, also. Some are below the soil line, some above. For those below the soil line, cut into the rhizome with a very clean and sharp knife, and treat it like "Division," which we described earlier.

Davallia and polypodium ferns (squirrel's foot, hare's foot, rabbit's foot, bear's paw ferns) have rhizomes visible above the soil that creep over the edges of their pots. If a bit of this rhizome, while still attached to the parent plant, is hairpinned down onto a pot of well-watered soil, the rhizome will often root and send up fronds. Once rooted, take a sharp, sterile knife and cut it from the main plant.

SUCKERS

Suckers are offsets; they get this unflattering name because they distract the flowering plant into this superfluous vegetative growth instead of making flowers.

They are really rootless little plants, often with several leaves, and if they can be carefully removed from the leaf axil, where they usually grow, they can be put into a prop box for rooting, and be expected to make a real plant in short order.

African violets often sucker—especially the miniatures—as do gloxinias and other sinningias.

We've described suckers and their removal in GROOMING AND PRUNING, Chapter 9.

If you've mashed the sucker so badly that nothing can be salvaged for propagation, don't be unhappy; you've at least added to the vigor of the main plant.

AIR-LAYERING

Here's a method of propagation that's a lot of fun, because you can keep track of it as it goes along.

Plants such as dracaena, cordyline, dieffenbachia, shefflera, ficus, ardisia, croton, monstera, large philodendrons, large coffee trees, and others that form thick but not woody stems can be propagated by air-layering.

In air-layering, you wound the plant, wrap the wound in dampened long-haired sphagnum moss, wrap the moss in clear plastic, then tie on the plastic with twist ties. After a period of time (weeks to months, depending on the toughness of the stem), there should be enough rooting from the stem into the damp moss to cut off the rooted piece and its leaves and plant it up, moss and all.

When? You air-layer when your plant is leggy.

Why? You air-layer because it's a sure method of propagation for thick-stemmed mature plants.

What? For air-layering you need: a sharp, clean knife; long-haired sphagnum moss; a piece of clear plastic (or a clear plastic bag); 2 twist ties. If you can't come by the moss separately, there is an air-layering kit on the market that has all the equipment (except the knife) and directions, but it is, of course, much more expensive than buying the parts separately.

How? Let's air-layer our top-heavy 7′ dieffenbachia—the one so leggy that we've had to loop a string around the door hinge to keep it erect on its broomhandle of a stake.

Clean your knife with alcohol.

Bring the rest of your equipment close to hand. After the cut, you may have to do all the rest with one hand supporting the top of the plant.

Thoroughly wet and wring out a few handfuls of long-haired sphagnum moss—enough so that when squeezed out it will form a pad around the stem, about 6″ high, and about 1″ thick at its middle. Wet up more moss than you'll need—it's easier to store the remainder than to wet more if you're in the middle of the project.

[200]

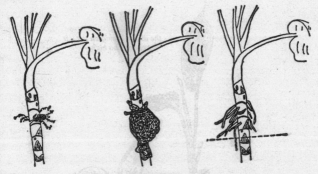

Air-layering.

Take a piece of clear plastic the size of a large plastic bag (you want it clear so that you can see if the moss should dry out, or if the roots should grow right out to the surface), and with a twist tie secure it to the stem about 4″ below where you will make your cut. Keep in mind that you are going to wrap the plastic around moss, stem, and all, but that you can readjust the twist tie and plastic after you've gotten everything else in place. Let the upper part of the plastic hang down.

Now you're ready to make the cut. The cut is made between two nodes, as close to the bottom leaves as you can get. Hold the knife parallel to the ground and cut upward at an angle into the stem, about *⅓ to ½ way through the stem.* It will not kill the plant. (See drawing below.)

With one hand hold the stem so that *the cut does not close,* and place a little of the damp moss into the cut—to keep it open and to encourage rooting.

Take handfuls of the damp moss and shape it around the stem into a kind of collar (tapering at top and bottom). Use as much moss as you need to make sure the area is well covered. When the moss is in place, bring up the plastic and wrap it around the moss, using a twist tie to close it off at the top. Be sure the plastic overlaps sufficiently to permit no open spaces. Open spaces lead to drying out, and drying out leads to failures at air-layering.

Readjust the bottom tie, wrapping the plastic securely.

And now all you have to do is wait. When roots have formed to a length of a couple of inches, cut the stem through just below the bottom roots, allow the bottom to cal-

*the dieffenbachia on the left
was cut off too high—*

so notch it here →

and air-layer again,

and lop it off here →

lus for a half hour or so, and plant it up, moss and all. It needs no hardening off and may be watered and treated just like a plant.

STEMS

After you lop off the top of the dieffenbachia to pot it up, you'll have left that long, leggy stem that bothered you in the first place. Look at it. You will see, between each pair of nodes, a raised bit like a tiny turtle shell in shape, but green. These are called "eyes" and they can sprout into new growth—even make an entire new plant. Cut the stem into about 2″ segments, each segment with two eyes. Allow these cuttings to callus for an hour or so, and lay them *horizontally* in an open prop box, only ½ *buried* beneath the medium. They may take a long time to sprout, but you should be able to get plants from most of them. When sprouts are a few inches high and some roots have formed, pot them up.

Other plants with similar dormant eyes can be treated the same way: monstera, philodendron, dracaena, cordyline, ficus, etc.

The bottom, what's left of the stem on the parent plant, will very often sprout near its tip. So be sure you cut the stem to within a few inches of the soil, to get a thrifty plant.

After the top was lopped off this Dracaena sanderiana *'Borinquensis,' the two highest nodes sprang into growth. It should have been cut lower.*

BULBS, CORMS, TUBERS, SCALY RHIZOMES

See Chapter 27 for a discussion of their general characteristics.

BULBS

Bulbs are made up of thickened scales or layers which join at a base plate. Any of these scales can be grown on into a plant and then into a bulb. Simply break off the scales and set them into an open prop box. They will sprout; then pot them up and give them good light. *Next season* you'll get flowers—live and be well.

Sometimes a mature bulb will form bulblets—smaller bulbs attached to the main bulb. With a plant like amaryllis, these offsets are quite easy to see. The bulb itself is grown half out of the soil, and the offsets are similarly visible, without digging down.

Sometimes a bulbous plant will form little bulbils in the leaf axils. When they come off easily, these bulbils can be treated like offsets or scales and potted up for growth until they are of flowering size. (There is a begonia that forms these bulbils also—*Begonia evansiana*, which is also hardy and a scented begonia, altogether an uncommon plant.)

CORMS

Many oxalis grow from corms, and *Oxalis regnali* and *O. deppei* make excellent pot plants, even under lights; *O. lasiandra* flowers beautifully on a bright windowsill.

Plants that grow from corms also can form minor "cormels" as well as the new corm; and these cormels can be grown along into flowering plants after a season of just foliage growth.

Bulbs and corms will *not*, in general, propagate from stem cuttings.

TUBERS

We've already discussed a bit about tuber propagation;

when gloxinia leaves are propagated, either as *petiole* or *wedge cuttings* (which see), they form a tuber before forming a plant.

Tuberous plants will, in general, propagate from stem and/or leaf cuttings; however, they, too, form offsets quite often—and those offsets, unlike offsets from bulbs and corms, will form flowering plants the first year. Your miniature *Sinningia* 'Bright eyes,' for example, comes from a tiny tuber and often forms an offset—an even tinier tuber. Break that offset off and pot it up, and you can have flowering within a month or so!

There is another way to propagate your tuberous plants quite easily. Most tubers eventually require a dormant period. For tuberous begonias or for gloxinias, this can be a period of several months. When your tubers come into growth

Now is the time to break off and propagate the secondary sprout of this gloxinia tuber.

again, the first sprout (or any extra sprouts) can be broken off when 1½"–2" tall and put into a closed prop box to root. Plants from these sprouts are usually very vigorous and will flower quickly (while simultaneously forming their own tuber). A gloxinia sprout and the tuber you broke it from will both come to flower at about the same time.

SCALY RHIZOMES

Achimenes, smithiantha, and some other gesneriads propagate from these propagules that look like tiny elongated pine cones. *Every scale on the rhizome can make a whole plant.* Set them in a closed prop box, spaced out and labeled, and when they sprout, pot them up.

At the bottom of this Pandanus veitchii *are several offsets.*

OFFSETS

Terms for propagules vary according to your expert, and lots of terms are interchangeable. "Offset" is a very general term applying to many of the means of propagation we describe. But here we're using it to apply to the "miniature plants" that grow at the base of two of our favorite houseplants: pandanus and beaucarnea.

These plants form offsets complete with leaves but without roots: the beaucarnea does it on the thick bulb at its base; the pandanus forms its offsets at its stem, just below its lowest leaves.

They will usually break off easily, or you might want to

use a clean knife—if you can keep from wounding the parent plant.

Propagate in a closed prop box until rooting develops, then pot up.

CACTI

True cacti cuttings must be allowed to callus—and the thicker they are, the longer they must callus. A stem cutting only ½″ thick must be left to dry for 3 days to a week; a thicker cutting must be allowed to dry for *weeks*, until there is no wet at all visible in the cut. (Put to root sooner and you take a good chance of rotting your cuttings.) Don't worry, that cactus cutting is full of life, and it is not dying for lack of roots and water.

Take your cutting with a sterile knife or razor and put it in a dry place, lying on its side, to callus.

Even after they have callused, cactus should not be treated like other cuttings and buried part way beneath the rooting medium: cactus cuttings are best barely stood *on* the damp medium, or even suspended just *over* the damp medium.

Using either an open prop box or an individual pot with rooting medium in it, we dampen the medium well, set a stake in it, and then *tie* the cutting to the stake with a twist tie, to hold it just on or just over the medium. We expect rooting rather quickly, but if it is slow to come and the medium needs watering, we dampen the top of the medium and allow any excess to drain off.

With any barrel-type cactus, the ball-shaped offsets or branches break off easily at the joints; they can then be callused and stood on the medium without a stake.

We try not to make cuttings across the barrels of these fat cacti, large or small. A cactus of this shape has so much surface area to callus that it may have to be callused for weeks before it's ready to put on the medium—and even then there is no guarantee against rot.

However, sometimes your cacti don't cooperate. If a mature plant is showing signs of basal rot, there's nothing you can do but to make the cutting well above the rot line, and try to root the top, after drying it off for weeks.

SUCCULENTS

With cacti, you know you have to let them all callus before you try to root them, but other succulents are more varied. With some succulents, you can lose them if you let them dry for more than a few hours. Ice plants (lampranthus) are that way; don't let them callus at all. The thin-stemmed sedums are the same way; they strike roots much more quickly if you don't let them go dry before inserting them in the medium. We root the ice plants and the thin-stemmed sedum in a closed prop box, just like coleus.

There are some crassulas that we propagate in a closed box, after allowing them a couple of hours to callus (though they will often strike roots in an open prop box).

However, most thick-stemmed succulents are best treated like cacti: let the callus form, but only for several hours, and then either stand on your open rooting medium or suspend it just over the rooting medium by means of a stake.

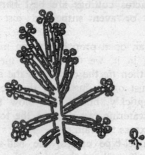

Each leaf of Kalanchoe tubiflora *is tubular; the plantlets are at the leaftips.*

Many succulents will propagate from their leaves. Break off a leaf (don't cut it—you want to include the part nearest the stem) by moving it back and forth, then lay it horizontally on the rooting medium in the same position it held on the plant. We've found that for leaves, in general the closed prop box is best.

Kalanchoe daigremontiana (mother of thousands) and *K. tubiflorium* make tiny plantlets along the edges of their mature leaves. The plantlet starts as a growth bud that develops a pair of leaves and a few filaments of roots and then a second pair of leaves ... and so on until it may reach a diameter of ⅜″. In nature (and in our apartment) these plantlets fall to the soil (of any pot that happens to be near) and root and grow. You can take them off yourself, though, as soon as you can handle them, put a dozen or so into one pot, and then transplant them as they mature.

The adult *K. daigremontiana* grows to a couple of feet and more, and can be leggy in a window. Lop a few inches off the top and allow the cut to callus, then put it into an open prop box. Crassulas and other upright succulents also propagate easily from tip cuttings.

Burro's tail sedum (*Sedum morganianum*) can make a plant from every one of its many silvery-gray leaves. They can be sprinkled about on an open prop box's rooting medium, or stood on the flat end, the bottom of the leaf. If the leaf (still on the plant) is wounded, a new little plant will form right in the wound.

Hoya and peperomia, both waxy and succulent, will propagate from single leaves. Just stick the petiole into rooting medium in a closed prop box, and new plantlets will rise.

If you have a succulent with long leaves, you needn't use an entire leaf for propagation. Cut the leaf into sections a couple of inches long and allow to callus for several hours, or overnight. Stand the bottom of the piece in an open box, as you would a cactus cutting. Gasterias and aloes propagate easily this way.

Similarly, a leaf cutting of sanseveria will propagate in an open box, although the new sanseverias propagated from leaf cuttings will not have the variegations of the parent leaf. For the variegations you'll have to include a bit of the root stock.

Two quite delightful succulents, echevarias and sempervivums, propagate by offsets that extend on thin stems from the base of the parent plant (hence their common name: hens-and-chicks). Cut the offsets off when they are about ½″ or more across, and pot up directly, without an intermediate stage in rooting medium.

Aloes and agaves will also put out offsets, but on underground stems. Dig down into the soil and cut through the stem—*when the soil is dry*—then pot up directly without using a prop box.

POTTING

Do not pot your succulent and cacti rootings into wet medium; don't even water them for the first two weeks they are in their new pots. This is true for all cacti and succulents (except for lampranthus and the thin-stemmed sedums we mentioned earlier). We speak from bitter experience, friends. Those cacti and succulent roots are very delicate and very easily damaged and very easily rotted. Let your medium be any more than the barest bit damp, and you're running a chance of rot.

PUPS AND KEIKIS AND BACKBULBS

Orchids and bromeliads have a propagation vocabulary of their own: with bromeliads the offsets that grow from the base of the plant are called "pups"; with orchids, the plantlets that form (and grow their own independent root system) on the stems of orchids like dendrobiums, are called "keikis"; with the monopodial orchids, the thickening at the base is called "pseudobulb," and you can propagate the plants from "backbulbs" (pseudobulbs of previous years' growth). For their propagation, see Chapters 23 and 26.

PART IV

THE PROTECTED ENVIRONMENT

18. Growing in a Protected Environment, or The Apartment Gardener Strikes Back

Our living room is like a lot of old New York apartments: the ceilings are high, which means that the summers are not unendurable; the heat in winter is fairly constant; the walls are thick, so that we usually don't hear the neighbors quarreling; and the growing conditions are a combination of Death Valley and the Black Hole of Calcutta.

PROTECTED ENVIRONMENTS

We've solved our living-room growing problems with the help of fluorescent lights (see Chapter 12) and protected environments.

You notice we say "protected environment," not "terrarium." Certainly, all terrariums are protected environments; but in order for a protected environment to qualify as a terrarium, there has to be some attempt at design, some reaching for elements of (you'll pardon the expression) art, something more than just sticking a plant in a plastic flying saucer or 12 plants in a fish tank or 6 plants in a bottle and calling that a terrarium. You can't make it a terrarium by just calling it that.

HOW DO YOU DO IT?

Let's start planting something together in a protected environment, and as we go along we'll discuss any problems that arise.

We'll begin with a container quite open and simple: let's

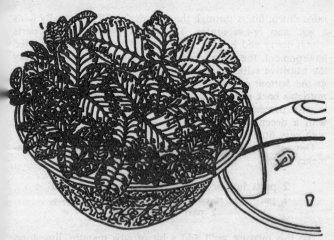

Episcia 'Helen O.' in a "flying saucer." Some of the outer stolons should be removed now and propagated.

first plant up our *Episcia* 'Helen O.' in that saucer-shaped planter.

Episcias are related to African violets and require high humidity to thrive. They don't flower nearly as freely as do the violets, but their foliage is often exquisite.

First, take your planter and wash it well in a solution of 9 parts water and 1 part chlorine bleach. (You say you can't see any reason for washing a brand-new planter? Well, more protected environments and terrariums have failed because of fungus than any other reason. The bleach will clean your planter.)

Rinse it well in hot water and allow it to dry.

Since you have no holes in the bottom of your container, you must have some drainage material.

With a 12″ diameter saucer, we use pea gravel—also washed in bleach and water—enough to be about 1½″ deep at the center.

Your soil is quite important in a protected environment. A too-heavy soil will cramp the roots of your episcia, while a too-light soil may not carry enough nutrition for those long periods between waterings.

(Let's take a side trip for a moment. A protected environment is somewhat like the earth—the completely closed system. In the earth, virtually everything recycles. The water rains down, filters through the soil, drains off, eventually joins a sea, and re-evaporates. The plants grow, lose old parts which decay and help to make new plants. In your protected environment, the "rain" washes past the roots, carrying away the nutritive salts not absorbed immediately—*but only as far as the bottom of the container*. There is some *return* of the nutrients back up toward the roots by capillary action—which is why protected environments require so little food. Start with a decent soil, and you've got something that will last with very little feeding for a long while.)

Our mix for terrariums, bottles, and all protected environments is this:

2 parts humus	**1** part topsoil
1 part peat moss	**1** part perlite
1 part vermiculite	

To this mixture we'll add a bit of cow manure, limestone, and bone meal. It's been a very successful mix for us. If you've been paying attention, you'll recognize this as our standard soil mix with an extra helping of humus (see Chapter 7).

Spoon in enough soil to come within about 2″ of the lip of your planter. If you are planting something of a different shape than a saucer—say a globe or an egg-shaped container—you'll have to make adjustments. A globe wants a little more gravel and a little less soil; an egg wants less of both.

Now you're almost finished. Take the plant and groom off any dead or dying material—that's very important. Rotten material left on a plant can promote rot in the good parts in this higher-humidity environment.

Before planting, do examine the plant very carefully for bugs: bugs can just destroy a closed environment.

Now, dig a hole for the rootball. Remove the pot from your plant and rub off some of the old soil. Set the rootball into the hole so that the plant sits a little *lower* than it did originally. Firm the soil gently around the roots, and water lightly.

If the plant won't stand upright (though, remember, episcias are mostly trailers and don't have an upright habit), don't hesitate to use a few small, temporary stakes to hold your plant in position. After a week or three, you'll be able to remove the stakes, and the plant will stand on its own.

Put the cover on, and place the planter under the light unit where it will live.

PLANT SIZE

This kind of planting isn't for today, but for a lot of tomorrows.

If you use a plant that fills the planter now and looks perfect now, what's going to happen when that plant starts to grow?

We understand the desire to have something good-looking right away, but if you're going to grow plants you're going to have to learn patience, and this is as good a spot as any to begin. Your plant should fill *less than half* of the available growing space—considerably less if you have the guts. (The prizewinner we have now went in as a 1" rooted stolen 4 months ago.) That way you'll have the pleasure of it when you make it, *and* while you see it grow and reach perfection.

SOMETHING EASIER

Apothecary jars are easier because you don't have to make so many decisions—there are fewer plants that will fit into a small jar.

Sinningia pusilla *fits easily into a small apothecary jar.*

Wash the jar and its cover with the usual solution of bleach-water, rinse and allow them to dry, then fill the bottom of the jar with ½–¾ " of fine drainage material—depending on the depth of the jar. We use bird gravel (a coarse, clean sand sold in pet stores) for this quite successfully, though fine perlite will do, also, if you don't mind the green algae that always seems so noticeable on perlite.

Spoon in 1½–2" of the soil mix.

With a teaspoon, dig a small hole to receive the rootball of the miniature you are planting—say a bit of *Begonia boweri nigramarga*—an appealing little stitch-leafed begonia, excellent for planting in larger terrariums to fill in some of the blank spaces.

Drop the plant into the hole and, with the spoon (or with those long, aristocratic fingers, if they fit), press the soil gently around the base to firm up the roots. We've never found it necessary to prop up a plant small enough to go into an apothecary jar.

There are some miniatures so tiny that several of them will go into a container even this small. But we'll name names later on.

You noticed, we hope, that you used no tools at all for the large open planter, and only a teaspoon for the jar. We now come to an area of planting which requires some special tools.

BOTTLE GARDENING

Bottles seem to be "in" now. You see them in the windows of virtually every florist, selling for what seem to us astronomical prices, generally planted with plants that don't need a protected environment, and often with plants that will soon outgrow the bottle.

One florist in our neighborhood had in his window a 5-gallon bottle, planted with laughable plants: a palm tree, aucuba (a shrub that will reach 6' with the least encouragement), and nephthitis—*which had already grown three leaves out of the neck of the bottle.*

You can make two kinds of bottle gardens: a bottle holding only one plant (simply, the protected environment) or a terrarium bottle (again, with some elements of design).

They both have their place. A single rex begonia, which will eventually grow to fill a 5-gallon bottle completely, is a lovely sight, and requires no supplementary planting. Rex begonias are excellent bottle subjects because they are so difficult to grow in a city apartment, without special humidity devices. Watch it, though: rex and other rhizome-type begonias sometimes go *dormant* for a week or so after bottling, dropping all their leaves. Don't panic, they will usually come back.

But, then, a planting of miniatures to make a garden within a bottle is also quite exciting—both to do and to see.

Bottle sizes make it difficult to speak of planting bottles in general by one technique. After all, it's a lot easier to get a well-rooted plant through the neck of a 5- or 10-gallon demijohn than through the neck of a miniature whiskey bottle. Not that you necessarily want to plant either. The tiny bottle is just a conversation piece (something we use when we do lectures and demonstrations on bottle gardening—just to show it can be done) and the largest bottles can be expensive, hard to come by, and difficult to light.

Let's start by planting a ½-gallon bottle. They are large enough to give growing room to a miniature, while not taking up much space under your lights.

TOOLS

You need tools for planting bottles, but they can be made at home.

The most important thing is a long tweezer. We made ours from an 18″ bamboo stake, splitting it most of the way down to the end, then tying it off with a rubber band to prevent further splitting, inserting a small peg to keep it open, and then wrapping another rubber band around the other side of the peg (see the drawing on page 217). It took us three stakes before we were satisfied, so do get yourself an extra or so for practice.

An X-acto blade wired and glued onto the end of another

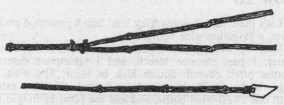

Bamboo stakes make good bottle tools.

For watering bottles.

stake is also a desirable tool: excellent for cutting off what got damaged while putting the plant into the bottle.

A largish plastic funnel is handy (the end of the spout can be cut off to make it larger) for pouring in gravel and soil—though you can roll a temporary funnel out of paper.

We also like a waterer we put together: a 3-ounce rubber squeeze-ball with an 18″ piece of ¼″ plastic tubing, which enables us to water right *at* the roots.

KNOW YOUR PLANT

Most plants behave in bottles the way they do out of bottles, only better. Miniatures stay small, large-leafed plants grow large. But some plants get into a protected environment and take off like giants. And some large growers stay quite small.

The *Begonia* 'Gay Star' we'll describe planting below is a moderately-large grower. We bought it as a baby, not familiar with it, because of the beautiful leaf shape. In our bottle, it has stayed small for more than 2 years.

A *Gesneria citrina* we bottled grew right out of the bottle, though it is supposed to be a miniature.

So, while it is important to know how large a plant is supposed to grow, be prepared for surprises, too.

HOW TO

Let's plant that *Begonia* 'Gay Star' into a protected environment, a ½-gallon wine bottle.

Start by washing the bottle in a solution of 9 parts hot water, 1 part chlorine bleach, and 1 tablespoon detergent. Bottles often contain liquids high in sugar, like wine, and sugar is the world's best food for fungus. We were careless with one sweet-wine bottle, and lost the plant to fungus liter-

Begonia 'Gay Star' has been in this bottle for 2 years.

ally overnight. So, wash and rinse well. Then reuse the same solution to bleach the pea gravel that is the most desirable drainage material for bottles.

Insert your funnel into the neck of the bottle and pour in gravel to a depth of about an inch, depending, again, on the depth of the bottle.

Bottle Color. Bottle colors range from perfectly clear to perfectly opaque. Spanish sherry bottles are a medium green and those are the darkest bottles we use for plants. We never use brown or blue bottles: the light they let through is poor for plant growth.

Still using the funnel, pour in about 2″ of *rather dry* soil (we'll water when we're finished, and that will wash the sides of the bottle down, too).

With your bamboo tweezers, reach into the bottle and even out the soil. (We'll landscape our *next* bottle.)

GENTLY, GENTLY

Take your young plant out of its pot and remove as much

soil from around the roots as you can—*gently*.

People sometimes ask if we start a bottled plant from a seed. It couldn't work: a seed requires intense light to grow into a thrifty plant—certainly much more light than a seedling would get in the bottom of a bottle.

You begin with young plants, but you don't want a baby. You want a plant that has a rootball small enough to go through the bottle's neck, and yet a plant well-enough established to survive. So, when you pick a plant for a bottle, have the opening of the bottle in mind. The larger the bottle's neck, the larger the plant you can get in.

Now, once you've put in soil and gravel, and unpotted your plant, the fun begins.

With the back of your tweezers, make a hole in the soil large enough to accommodate the rootball.

Lift the plant, roots down, to the opening. Then gather the roots together and lift the ends into the opening. So far no trouble: those ends go right in.

Now, *gently* squeezing the rootball together, continue to feed the roots in through the opening with your fingers. If your plant is young and has little root system, the ball will go in without difficulty. If the root system is well developed, much handling and compressing may be necessary (nervous?).

You will shortly reach the point where the roots are in the bottle neck and only the leaves stick out (nervous, nervous). At this stage you will realize that the leaves are at least twice as large across as is the opening and they can't possibly go in.

In effect, what you have to do is *roll up* the leaves so that they are in a funnel shape and will pass through the opening. Once you have the point of this leaf funnel into the opening, the rest is simplicity itself.

With your little finger or with a pencil (eraser end, please), push down gently on the rootball (keeping the leaf-funnel tight) and the whole affair will plop right into the waiting hole. If your hole was a bit off center, a little nudge with the tweezers will push the plant into position or will dig a new hole.

With the back end of the tweezers (they are a busy tool), press the rootball into the waiting hole. Don't be afraid to be firm.

Nudge enough soil over the roots so that the plant will stand in the proper position. If it is too floppy for you, use a stake, one long enough to stick out of the neck of the bottle: you'll be able to remove it after a week or so.

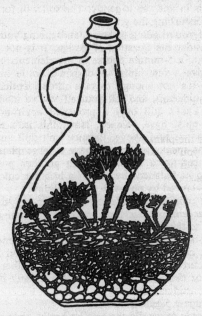

Begonia 'Black Falcon' in a bottle for 18 months.

All that remains now is to give a shot of water at the roots of the plant and a thin stream down the insides of the bottle with the watering bulb. Water gently, but make sure all the soil is off the sides of the bottle.

There should be a small amount of water in the gravel. If not, look for dry spots. If you have watered too much, carefully tilt the bottle on its side and, with the same squeeze-bulb, suck out the excess.

Now, label the bottle—and that's it. Just place your finished masterwork under fluorescent light, or in a very bright north window.

A LANDSCAPED BOTTLE

It's possible to landscape even a small bottle—say, a ½-liter wine flask—if you're dealing with some true mini-miniatures, such as are found among gesneriads.

For the simplest kind of landscaping, just tilt the bottle

after the soil is in and tap it gently. The soil will form an incline without disturbing the gravel.

However, if you're going to begin landscaping your bottles, you must consider the question of design. It is not our plan here to give you a 5-minute course in the elements of design, but we can give a few hints: A designed bottle must have some *variety*. It's not enough to take three identical plants, place them equidistant, and tell yourself you've made an artistic design. That's still only a protected environment.

The bottle must have *balance*. Now, this isn't a contradiction to what we said above. Balance isn't dull and it isn't just equidistant spacing. You can have a large plant in one position balanced by a smaller one in another position—a large plant can be balanced by one of a brighter color, a thin plant can be balanced by one with more solidity.

And, in our opinion, a bottle terrarium (or any terrarium) should have *accents:* things that break away from and give added interest to the design.

There is also the question of non-natural elements in the bottle: that is, china deer or ballerinas, bridges and Japanese boatmen. We are against ballerinas, but we rather like an artificial bird or two—as long as the bottle doesn't become a story about an artificial bird.

Let's landscape a 5-gallon bottle.

Wash the bottle as we did the smaller bottle, rinse well, and allow to dry.

Pour in about 2″ of bleached and washed gravel.

Now, while tilting the bottle slightly, pour in (through the funnel) what would be about 3–4″ of soil, if the bottle were level. If you are not pleased by the angle, tilt a bit more (or less) and tap the bottle until the soil gets to the angle you want.

So here we have a bottle with a raked stage: what do we plant, and what do we plant where?

First of all, we want to make sure that none of the plants we use are likely to outgrow the bottle—at least not for a year or so—so we use none of the aroids (syngonium, nephthytis, etc.), no philodendrons, no dieffenbachias. There are a couple of odd dracaenas that are rather slow-growing, but we refuse to put anything into our bottles which in nature becomes an 8′ shrub, so we'll eliminate the dracaenas, too, and the palms—even the dwarfs will outgrow a bottle rather quickly.

How about ferns? Actually, some ferns are quite good for bottles: they like the high humidity and the reduced light.

But which do you use? There are some miniature ferns which will stay small for quite a while: miniature maidenhair, for example, can't be grown in an apartment *except* in a protected environment. There is also a slow-growing *Asparagus meyeri* (not a true fern). But one we like especially for large bottles is *Pteris cretica:* its sterile and fertile fronds are of different heights, so that the plant provides its own accents.

For ground cover, we'll use some *Pellionia daveauna*, another slow grower which has trouble outside a protected environment, a bit of fittonia, and a miniature begonia. In addition, we'll try a couple of offsets of slow-growing cryptanthus (earth star). Cryptanthus is the only bromeliad we'd put in a bottle—none of the others would do well in contact with the soil. And, as a final bit of ground cover, *Sellaginella kraussiana*, a tiny moss that loves protected environments.

For an additional accent or two, we might use a *Peperomia obtusifolia variegata*.

But, you ask, what about an African violet? What about those miniature gesneriads we were talking about just a little while ago? Can't we include them?

We wouldn't. In order to keep your bottle healthy, you must keep it well groomed. A plant that flowers profusely, like an African violet or its relations, the miniature gesneriads, requires a great deal of attention to keep the deadheads off. You would have to groom your bottle every few days if you grew a violet in it and wished to keep the plant healthy and free from fungus.

In smaller bottles, the grooming problem is less acute—especially if you have a long scissors to reach in and clip off the deadheads, which can then be pulled out easily with the tweezers. With a large bottle, it's much more difficult to cut off the deadheads. It can be done with the blade, if you're careful, but we prefer not to have the bother and seldom put a free-flowering plant in a large bottle.

PLANTING THE PLANTS

The insertion of the plants is much easier in a bottle of this size, as no plant you'll want to use will have a rootball larger than the neck. In fact, often you won't even have to break up the rootball to get it in. Just poke out a hole large enough for the plant, tilt the bottle so that it will land right in the hole, and drop it in. Firm the plant into place as you did for the smaller bottle, and continue until you're well planted. If you don't like what you wind up with, use your tweezers to remove the offending plants, and redo.

Water as you did the smaller bottle.

A bottle this size is hard to light with a 2-tube fixture. Because of its height, the tubes sit at least a foot above the plants—too far for best lighting. That brilliant north window will do, or a 4-tube fixture, or a 2-tube fixture set perpendicular and kept next to the bottle. But you'll have to turn the bottle frequently.

PLANTING A TERRARIUM

As part of a demonstration for a plant society, we planted up a fish-tank terrarium with rocks, a mirror-pond, birds, the works—oh, yes, and plants, too.

Now, *here* was where we used an African violet: as long as you can reach in and groom, great. Also, here was where we were happy to use any number of other gesneriads—including ones that don't hold their flowers too well and so need frequent grooming.

A terrarium—as are all protected environments—is not forever; it is for a limited period of time—months, a couple of years if you're very lucky and very good.

One of the ways of keeping a terrarium going, and healthy, is to change the plants from time to time. If that violet is going downhill—change it for one about to come into bloom —if your tuberous miniature gesneriads insist on a rest period (they don't really go dormant), let them rest somewhere else, and move in some plants willing to work for the terrarium.

WHAT ABOUT WILD PLANTS?

We don't use wild plant material in our terrariums, except for certain "sidewalk" mosses which establish themselves readily. (These are the mosses you can dig out from between the cracks in the sidewalk.)

For one thing, most wild plants either are protected or *should be* protected and should not be taken from their natural habitat. Moreover, we have never seen a terrarium with wild plants that did anything but *exist*. All the wild plants in the northern United States and Canada are winter-hardy, which means that they must have a cold winter's rest—and how do you do that with a terrarium?

Those plants in a terrarium are rather like wild birds and animals in cages: beautiful, but sad.

LET'S DO IT

To get back to making our terrarium-fish-tank, the preparation is the same as with the bottles, so let's pick up at the point of spooning in the soil. We use the same soil mix, of course, but now we can moisten it slightly. We only left it dry in the bottles and jars so that we could wash the extra bits of soil down as we watered.

Spoon in a minimum of an inch or so of soil, but spoon in as much as, say, 6″ to be a hillside or as a raised area for variety and accent.

To make a "pond," simply take a small mirror, bury it at soil level, and cover the edges with soil.

To make a stream, bury the mirror a bit below ground level and leave only a thin ribbon of it uncovered.

Interesting stones or petrified wood can make handsome boulders or cliffs.

We like to use a porous volcanic rock called *feather rock* in a terrarium. We hollow out the rock very easily with a screwdriver and hammer, and set a shallow-rooted plant into the hollow in a bit of soil. But the rock dries out very quickly—more quickly than the rest of your terrarium—and will require more frequent watering.

These are just a few ideas you can use to give your terrar-

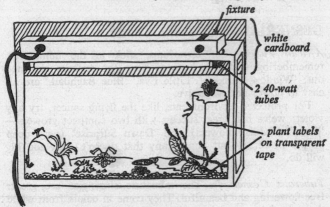

Rear view of a fish-tank terrarium. Cardboard is stapled to the front of the fixture to mask the light tubes.

ium a distinctive design. But, you can have a beautiful terrarium without using anything but soil and plants.

Let's start choosing plants for a fish-tank terrarium:

A miniature tillandsia (a group of dry-growing bromeliads) is great for the rock, because it likes to dry out well between waterings.

Miniature calathea.

A SMALL *Dracaena godseffiana* (thought not a miniature, this plant is slow growing and fine if you'll take it out of the terrarium and replace it before it grows out).

Several miniature gesneriads, like *Sinningia* 'Freckles,' and the charming *Koellikeria erinoides*.

A miniature African violet.

A couple of compact begonias.

Together a very interesting combination of foliage and flowering plants.

After the plants are in and watered, we cover the top of the tank with a piece of plastic or glass, *most of the way*. We want to leave an opening for air circulation.

PLANTS FOR A PROTECTED ENVIRONMENT

We've mentioned a few plants, but let us list some of the named and unnamed varieties of plants we've grown protected, for your guidance.

GESNERIADS

African Violets. For terrariums, stick to the miniatures, remembering that you have to keep the suckers groomed out: 'Window Wonder,' 'Little Eva,' 'Blue Baghdad,' are all easy to flower and attractive.

For protected environments, like the flying saucer, try any violet: we've had great success with two compact growers—'Rusty' (reddish flowers) and 'Dawn Surprise' (very deep purple flowers)—but almost any that doesn't grow too big will do.

Tuberous Gesneriads. The miniature sinningias are great: free-flowering and beautiful. They come in colors from white through pink to purple—solids and spotted and striped. They are easy to flower in a terrarium—easier than any other plant group—responding even to the minimal light down at the bottom. Do look for *Sinningia* 'Bright Eyes,' *S. pusila*, *S.* 'White Sprite,' *S.* 'Snowflake,' *S.* 'Freckles,' and *S. concinna*, all great.

We stay away from most of the larger growers, but the medium-sized *Sinningia* 'Dollbaby' and *S.* 'Cindy,' which makes plants 8–10″ across with good culture, both do well.

Other Gesneriads.

Koellikeria erinoides is a tiny gem, rarely growing more than a few inches high, with speckled leaves and many maroon-and-cream small flowers held high (so make sure there is room above the plant). It is a little slower to flower than some, but a beauty to have when it does.

Phinea multiflora gives many charming white flowers, but it needs a lot of grooming: the dead flowers look unsightly. Also very small—though we have seen some that forgot they were true miniatures.

Streptocarpus rimicola is very desirable, and may self-seed for you right in the terrarium. It is monocarpic and dies after flowering, but this tiny thing is still worth trying in a terrarium.

Smithiantha is a lovely, velvety plant, but it is pollution-sensitive, and often won't flower in cities. Be certain you get one of the new miniature hybrids.

Pieces of aeschynanthus, columnea, and hypocyrta can be tried, but they are large-growing trailers, usually, and must be replaced before they grow too large.

Diastema: there are several species of this small grower that you might want to try, if you can find them.

Episcias are the greatest, but they grow rapidly. If yours outgrows its protected environment, take out the main plant and start over with a rooted stolon (give the parent to your favorite plant society). There are a few miniatures around, though not widely available. Episcia foliage makes them very desirable for color accents.

Gesnerias are miniatures that grow in rosette shape and do very well in high-humidity environments. Flowers easily.

BEGONIAS

Begonias will often be shy of flowering in protected environments, but they grow well in high-humidity conditions and should certainly have a place in any terrarium you try.

Of course, when we speak of begonias in terrariums, we're not speaking of the semperflorens types, or the tall-growing canes and uprights.

Here are some of the varieties we've tried, and which you may be able to order from the growers listed in the back of this book:

B. 'Gay Star'—grows smaller inside a container than out.

B. herbacea—doesn't really look like a begonia, because of the long, uncut leaves, but it makes nice tufts in a terrarium.

B. masoniana (Iron Cross)—grows too large for any but the largest bottles, but it looks beautiful.

Rexes—there are hundreds of rex begonias in beautiful colors, but they are mostly big growers and have to be removed from a terrarium before they crowd out the other plants. One miniature delight is *B.* 'Peridot,' available from Mike Kartuz, one of our favorite growers and hybridizers.

B. versicolor—quite slow-growing and therefore excellent for terrariums, but it will eventually make a plant a foot or more across.

B. boweri nigramarga and *B. boweri nigramarga minima*—both are small-leaved, though they will spread. These rhizomatous begonias should be clipped to keep them small. We use them a great deal for ground covers.

B. 'Black Falcon'—will stay small enough to keep in a ½-gallon bottle. (Try any of the small rhizome types.)

B. 'Chantilly Lace' and *B.* 'Maphil' ('Cleopatra')—have similar growth habits, and are of intermediate size. The rhizomes must be kept clipped to keep the plants compact.

B. prismatocarpa is a delightful yellow-flowered miniature. It will propagate from the tiny leaves.

There are too many begonia possibilities to try to cover them all.

BROMELIADS

Cryptanthus make for a nice bit of variety on your terrarium floor.

Miniature tillandsias are great, if you are willing to mount them on a bit of cork or in a bit of sphagnum moss, and then use them to fill holes in rocks: those that have roots don't care for contact with soil.

ORCHIDS

Lockhartia does well in terrarium conditions, and its small, tight, overlapping leaves make for a very unusual growth pattern.

Vanda miniatures look well, but they must be removed if they show any sign of fungus developing.

MOSSES

There are mosses one can find between the cracks of bricks or the sidewalk, if you're willing to gather them. If you don't care to bend, there are several varieties of selaginella that do very well in terrariums.

There's hardly a terrarium we make that doesn't grow some volunteer moss.

CACTI AND SUCCULENTS

Don't! Cacti and succulents generally rot in these high-humidity planters.

MISCELLANEOUS

Marantas. These are fine—if you don't mind an entire terrarium full of prayer plant. (You'll often find marantas sold stapled to a totem, but they're not happiest that way: these are spreaders, not climbers.)

Calathea. We have a miniature of this lovely plant, doing quite well in a terrarium. We have a friend with a 4-by-2′ terrarium, growing several varieties happily under quite low light.

Ferns. There are excellent miniature ferns (some maidenhairs for example), but some ferns grow quite large. Staghorn ferns (platycerium) start out, as do all ferns, as tiny sporophytes and can be had as tiny plants. But in a greenhouse they can easily grow to a diameter of 3′. The polypodiums and daviallia do fairly well in a moderate amount of humidity, but they spread by hairy rhizomes—not appropriate for a terrarium. Almost any fern is suitable to a large terrarium for a short period of time. If, however, you want to keep a fern small, you're going to have to use the minis. Try the button fern, *Pellaea rotundifolia*—its round leaflets hardly look like a fern's.

Bertolonias. These are most handsome in a terrarium—slightly hairy-leaved with a good sheen—but they'll take over if given the chance, with a spread of almost 12".

Pileas. There are several pileas, small plants making small flowers.

Peperomias. These are unlikely to flower outside a greenhouse, but their shiny foliage (sometimes variegated) make nice accents.

Pellionias. Pellionias are spreaders with muted foliage, especially handsome in young plants.

Fittonias. These are bright and beautiful in two-color combinations.

Oxalis. The tropical oxalis will flower for you in a terrarium: *Oxalis hedysaroides ruba* (firefern) and *O. martiana* 'Aureo-reticulata.' The former is red-leaved and the latter laced with gold.

Ficus pumilla. Creeping fig has to be kept cut back or it will take over the world.

Hoya bella. This is the smallest-leaved of the hoyas and needs the extra humidity of an open or semi-open terrarium.

Saxifrage. You might want to try a saxifrage on a high place, leaving room for the stolons to hang down.

LIGHTING YOUR PROTECTED ENVIRONMENT

Some plants need less light inside a protrected environment than out. We've had *Sinningia* 'Bright Eyes' flower for us under a single tube about 12" away.

Certainly some bottled begonias seem to require less light

to stay compact than their cousins in the open (though others reach for the light, no matter how close you try to get them).

We grow all our protected plants under 16 hours of daily fluorescent light, as close to the tubes as we can get them. Brandy snifters and mustard jars can get quite close.

Our fish-tank terrarium is too tall to fit into our regular light set-up, so we put together a 2-tube 18″ fixture that fits right on top of the tank, with a little room for air circulation (see drawing, page 225).

WHAT ABOUT NATURAL LIGHT?

We said at a lecture one evening that you can't really grow a good, healthy, flowering or foliage terrarium in a window in New York City, and of course, as soon as we said it, several growers came running up to say they did.

Generally speaking, any window with sun is too hot for a protected environment. The heat builds up inside of the container, the water in the soil and in the plants is cooked out, and you kill your plants.

If you have an east window which gets only the barest morning sun but good light the rest of the day, you may find that you can keep your containers alive, but the plants will usually get leggy.

In general, all but the most brilliant north windows are just too dim: but those ladies who came up to tell us that their terrariums were doing well in windows all lived in the same co-op in the Bronx (where the air is a bit cleaner), and all had absolutely brilliant northern exposures.

If you live where the air is relatively clear, and your window is a brilliant northern exposure and not blocked by other buildings, then you, too, can try your terrarium in your window. Otherwise, we strongly recommend you read Chapter 12, GROWING UNDER LIGHTS.

MAINTENANCE

Do you keep the cover on your fish tank, or take it off? Are your bottles corked or open? How often do you water? Feed? Here's what we do with a variety of containers.

Flying Saucers. The plastic saucers have a top and a bottom, with a 2–2½″ hole in the top. (Spheres and egg-shaped planters also come in two parts, but without the hole.) The hole means that the humidity is not quite 100% though it is very high—80% or more. Some plants, like episcias and African violets, do better in this "lower" humidity.

Also, it means that the medium does dry out somewhat between waterings, which come about every month, on the average, though perhaps more often in the very hot months.

Feed very dilutely with every other watering.

The removal of the top makes for easy grooming—and do remove all deadheads and dead or dying foliage.

Small Jars. These sometimes go for more than a month between waterings, but in general, treat them the same as flying saucers.

Bottles. We leave our bottles open all the time—for the tiny amount of air circulation—and find their need for water varies. We have had some go almost a year without needing water and some that needed it every few months—but none more often than that. Keep an eye on the soil. If it begins to pull away from the sides of the bottle, water. But never water heavily. Water a bit, then a bit more if it still seems to need it.

Sinningia 'Petite Fleur' in flower in a 4″ snifter.

Screw the handle off the bottom of an old Silex coffeemaker.

Feed with very dilute chemical food at every watering.

Use the tools described earlier in the chapter to groom, but do it carefully.

Fish tanks. Even with a partial cover—the way we prefer growing fish-tank terrariums—they dry out rather quickly and need watering every two weeks or so, especially in the hot weather.

Feed once a month with very dilute chemical food.

Groom frequently, and don't hesitate to change plants if you've got someone in there not holding up his end.

Snifters and Things. Mustard jars, silex percolators, chemical flasks, rose bowls, brandy snifters, clear vases—there are more containers that can be used as planters than you could imagine or we could describe. If they are open, cover them (perhaps with clear plastic or watch glasses), and treat them like the flying saucers.

PART V

THE KITCHEN

19. Avocados

Even people who can't grow one other thing can often grow avocados because, in many respects, this tree is an ideal apartment plant.

It is semitropical and likes the warmth of an apartment, without being too bothered by its dry air.

Though a tree, it doesn't require full sun; it can, in fact, be trained to get along on moderate sun, so long as it gets good light.

It grows quickly during its first couple of years. But, unlike the herbaceous fast-growers, it is not subject to every bug going around.

The huge seed aren't susceptible to damping-off, so that when one does sprout, you're going to get your tree.

And it is the cheapest plant you can find, costing exactly nothing to buy (it comes free with the avocado), though you'll have to pay for those large pots your friend requires when it gets big.

Because it is a moisture-lover, it isn't bothered by the heavy soil that many novices seem to like. (This can be overdone, though, so don't plant them into pots without drainage holes.)

In many respects, an avocado is *the* plant for the beginning apartment gardener.

DID YOU HEAR THE ONE ABOUT THE GLASS OF WATER AND THE TOOTHPICKS?

We used to start avocado seeds that way: stick toothpicks into them and suspend them in a glass of water. And sometimes the roots came out and a bit of shoot, and sometimes the whole thing turned into a stinking mess.

Until one day a funny thing happened.

This one seed had failed to root; it had shriveled and

turned black, and we were going to throw it out; but we were potting up a beefsteak begonia at the moment and so we broke the dead seed in half and threw the halves into the bottom of the 6″ pot. We're not really sure why we did it, now; perhaps we had some idea of providing some organic food for the begonia.

The begonia took and was thriving when we noticed a pencil-thick stem coming out of the center of the begonia. No, it wasn't part of the begonia, it was the avocado, springing from the dead, and making a sprout that made all the other avocados we'd ever tried look sick.

Let us tell you that "science" took a great leap backward that day. After all, we'd been sticking toothpicks according to the best advice available. And now, like the guy who burned down the shack, we'd discovered roast pig.

WHICH KIND?

Avocado seeds vary, depending on their species and national origin. For us, the seeds from the green-skinned fruit sprout faster than the seeds from brown ones, but aside from that, we've been unable to determine whether big are better than small or very pebbled seeds stronger than rather smooth ones.

WHAT DO YOU DO?

Remove the seed from the oily flesh, wash it, and scrape off the paper-brown covering. Soaking overnight in warm water helps get that wrapper off.

Prepare a 6″ pot with crock and our standard potting mix (see Chapter 7) with an extra helping each of topsoil and of humus.

Now, set the seed and cover with soil so that the top of the seed—the pointier end—sticks out of the soil. Yes, you can bury the seed deep in the pot and it will make the thickest and strongest plant you've ever had, but it takes longer to come up.

That's right, no toothpicks, no glasses, no cutting off bits of the seed.

Water well, and put the pot where you will remember to keep it watered.

As long as the seed stays pink and firm, keep on watering. If it's shriveled and black, heave it out and start over: you don't want to go on watering a dead seed for the rest of your life.

A 6" POT?

Yes, we start our avocados in big pots, even though we recommend small pots for other young plants.

You see those great big sturdy-looking roots your avocado makes? Well, it's all a bluff. Those roots are especially delicate and susceptible to damage. And what those roots like least of all is the kind of manhandling they get during repotting. And, since they are moisture-lovers, they don't mind the extra soil around their roots. (In many other plants, such overpotting would cause rot.)

LIGHT

Once the avocado is sprouted, you have to decide on a place for it. They are trees, remember, sitting out there in the Florida sunshine, making flowers and fruit like crazy, so they obviously like a good deal of sunlight. But, if you raise an avocado in a dim corner (where it will live, though never thrive), and then put it into the full sun, you will burn the leaves.

We have met most attractive avocados growing in north-light-only apartments.

Recently, we have taken to *starting* some seedlings right out in the full sun (that is, as much full sun as our obstructed-east balcony will allow) and they were thriving up to a 10-day heatwave, when a few young leaves burned. We think it wasn't the sun but the heat, because up to that time, all through July and most of August, they seemed very happy in the sun. You might try it: they are making very stocky growth, something that isn't always easy to achieve with an avocado.

FOOD

Yes, by all means, feed your avocados as heavily as anything you grow: every 2 weeks, at half strength, alternating fish emulsion and 15-30-15. They are heavy feeders.

REPOTTING

(For general technique, see AND POTTING, Chapter 11.)

With most repotting, we move up only an inch or two; with avocados, we go right from that 6" pot into a 10" pot so we won't have to repot for a good long time. And remember to handle those tender roots as little as possible.

WATERING

Keep your avocados pretty much evenly moist, watering when the top of the soil *begins* to go dry. If you allow it to dry out, it will cost you leaves.

PROBLEMS

Allowing the plant to get potbound will also cost you leaves. So, if you find yourself losing leaves, check the rootball (Chapter 11 tells you how).

Avocados are prone to scale, but they aren't much troubled by it—an advantage of being a tree—and they are very susceptible to root damage, which can kill your plant off quickly. (Chapter 14 tells you what you can *try* to do about root damage.)

TO PINCH OR NOT TO PINCH

You can't change a plant's genetic character by lopping off its head. You can *shape* a plant after it is growing well: that's pruning. But lopping off that head is a terrible setback to the plant, and slows it down.

Your avocado will do its own thing. If, genetically, it is a brancher, it will branch, whether you pinch it or not. If, genetically, it is a single-stemmer, then it will stay a single-stemmer, no matter how many times you pinch.

If you don't like the basic habit of the seed you are growing, get one of a different variety or from a different state or country. We've had avocados that put up multiple stems, those that branched, and those that reached for the sky. (Make sure it's not just reaching for the light.)

THE AVOCADO SYNDROME

The fact is that most avocados in apartments in cities have a limited life. If your avocado is more than 2 to 3 years old, you're ahead of the game, because most just pack it in long before then.

Why? We don't know. And some of the biggest guns in horticulture don't know either. But the leaves begin to darken and go papery from the leaf edges inward, and leaf after leaf shrivels and falls.

Examination of thousands of avocados with these symptoms showed no disease, no bug, nothing but dying plants.

Perhaps it's something in the city air or in the city water. Whatever it is, it now seems to be attacking younger and younger plants.

Now, about *your* avocado that is a glorious 10-year-old beauty—congratulations: it's one in a thousand. But for the rest of us, it pays to have a new avocado seed coming along all the time.

20. Garbage Gardening

Garbage is great—let's recycle more of it. Some of what we throw out after preparing or eating a meal or find lying around in the world can be grown on into quite satisfactory plants.

Certainly, last chapter's avocados are the greatest examples, but there are many other good garbage plants.

CITRUS

Seeds from lemons, grapefruit, and oranges sprout very readily, and we doubt that there is a lovelier plain foliage in the plant world than the shiny green of citrus plants. (We've never tried lime seeds, and are curious if they will sprout. The limes we get in the market are not ripe—that's why they're green—and so the seeds may not be mature enough to germinate.)

DON'T DRY THEM

The secret of success with citrus seeds is to plant them fresh: that's right, don't let them dry out. Dry, we've always failed with them; wet, we've gotten good germination. So, if you don't have time to plant your breakfast today, put your grapefruit seed in a saucer with some water for a day or so.

The citrus are all acid-lovers, so put several of the seed to sprout in a 4″ pot, buried just beneath the surface of an acid soil (our basic soil mix with an extra helping of peat moss; see Chapter 7). With tree seed, or so it seems, damp-off isn't a problem, so you don't need any special sowing techniques.

As soon as your seedlings are showing green, move them into good light, though not directly into bright sun. Thin to 2 or 3 seedlings in the pot when they are big enough to handle. Then you can move them into more sun. Citrus, like avocados, also resent repotting.

WATERING

The most important thing with citrus is that they *never dry out*. Keep them evenly moist at all times, watering whenever the surface of the soil begins to show any signs of drying.

MINIS

We have successfully sprouted seed from our own miniature orange tree, and have grown the plants on to a moderate size before giving them away. But we've never gotten flowers on a miniature orange grown from seed.

GRAPEFRUIT SPECIAL

Of the citrus, we've found grapefruit the quickest to sprout, with the highest percentage of germination, and making the most vigorous plants.

On all your citrus, though, remember to keep the soil acid, feed with an acid food occasionally, keep in good sun, mist the leaves with water as often as you can, and keep well watered.

Watch for scale, and for spider mites.

SQUASH AND FRIENDS

Squash and melons (all members of the cucurbit family) sprout readily and have only one drawback, really; they are vines, and so they take up a lot of windowspace and require a lot of soil to do their best. All cucurbits are heavy feeders—which makes them not too practical as apartment plants. They love hills of manure and compost.

They are grown strictly as annuals, but you can have a lot of fun with them for one season. We've had success with butternut squash, cantaloupe, watermelon, and cucumbers.

We wash the seed to remove all extraneous stuff clinging to them and then spread them on a dish or a paper towel to dry. Yes, we do dry these seed, though we don't dry citrus seed. Either we use them as soon as they are dry, or store the seeds in the fridge for next spring.

Watermelon seed are especially fast to come up, and so vigorous to grow that they make a good project for schoolkids; their progress can be easily marked from day to day (or from morning to afternoon). And we've even gotten a cucumber or three from a planting of our own cucumber seed. But our favorites are cantaloupes and butternut squash. On our windowsill, in 4″ pots, both have flowered for us: *big* yellow flowers that lasted only a day each, but still very exciting. We got no squash or melons, but we did get those lovely flowers.

These vines are all heavy feeders and heavy drinkers, but they don't require being evenly moist, so allow the soil surface to go dry before watering again, but then water well.

Give good sun for best growth, and as much root room as you can afford. We put the cucumbers into a foot-square wooden box full of soil—which is why we got any cukes at all. Those 4″ pots could give us flowers, but they didn't hold enough nutrition or space for fruit.

You can start the seed as described in GROWING FROM SEED, Chapter 17, though watermelon seed will sprout in any medium.

OTHER FRUIT

APPLES

Apple seeds sprout quite readily, especially toward the autumn, when the apples we get in city markets are a bit overripe. Seed from green (sour) apples won't sprout at all; and always remember that apples are hardy trees, and unless you can give them a very cool winter rest, you are not going to be able to keep them over the winter. They are deciduous, so don't panic when they drop leaves.

Plant the apple seeds moist, right from the fruit if they've begun to sprout already, using any of the methods described in Chapter 17.

HARD SEEDS

We've had some fun with apricots and peaches, but never grown them on successfully. They *may* germinate, if you give them enough time. What we've done is to sometimes throw a cleaned peach or apricot pit (hard shell and all) into a pot in which some houseplant is being potted up. That way we don't have to sit around and wait for the seed to germinate. But we put a label into the pot so when a sprout finally does show itself, we are not completely befuddled.

MANGO

Mangos make good plants, if you can get them out of their jackets and sprouted. We've had one in leaf for over a year,

Mango trees are slower-growing than avocados.

now; it stays much more compact than an avocado, and the new leaves come in *red*—very attractive.

When you've cut away all the flesh of the fruit, allow that large seed to dry enough to harden the fibrous outer jacket. Then, hold it up to the light and look for the seed. With a scissors, cut off a part of the jacket *away from the seed*. Then, with fingers or a scissors or knife, peel or cut away the rest of the jacket and discard it. There will be left on the seed a partial covering, brown and papery. Peel away what you can but don't hassle it. Plant the seed about an inch down in rich potting soil, horizontally. It's not so easy to tell top from bottom with mangos, so let the seed work it out.

Germination is slow and chancy. Only about 30% of our mango seeds germinate. Don't allow the soil to dry out while you're waiting.

Once up, treat just like an avocado.

DATES AND PERSIMMONS

These are trees from different climates that work the same.

Soak the seeds overnight and plant them as described for large seeds in Chapter 17. Seeds from "pasteurized" dates will not germinate.

Once the seedlings are up (you may get 50–60% germination), transplant to individual pots, water well, and give good light. Once established, you can give them more sun and reduce their watering slightly, allowing them to go surface-dry between waterings.

Will It Fruit? We read in a gardening column years ago, this question: "Will my windowsill date palm fruit?" The reply was, "Yes: the plant will make fruit when it reaches 40′ in height and meets a date palm of the opposite sex."

POMEGRANATES

We especially like these because they make such nice houseplants, staying compact under lights, and even flowering.

Remove the fruit from around the seeds and soak them overnight. Lay them on the surface of your seed medium and press the seeds down into it to their own thickness. Germination will probably take only a couple of weeks.

When large enough to handle, pot into our standard soil mix, and set under strong fluorescent light or in a moderately-bright window.

Pomegranate is a favorite subject among bonsai fanciers.

EXOTICS

Actually, an exotic is anything that comes originally from an exotic climate, and many of our everyday fruits and vegetables would fill that description.

The fancier fruit-sellers have some wild-looking and wildtasting fruit on their shelves. We got something called a cherimoya that tasted like a cross between a banana and a pineapple, and now we have several lovely little cherimoya plants on our windowsills and under lights. Once you've enjoyed the fruit, what have you got to lose by trying to plant the seeds?

For the cherimoya, plant at once in a Jiffy-7, or soak overnight to trigger them (no longer or they will rot).

With untried exotics, treat the seeds as you would "Citrus," described above. And most tropical trees are not deciduous.

NONSEEDS

You can get interesting if temporary plants from some root vegetables, which can be fun for the kids.

Growing a sweet potato is a good way to have kids understand *tubers*. Using those toothpicks you no longer need for your avocados, suspend a sweet potato half in and half out of a glass of water. Roots will grow into the water and quite a bit of top growth will grow out of the dry-air half. In soil of course, you'd get a more vigorous growth, and plants watergrown like this will peter out, but the kids love to see what's going on.

A carrot top, also toothpicked over a glass of water, will give you some interesting growth, too.

Pineapple tops make attractive, long-lasting houseplants. In Chapter 23, BROMELIADS, we will detail the rooting of them; this is one bromeliad that everyone can have.

FREE TREES

When you go to national forest or national seashores, the

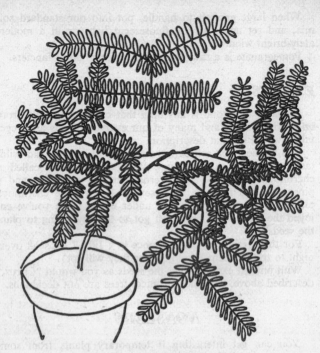

Albizzia is a fun tree.

rangers say that you can pick flowers or fruit or seeds, but not the plants themselves. It's a healthy attitude, and one we might carry over into our city parks.

We've mentioned the powderpuff tree (albizzia) before, and it is a favorite of ours for a houseplant (we have a friend who uses it for bonsai). Start it like any large seed (see Chapter 17), but give it a soaking overnight in water, first. The leaves of this charming plant close at night and open in the morning. There are seedpods on the tree, or lying on the ground under it all year round, and you can plant them at any time.

Gingkos are also great fun, but only the female trees bear seed; the ripe seed has a very cheesy smell. In the fall, you can find a female tree by the smell. Be sure you wash all the soft matter off the seed before you plant it.

Locusts and magnolias will also do well for you in an

apartment, for a year or two. We have a friend who tells us she flowered a small locust on her windowsill.

Trees growing in an apartment (except for albizzia) must be kept quite *cool* in winter.

Try any seed: shrubs, trees, vegetables, fruits. The plants you get can be very rewarding. But don't expect all seedlings to jump up at you; tree and shrub seed may take months to germinate.

21. Salad on Your Windowsill

When we first planned our windowsill salad-gardening course for the Horticultural Society of New York, we figured that while a lot of our salad stuff was fun, some of it was just not economical. And then prices began to rise and rise and ... And all of a sudden lettuce was 69¢ and the lettuce we were growing, while still fun, had become a bargain.

Always ahead of our time.

There is a limit to what you can grow to eat on your windowsill (or on that small balcony or fire escape). A parsley plant requires a 4″ pot to grow to full size, so does a "Tiny Tim" tomato (our favorite among the miniature vegetables). And, there is room for only just so many 4″ pots on any windowsill, as well as a limit to the crop you can harvest from a single plant.

Also, some salad vegetables are just inappropriate to window culture: cucumbers—even the miniatures—require a lot of soil and a lot of room. We planted cucumbers one year and got 3 cukes—out of almost a cubic foot of soil—hardly sound agronomics. Green peppers are so sensitive to air pollution that they just aren't practical in the city.

But rather than dwell on the cannots, let's look at the cans.

SPROUTS

Here's the easiest way to get fresh, unsprayed salad stuff in your apartment: sprout it.

Bean sprouts, an excellent food and popular among Oriental cooks and health foodists, are ready to eat just 3 to 5 days after you put them up. Can you imagine? An edible crop from seed in just 3 days!

Garlic sprouts—the sprouted tops of garlic cloves—are ready to use as seasoning in *2 weeks*—as are the sprouts of other edible bulbs.

BEAN SPROUTS

Even if you live in a closet, you can grow some salad stuff in your apartment—without soil or plant food or lights—with bean sprouts.

Sprouted mung beans ready to eat.

Many different beans and seeds can be sprouted: radish seeds, alfalfa seeds, mung beans, soybeans, wheat, buckwheat, cress, most any seed or bean will give you a sprout.

Among the easiest, quickest, and most nutritious is the small green "mung bean" (you find it with pale tails in your chop suey). You can buy these beans already freshly sprouted in Oriental food stores, and canned in supermarkets. But the canned have been heated and so are of poor texture and small nutrition. It's much more economical, nutritious, and exciting to sprout them fresh yourself.

Start with about 2 ounces of dried beans, a 2-cup glass jar

with a cover, and a strainer. Pour the beans into a strainer and wash with running water. Scrape the beans into the glass jar and add 1 cup of water (whether cool or warm doesn't matter). Cover the jar (do not seal it, but cover it well enough to keep bugs and dust out), and let stand out of the way (light or dark doesn't matter) overnight—no more than 24 hours.

Next day, pour off any excess water and add a cup of fresh water and drain it off again, leaving no extra water in the beans—the *moisture* will be enough. Cover the beans again. Do the same thing the next day.

Repeat until the beans are ready. They are ready when the tails (the roots) are about 1″ long, though they may be eaten when the tails are shorter than that. Eat at once or store in the fridge.

These little things are so nutritious that it's hard to believe—much more so than the dry beans themselves were. But don't let the sprouts stay in the fridge for more than a week before eating them—their vitamin content goes down if they are kept around.

These crisp and delicately-flavored sprouts make a delightful addition to a salad.

Our second-favorite seed sprouts is a medley of mung beans, lentils, and alfalfa. The alfalfa are much smaller, so don't put them in the strainer—just add them right to the dish. They fill the spaces between the larger beans.

WHEAT GRASS

Lots of health-food folks have gotten quite interested in wheat grass lately.

Take a baking pan and put in a layer of about ½″ of damp soil. Sow the wheat berries thickly over the surface. Don't bury. Water lightly if needed.

Harvest after about a week by clipping the green wheat "grass," and add raw to a salad.

BULB SPROUTS

You can plant garlic, onion, or shallot bulbs in the spring and harvest a crop of green sprouts to season your salads all summer and fall. (You can also grow these on to maturity, and we'll discuss that later—the planting technique is just the same.)

If you are staggering your plantings, store your extra bulbs in the fridge—this gives them the message that winter has turned to spring when you bring them out, and they get going fast.

Garlic Sprouts. These are great to grow because they have the same taste as garlic in the clove, but with much less bite. You know what happens if you leave garlic bits in a salad— someone always makes a face; well, garlic sprouts are the answer.

To grow, crock up a 4″ pot and then fill it to the neck with soil (your standard potting mix). Then, tear a garlic clove off of the hand (a hand is that group of cloves, joined together at the base, that you buy at the supermarket). Poke a hole in the soil and bury the clove, *pointy end up.* Close the soil over the top. Repeat three more times, until you've a total of 4 cloves of garlic in one pot. Water and put under lights, or right on your windowsill. In the spring you'll often see green buds pushing up through the soil within 3 days. When the sprouts are 6″ high, you can begin to cut them for a salad.

Shallot Sprouts. Shallots are a favorite seasoning of French cooks, but they are quite dear in the States (though it's true

Break up clumps of shallots before planting.

they haven't gone up as much as onions). Still, you can buy a few ounces of shallots and have enough sprouts for seasoning all season long.

To grow, plant like garlic cloves, except that you bury the shallots only halfway under the soil—that is, leave the neck of the shallot well exposed. Water, and put in the sun or under lights. Shallots make multiple sprouts, and you can cut them when they reach about 4″.

Shallot sprouts, ready to clip.

Onion Sprouts. Onions don't even need soil or water for sprouting—or light either, for that matter. If you've ever kept onions too long in a bag out of the fridge, you'll have noticed that the onion has sprouted on its own, without any encouragement. The sprouts taste much like scallion greens (and why shouldn't they—scallions *are* onions, at a younger stage of development: we'll go into that later), and are a welcome addition to a salad.

ONION SETS AND SCALLIONS

All right, how *can* you grow onions on your windowsill? From onion sets, of course.

From seed to maturity, an onion takes about 6 sunny months. Which is way too long for northern farmers. So, starting latish in the season, the seedsmen grow onions from seed for a few months and get little onions. These babies are dug up and stored until the spring—they are great storers.

In the spring, the farmers plant those onion sets which they have bought from the seedsmen. If they wish, they may make a harvest in about 4 weeks, and what they will harvest is *scallions*. Or, they may let the set grow on until the fall, in which case they harvest *onions*. Honest.

To Grow Onion Sets to Scallions. Use our basic soil mix, but with an extra measure of topsoil (see SOIL, Chapter 7). Crock a 4″ pot and fill it with soil to the neckline, then poke holes and plant 4 onion sets to the pot—only about ⅔ covered: that is, some of the onion set should show above the soil line. Water, and put into a sunny location. For scallions, pull after about 4 weeks; for onions, start in a larger container (or 1 per 4″ pot) and grow on until the fall. Don't be surprised if the tips of the sprouts turn brown—they do that for farmers, too. That's why you usually get scallions with the tips cut off the greens.

Onion sets can be bought from seedsmen at quite a reasonable price (try Field's), but don't order more than you and your friends can use—even refrigerated they are hard to hold back once the spring comes. Also, be careful in handling them—the sets are often treated with a fungicide to keep them better in storage and transit.

WINDOWBOXES

All of these bulb sprouts can be grown in windowboxes, as long as the box has appropriate drainage. One thing all bulbs hate is to sit in soggy soil. Holes drilled into the bottom of the box, or an inch or so of gravel, will do. Just remember, heavy spring rain will accumulate in the bottom of a windowbox as in any closed container.

To plant up a windowbox with these, or any of the salad stuff in this chapter, we recommend that you keep the plants in flowerpots, and pile up some mulch over the top (peat moss or bark chips or broken peanut shells or the like). This will hide the pots, but it will allow you to take out a single pot of something for harvesting, without disturbing the root systems of neighboring plants.

However, keep in mind that onions and garlics, while they taste great, don't make the handsomest foliage for a windowbox, so mix them with nasturtiums or herbs.

CHIVES

Have you wondered why it is that those pots of chives you buy from your produce market look so shabby and die so quickly? Or did you think it was something *you* were doing?

No, the way they are sold is a rip-off. Those pots of chives are so crowded together when you buy them that the wonder is they live long enough for you to get them home.

But you can save them and grow them on if you divide them up immediately.

Water the chives and knock them out of the pot. See how the whole thing seems to be one large clump.

Hold half the clump of chives in each hand, and pull them apart—go on, don't be scared. Now you have 2 smaller clumps. Now, do it again, and again, dividing down until you have many clumps of only 2 or 3 little bulbs. Throw away any material that seems dead, rotten, or squishy. Plant up, say, 6 of those clumps to a 3″ pot (with standard soil and crock), put into the sun, and you've got a good chance of having your chives live a good healthy growing season. You're unlikely to keep them over the winter unless you can give them a quite cool window. But, come the fall, do divide again, and see if you can't get some of them to live over.

Of course, chives can be grown from seed; they are slow that way, but not difficult. (See Chapter 16, GROWING FROM SEED.) Keep in mind, though, when growing chives from seed —the seedlings look like grass: don't weed them out. You can clip the young chive seedlings for your salads, especially if you've made a heavy planting.

HERBS

Many delicious herbs will grow either on your windowsill or under lights.

BASIL

If we grew only one herb that would be basil.

If we cooked with only one herb, that, too, would be basil.

Basil is very quick from seed (see Chapter 16, GROWING FROM SEED). You can take your first serious crop after a month, which is great.

This year, we are growing Greek basil, from seed brought to us from a friend's trip to Greece. It is quite different from the broadleaf basil which is most common; but last year we ordered basil (just basil) from a major seedsman and the basil seed we were sent turned out to be another kind of small-leafed basil identified as French basil.

There is also a purple-leafed basil, not quite as pungent as some of the others, but very handsome.

But the basil most commonly seen around and most commonly grown (we recently saw a plant 18″ tall and in magnificently full leaf, growing in a concrete urn outside an Italian restaurant) is broadleaf basil, *Ocimum basilicum* to give it its Latin name.

Keep basil well watered and it will follow you anywhere. It will flourish in any soil and in any good light. If you do let it dry out, you will get recriminations from the sorriest-looking plant you've ever seen. Sometimes, prompt watering will bring back even a dead-looking plant. But try not to make a habit of it: each drying costs you leaves.

Pinching out the growing tips will encourage branching and give you a bushier plant and a bigger crop. Eat the pinchings. Later in the summer, keep the flower buds pinched out also, for once this lovely herb goes into flower it changes from a beautiful bushy creature to a scraggly bum. Being an annual, once it has flowered it feels that its life work is done.

While the plant is still in good growth, take 4″ cuttings for your prop box (see Chapter 17). Cuttings taken from young growth will show roots in a few days and be ready for potting in 10.

We often prefer to grow basil under fluorescent light, where it is slower to flower—and so gives us a longer harvesting season.

For drying your own basil, look to the end of this "Herbs" section.

DILL

Dill is a good strong grower on your windowsill. Fairly easy to grow from seed (see Chapter 16), it is usable as a quite young plant. But remember, this is not a bulbous plant, and so you can't clip most of the plant for seasoning and then expect it to grow up to be a mature plant.

We grow dill only for the greens, preferring to buy the seeds when they are wanted. For drying dill, see the end of this section—though this, like most herbs, is really tastier when fresh.

But watch it; since most of a fresh herb is water, you must use, by weight or by volume, *more* of a fresh herb than a dried herb to achieve the same flavoring in a particular recipe.

Try one large plant to a 4″ pot.

Sometimes you will find dill very fresh at your greengrocer, with the roots intact. Try to pot it up. What can you lose?

NASTURTIUMS

These annuals are triple-threat plants. The flowers are

quite lovely, the plants are excellent for companion plantings (they attract bugs away from other plants), and the leaves make a fine contribution to your salad. In fact, even the flowers are edible.

They are easy to grow from their very large seed (see Chapter 16), and grow rapidly and flower young. You will find these plants rather sprawly, so you may want to stake them while they are young. Try one plant to a 3″ or 4″ pot. Make certain you buy the dwarf varieties, or you'll have more than you want for your windowsill.

Wash off any aphids before using as salad.

PARSLEY

Parsley is a real winner on your windowsill. A couple of mature parsley plants in 4″ pots will provide lots of greens for your salads, but they require watering every other day.

There are several old-wives' tales about the germination time of parsley, and it certainly is true that if left to its own devices it may take weeks to germinate; but why wait? Simply *soak the seed overnight in a dish of water*. The next day make up a seedbed, as described in GROWING FROM SEED, Chapter 16, and pour the seeds and the water over the bed, and you'll get good germination in 4 or 5 days (3 is our record).

Don't cut the parsley before the plant is beginning to mature—which won't be for a couple of months. It grows in a rosette, like an African violet, so new leaves come from the center; clip the outer leaves first.

Parsley is a biennial, which means that it goes through its life cycle over the course of 2 years. It will sprout, grow on, mature, and, finally in the next year, flower and die. So you can carry it over in a cool window (but don't clip it while it is dormant).

Try to cut your parsley only as you need it—the flavor really is superior fresh.

ROSEMARY

Rosemary is a perennial: a plant that will live on through several years and several growing seasons—if you don't kill it.

It should be happy for years in a 4″ pot (5″ if it grows

quite large), and since the herb has quite a strong taste, not much of it is needed to season something.

The prime cause of death among rosemary plants is stupidity: not watering. Though the plant is native to several dry regions, you cannot let it get very dry in a pot, or you can lose it. When the soil begins to feel dry on the top, water well, allow to drain, and then don't water again until the top begins to feel dry again.

Rosemary is slow from seed; the easiest way to get plants is to buy them—they are widely available during the summer.

SAGE

Sage is our favorite perennial herb. It comes easily from seed, and is *not* readily available as plants. Sow seed as described in Chapter 16. Germination is fairly quick. Give as much light as you can.

You may want to provide a little trellis for the maturing plants, as, at least for us, the growth tends to be a little sprawly.

One or two plants to a 4″ pot should do well. You probably will want to cut the plants back before bringing them inside for the winter. Do try to provide a cool window and good light for wintering.

This herb keeps its flavor quite well after drying.

SUMMER SAVORY

This plant is a hardy annual—that is, a one-year plant which *can* take frost—(to distinguish it from winter savory which is a perennial shrub, but not as flavorful or useful as seasoning). It is easy to grow on your windowsill provided you don't let it get too dry; you can clip it quite young, or wait until it has matured and dry the whole plant. Give it a rich soil and as much sun as you can.

SWEET MARJORAM

This is a fine seed, so be sure you sow it on milled sphagnum as described in GROWING FROM SEED, Chapter 16. It is a rather tender perennial, usually grown as an annual, though you may be able to carry it over the winter in pots.

Shade it from the hottest of the summer sun, if you have it in a south window.

TARRAGON

This perennial is propagated readily from a thickened root. The tarragon *seed* you see offered in most catalogs is for Russian tarragon, a plant with little flavor, not for French tarragon, the desirable herb. We've never gotten a satisfactory explanation for the rip-off.

Whatever the reason, whether the French is difficult to flower or just very slow from seed, be sure you buy the herb either as a plant or as a bit of this root.

A large tarragon plant will want a 4" or 5" pot.

All we've given you here are a few of our favorite salad herbs, but for a smell-freak there are many others. There are many, many mints (some of them not called mints): spearmint, peppermint, lemon balm (all as easy to grow as coleus and basil—which are in the same family), and corsican mint (keep it wet all the time or you'll lose it).

Coriander is an easy little plant to grow and flower. Lemon verbena is more of a challenge. We don't eat tansy or roman wormwood or lavendar—but what exciting aromas!

DRYING HERBS

It's really quite simple to dry your own herbs.

Take the herb, stem and all, wash well, and either pat dry or allow to drain well. Take a clean shopping bag and spread the herb over the bottom. *Hang the shopping bag over a doorknob.* After a couple of days, stir the herb up, to allow any dampness on the bottom to come to the top. Allow a few more days for the herb to dry thoroughly. It's important to allow for thorough drying; any dampness may cause mold when you bottle the herb.

Once the herb is quite dry, crush, and bottle in jars with very tight-fitting lids, and label clearly. Discard the stems if you wish. And that's all there is to it.

VEGETABLES

Your choice of windowsill vegetables is more limited than

your choice of windowsill herbs. Only those with relatively shallow root systems and relatively low height are appropriate to apartment culture. We've already mentioned our 3-cucumber crop—though those 3 cucumbers were incredibly sweet. Also, an attempt to grow miniature corn was defeated because the balcony wind was too strong for the plants, though they didn't grow any taller than the 2 feet or so advertised.

And there is this big difference between growing vegetables and growing herbs on your windowsill: one or two pots of sage will be enough sage to last you for a year; a few pots of basil will flavor up dozens and dozens of dishes; but one pot of lettuce gives you enough lettuce for a single serving of salad at a single meal, and one 4″ pot gives you no more than a couple of radishes.

Why then, grow vegetables at all?

Aside from the price of salad stuff today, the reward of seeing something you've nurtured grow, sometimes flower, and then brought to table is one of the richer moments of life.

If you want satisfaction, grow vegetables on your windowsill.

CARROTS

Read your seed catalogs; they'll tell you of the expected length of various carrots. You cannot grow a 6″ carrot in a 4″ pot, but you can grow a 3″ carrot in a 4″ pot. We recommend 'Tiny Sweet,' which should be ready as adults after about 60 days, but which can be eaten as babies as you thin them out, or anywhere along the way.

These are biennials (they flower the second year), but we eat them the first year. And don't throw out the greens, they are full of good nutrition.

Try several seedlings in a 4″ pot, and then thin them out to 2 carrots per pot as the seedlings mature. Remember to eat the thinnings.

CRESS

What you see in most supermarkets is watercress, but this isn't really suited to apartment culture: it requires constant running water—as by a running brook.

What we grow and recommend is garden cress (*Lepidium sativum*), a variety of which seedsmen sell as 'curlycress.'

The seeds germinate in just a few days, and the plant can be clipped and eaten as a sprout shortly after that, or grown on into a plant, a few to a 3″ pot, in our standard potting mix. (See Chapter 7.) Plant some every 3 weeks—any time of year—and eat it when it's an inch or so high.

LETTUCE

The 'Tom Thumb' we've grown makes small heads about the size of tennis balls, which will come to a maturity either on your windowsill or under lights in a 4″ pot. Even this windowsill lettuce prefers the cooler weather, so plant in the spring, and then again in the late summer or early fall.

One head makes one serving for one person.

MUSTARD GREENS

Also sold as 'Tendergreens,' this crop is a winner and can provide more greenery for your salads than lettuce—and at a smaller space investment. It will do well under lights as well as on your windowsill. A crop should be ready in about 4 weeks, so make several sowings through the growing season.

This is not the plant from which you get mustard seeds, though it is related and the greens do have a bit of a bite. The plant will show best growth in a soil less acid than most—so omit the peat moss in the soil mix for this annual. (See Chapter 7.)

RADISHES

Radishes are fun, and they are supposed to come to maturity in about 3 weeks in the garden, but our experience has been that they take a little longer on a windowsill. At any rate, 3 or 4 plants to a 4″ pot will allow them room enough.

When transplanting seedlings to their final pots, be sure you get the bottom portion of the stem well buried. It is this part of the stem, just between the lowest leaves (the leaves come out in a rosette) and the roots, that swells into the part that we eat.

If you're going through a hot spell, don't expect your radishes to thrive.

SPINACH

Spinach, like most leafy thin-leaved vegetables, needs lots of water in hot weather. Some varieties will "bolt"—that is, flower and go to seed instead of making the good leaf growth we eat.

Try 'Bloomsdale Long Standing' spinach, as having less of a tendency to bolt and being more heat-resistant. You should get a full crop in about 7 weeks, but you can sample leaves before then. What? You've never had a raw-spinach salad? Then you have a treat in store.

To beat the heat, sow in earliest spring and make a second sowing in August.

TOMATOES

Tomatoes are the star of any windowsill salad garden.

They must be kept well watered, and exposed to no frost at all, because they are *very* tender.

There are several small-growing varieties suited to pot culture. 'Tiny Tim' is probably the most popular. We have one in a 4″ pot in our obstructed east window which we started indoors, under lights, and didn't put out until all danger of frost was past. Two and a half months after sowing, it is in heavy bud; not bad for a plant only 10″ high. The tomatoes will be a bit smaller than the cherry tomatoes you get from your produce man.

'Atomic' is another good midget.

'Pixie' is a fairly new hybrid which gives larger tomatoes, in a 5 or 6″ pot, and from a slightly larger plant. If you can spare the space, the crop is heavier than the smaller midgets.

Tomatoes (the only flowering and fruiting crop we grow) are heavy feeders. We feed ours at every watering, with 15-30-15 plant food at about one quarter the strength recommended on the label. Since they are acid-lovers, a once-a-month acid feeding at quarter strength will help. (See FEEDING, Chapter 8.)

Tomato plants should be pinched young to make them branch. If you take off as much as an inch of tip growth, these tip cuttings can be rooted and grown on into fruiting plants—though they are slower than plants from seed. The cuttings root rapidly—within 2 weeks (see Chapter 17, VEGETATIVE PROPAGATION).

'Tiny Tim' tomato plant in bud.

We never use "blossom set" hormone to set the fruit on our tomatoes. On our windowsills the wind does the job of pollinating. Under lights or out of the wind, we give the plants a *shake* when in flower, and we get our pollinating done that way.

AFTERTHOUGHTS

Most of the plants we've described in this chapter are grown as annuals, though some few of the herbs can be carried over the winter in pots on a cool bright windowsill, or some can be started in the fall from cuttings (like basil).

Annuals, and any really fast growers, suffer from specific growing problems: lack of water or lack of light, even for short periods, may well stunt them forever. Also, their rapid growth attracts all kinds of insects. But plants can live with the depredations of a *small* insect population.

If the insect population on your edibles gets out of hand, throw the plant out. *Don't spray your edibles with insecticides.* (See Chapter 13, PESTS AND PROBLEMS—INSECTS.) One of the best bug deterrents is to mix herbs among your other plants: the alliums (onions, scallions, chives, garlic) and all the strong herbs are distasteful to certain bugs.

To repeat, annuals require lots of water. In limited space, they often cannot be given as large pots as they may need to hold moisture for a few days. If you have a space problem, keep your annuals where you can water them daily in warm weather; don't hide them in some corner where you may forget, or you may awaken to find them not just drooped but dead.

Vegetable and salad growing on your windowsill can present some problems, but it does provide a lot of delicious fun.

PART VI

SPECIAL
FRIENDS

22. Gesneriads

Gesneriads are a joy. They are the most delightful family of flowering houseplants, and easy of success once you understand and fulfill their requirements.

In general, they require higher humidity than is "normal" in an apartment or house, but if you provide that extra humidity, you'll find no family of plants more rewarding for less trouble.

SAINTPAULIA—AFRICAN VIOLET

Probably no flowering houseplant is known and grown as widely as African violets, and with good reason.

In the nineteenth century, gardening was extremely popular, and everyone had some parlor plants—generally, ferns or other plants that don't require much sun.

As the century turned and things went "modern," plants didn't fit in as well, and they seemed to drop out of peoples' scheme of indoor things. Then, along came the saintpaulia, and all that changed. Because here was a plant that would *flower* indoors, in a window, *at any time of year*, and without the sharp evening temperature drop that many other flowering plants require to set bud. (Apartment heating just doesn't give you that kind of drop.)

We can't deny that many of the new hybrids are lovely—we have Lyndon Lyon's new miniature, 'Tiny Dots,' which has the most beautiful spots on its petals—but in some respects, saintpaulias have been *overhybridized*. There are so many that competing hybrids may look very similar, and no one can know them all.

Learn their general nature and pick the hybrids you like by their flower color and form, their foliage color and form, and their general habit. Variegated foliage has been popular recently, but hybrids with curly-edged flowers may come into greater popularity, as may the trailing saintpaulias, when they become more available.

African violets are not violets, though their native habitat was originally Africa.

Some growers of exotics turn up their noses at saintpaulias—so did we, until we began to grow them and know them. They are easy to flower and to keep in bloom under many conditions, easy to propagate, and resistant to many bugs.

CULTURE

Saintpaulias are simpler to grow in an apartment than are many other gesneriads.

They will be content in a minimum humidity of 40% (see Chapters 4 and 5, HUMIDITY and RAISING HUMIDITY). Even a daily misting will help.

They flower on your bright windowsills or under about 14 hours of fluorescent light (keep the plants about 6" from the tubes). Summertime's bright sun will, however, burn your leaves, so some protection (perhaps a thin curtain) is desirable for the hottest days. Turn the plants frequently under natural light. Almost any sunny window will do, as long as it isn't too hot, though saintpaulias will be happy in a wide range of temperatures.

Clean the fuzzy leaves occasionally with a soft brush or a pipecleaner. But the foliage can be badly damaged by a stiff brush.

When the plants are in growth or in bud, feed every other week with a ¾-strength solution of fish emulsion alternated with a 15-30-15 chemical food. (They are heavy feeders, so you can give them *almost* as much as the plant food manufacturers say.) If, after flowering, a plant decides to take a vacation, reduce the feeding by half until new growth begins.

African violets like a very light soil, only slightly on the acid side. (Our basic soil mix will do quite well, see Chapter 7.) It's a good idea to repot any plants you get from a greenhouse or local florist, because the commercial growers tend to put them in too heavy a soil for apartments. Soils that work fine in a greenhouse can be a dismal failure in the apartment or home.

If you are growing your African violets in wick pots, they will stay evenly moist; if you are growing them in regular pots (azalea-shape is best because they are shallow-rooted), allow the surface of the soil to go barely dry before watering again. And water only with tepid water; cold water on the leaves will spot them.

Saintpaulias in protected environments not only thrive in the extra humidity, but also tend to hold their flowers better.

MINIATURE CULTURE

Miniature saintpaulias are a little fussier than the standard sizes: they want higher humidity, and they are very prone to sucker, which means that you must be constantly grooming them or they won't flower for you. Of course, you can grow these suckers on to plants, but if what you want is flowers, groom.

VARIETIES

Saintpaulias come in too many varieties to list; to name a few of our favorites: *S.* 'Blue Delft' is a winner with wavy leaves, and *S.* 'Persian Delight' is a rich pink, *S.* 'Triple Threat' is a very double saturated pink; *S.* 'Happy Harold' and *S.* 'Nancy Reagan' have lovely variegated foliage, but they are shy to bloom; *S.* 'Rusty' is an excellent red-pink, and a compact grower. *S.* 'Little Eva' is a smashing miniature, and *S.* 'Blue Baghdad,' *S.* 'Window Wonder,' *S.* 'Snoopy,' *S.* 'Star Daisy,' and *S.* 'Tiny Pink' are also lovely little plants.

The whole series of so-called "Rhapsodie violets" is worth having; and of them, we find the compact *S.* 'Gisele' especially attractive.

For years, growers have been crossing for double flowers, but, in general, single flowers last longer on the plant.

There are new sports with flowers edged in lighter colors, and there are hybrids with streaked, spotted, and mottled flowers.

Hybridizers lately are concentrating on some lovely trailing African violets.

In fact, visiting a greenhouse that specializes in saintpaulias can be an unsettling experience: there are so many plants to choose from, we find it difficult to choose.

PROPAGATION

Saintpaulias are most often propagated from petiole cuttings (see Chapter 17), but they can be had from suckers, or, if the neck of the plant has grown impossibly long, from a tip cutting.

Young plants can sometimes be had from division.

They are slow from seed.

LONG NECKS

If you've lost too many of your lower leaves (or if you've had to groom them off) and your plant is showing a long, bare neck, turn the plant out of its pot and reset the plant lower in the pot—removing soil if you have to, to get the plant lower.

If the neck is just too long, and after resetting you can still see bare neck, then surgery is the answer.

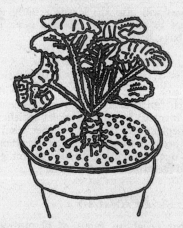

This long-necked African violet needs to be reset.

Remove the plant from the pot again, and feel up there in the middle of all those roots. If you feel high enough, you will find the *bottom* of the neck. It feels like the above-ground neck, but a bit moist from the soil.

Clean a knife with alcohol, and *cut off the bottom inch of the neck*. That's right, just cut if off. It sounds cruel, we know, but sometimes it's the only way to keep a favorite African violet presentable.

Now, dust the wound with mineral sulfur or fermate (a fungicide), allow it all to dry for a few minutes, and repot the plant, setting it so the bottoms of the lowest petioles are level with the soil.

Most times your plant will survive the surgery without difficulty. However, don't think you can change the neckline with all plants: this will kill cacti, for instance.

OTHER PROBLEMS

•If your leaves begin to point up, they are not getting enough light.

•If they curl under, they may not be getting enough humidity.

•Crown rot, a fungous disease, can come from overwatering. Take a leaf cutting (see Chapter 17) and throw out the rotter.

•Cyclamen mites will give the leaves a curly and hairy look. See Chapters 13 and 14 for this and other pests and problems (mealy bugs, botrytis, fungi).

JOYS

It's not fair to end with a listing of problems without telling you how much fun it is to grow African violets: there are more people involved in African violet societies than in all the other houseplant societies put together. And they are popular not just because they are easy, for certainly other plants are easier. But they are beautifully rewarding, and exciting to grow, and real winners under lights.

EPISCIAS

There is another delightful genus of fibrous-rooted gesneriads. It is usually grown for its gorgeously varied and textured foliage, but it makes colorful flowers, too. And these are the only plants really happy in an apartment during a heat wave. In fact, *cold* can be a problem: a cold window—below 55°—can be fatal for them.

Humidity is the kicker with episcias; they will just fold up and die in a desert-dry apartment. But they thrive if you can provide the humidity. See Chapter 18, GROWING IN A PROTECTED ENVIRONMENT, for episcias in flying saucers.

Compared to African violets, episcias need higher humidity, but are content with less light.

Aside from their humidity needs, these plants are perfect

for a city apartment: they love the warmth, their foliage colors will come out beautifully under rather subdued light, and they won't be burned in a somewhat bright window (though any plant will scorch if left in a very *hot* window unprotected). Keep in mind that the darker-leaved varieties will stand more direct sun than will the paler-leaved.

Episcias are sometimes called "flame violets," perhaps to cash in on the public's love for African violets, and certainly, if you can grow saintpaulias, you should have no trouble with these close cousins.

They spread by means of stolons (see Chapter 17), which means you can get a bushy plant quickly.

Like saintpaulias, most of them can be had in flower any time of year.

SOME VARIETIES

There are many fewer episcias in cultivation than there are saintpaulias, but the hundreds that exist give you a wide choice.

Among the most spectacular, certainly, are *Episcia* 'Ember Lace,' *E.* 'Lady Lou,' and *E.* 'Cleopatra,' sports which show multicolored foliage, some of which will be in pink-and-white flesh-tones. (However, with the first two you take the chance that they will revert to a more normal foliage. 'Cleo' doesn't revert.) All three are among the most difficult of episcias to grow because there is little chlorophyll in the leaves.

E. reptans is found in several forms with red flowers. Usually, the leaves are dark green veined with light green.

E. cupreata is another red-flowered species with a variety of foliage forms, though usually it is a pale green around the veins, with darker green elsewhere. The outside of the flower tube is usually somewhat hairy.

E. 'Chocolate Soldier' has brownish leaves and those of *E.* 'Tricolor' are multicolored, and both are fairly easy. *E.* 'Acajou' comes in shades of metallic green, and flowers quite easily. *E.* 'Shimmer' and *E.* 'Silver Sheen' have metallic-looking glowing leaves.

E. 'Pinkiscia' requires higher humidity than most, and we really wouldn't try it except in a protected environment. It makes lovely pink flowers, though, and is a slower grower than many.

E. dianthiflora and its offspring *E.* 'Cygnet' can both stand more cold and less sun than most. *E. dianthiflora*, with small leaves and pure white flowers, is very shy to bloom, and then only on quite mature plants. *E.* 'Cygnet,' whose leaves are slightly larger and whose flowers are white, fringed, and spotted with purple, is a bit easier to flower, but still not what you'd call floriferous.

E. 'Tropical Topaz' has light green foliage and yellow flowers.

Our current favorite is a new hybrid called *E.* 'Helen O.' It is a somewhat compact grower (though you wouldn't know it from the speed with which a 1″ stolon grew to fill a 12″ flying saucer), with young leaves having the varied purples and greens of a rex begonia. It should be more widely available by the time you read this.

There are some episcias that don't resemble the lovely foliage plants we've been talking about. *E. melitifolia* looks quite succulent and has more of an upright habit. It's strictly a terrarium plant in an apartment. *E. decurrens* is another upright. Neither of these is as easy of culture as the more colorful (and more readily available) spreading kinds.

CULTURE

Pot into our basic soil mix, in an azalea pot (they are shallow rooted), or into a terrarium or other protected environment.

Water well, and keep well watered, barely allowing the surface of the soil to go dry between waterings. If you allow it to dry out, you'll lose leaves.

Feed at half strength alternately with fish emulsion or 15-30-15 every 2 weeks, when in active growth or bud. Reduce the feeding, but not the watering, if the plant slows down for a while.

Since episcias spread by means of stolons (runners), you can handle them in one of two ways. You can cut them off and propagate them, or you can take some dark hairpins and pin them down to the soil. The stolons will root and new "plants" grow from every pinned node. You can get incredibly bushy plants this way.

LIGHT

You've got your choice with episcias: you can grow them for flowers or you can grow them for foliage. Strong light with good sun will encourage flowering but tends to pale the leaves and dull the colors. Fluorescent light or good window light without sun will bring out the wonderful colors, but won't give you as much in the way of flowers. The choice is yours.

PROPAGATION

Episcias propagate by those stolons we mentioned before or by petiole cuttings (see Chapter 17). They are difficult to get to set seed, and then slow from seed if you do get it.

PROBLEMS

Episcias are not really attractive to bugs, at least not in our apartment. They will succumb to certain environmental problems, though. Their leaves will sunburn, for example, and if you let them dry out, the wilted leaves will sometimes not come back.

JOYS

Gorgeous foliage, very attractive flowers, a unique habit, and the easiest propagation. And not attractive to bugs. Enough?

TUBEROUS GESNERIADS

Saintpaulias and episcias are fibrous-rooted, and we'll get to the other fibrous-rooted gesneriads later, but now we turn to our favorite houseplant, the plant that got us involved in *horticulture*, not just growing: GLOXINIAS.

SINNINGIA SPECIOSA—GLOXINIA

Picture large velvety bells in solids or mixed colors, edged or speckled, held high over large velvety leaves. Got the picture? That's the most modest description of a gloxinia.

They are not easy, but their culture is simple. In other words, it's easy when you know how.

The "bell" type gloxinia flower usually grows upright.

THE TUBER

A gloxinia tuber grows from year to year, reaching a diameter of 9″ or more, eventually. However, the size of your plant doesn't really depend on the size of your tuber. Whether a 1″ tuber or a 9″ tuber, you get about the same foliage spread. A large tuber means more *flowers* though, and certainly that's desirable.

Plant size is more determined by pot size. It seems that when a glox finds room around its tuber, it makes a larger plant. We had planted the tuber for a lovely pure-white double in a 4″ pot, and got a plant almost a foot across, and we were happy enough with it to enter it in a show. Diantha Buell came by and said, with perhaps more than a trace of superiority, that they would have put it in a larger pot and gotten a plant half again as big. (She had the right: it *was* a Buell tuber.)

The tuber had come unnamed: just labeled "double white." Unlike the saintpaulias on the market, most gloxinias are unnamed—just described: "purple slipper," or "deep-red double." Gloxes hybridize so easily (and come so quickly from seed) that it would be impossible to try and name them all. At a recent show, one of the members of our local A.G.G.S. chapter brought in a dozen unnamed gloxinias. It wasn't ignorance: they had all been grown from seed and none of them had variety names. They were all just *Sinningia speciosa* hybrids.

Get the best tuber you can. And the best tuber is one you've propagated yourself from a leaf (or a hybrid you've crossed). Barring that, buy a tuber from one of the very good American hybridizers: people like Michael Kartuz and the Buells, who are members of the American Gloxinia and Gesneriad Society, and involved in the scientific work the society is doing.

You'll sometimes see newspaper or magazine offers for very inexpensive tubers: they are usually imported, and only half alive when you get them. We've spoken to people who gave up on gloxinias because of failure with those cut-rate tubers. Don't buy them! Gloxinias are really wonderful plants, and should flower for you about 3 months after your tuber goes in; and a champion tuber will cost you about $1.

MINIS, COMPACTS, AND DWARFS

There is a lot of hybridizing going on here and abroad to find smaller versions of these large gloxes: not plants kept small by being potted in small pots, but real dwarf plants, with full-sized gloxinia flowers.

We've grown some ourselves, and find the hybridizers (especialy Lyndon Lyon) have come quite a way: one unnamed deep red dwarf makes full-sized flowers on a plant only 5″ across.

However, we've found them more finicky about humidity, requiring more than the standard-size plants—as much as 70–80%, which falls near the terrarium range.

We got some Scandinavian seed from Park's for our propagation course, and they reached flower for our students in about 5 months, keeping the dwarf habit.

But, be certain that your "dwarf" is really a small grower, and not something kept dwarfed by a small pot.

There is the unfortunate habit among some growers of calling the miniature sinningias "miniature gloxes." We'll cover the miniature sinningias in the next section: they are delightful plants and should be grown by the dozen. But here, we're discussing the florist gloxinia (*Sinningia speciosa*) only, and dwarfs of it.

(For a discussion of tubers, see BULBS, TUBERS . . . , Chapter 27.)

CULTURE

All right, let's assume that you've bought a tuber by mail order from Al Buell.

First, you must distinguish the top from the bottom. (See drawing, page 349.) It's best to plant the tuber with the top up and the bottom down, but we've seen tubers work it out for themselves.

For an apartment-sized plant, prepare, say, a 4″ azalea pot with crocking and soil (our basic soil mix, Chapter 7). Bury the tuber so that its top is about ½″ under the soil. Water well, and set in a warm place (light is not needed yet). Continue to water lightly until the tuber sprouts.

There is no mistaking when that sprout comes up: you see a pair of tiny pink fuzzy "ears" pushing their way through the soil—that moment has always been exciting.

Once the sprout starts, you must give it light.

We prefer fluorescent light for our tuberous gesneriads. Our windowsill light is not bright enough to keep the plants compact. If you have a very bright window (shaded in the middle of the hottest summer days), by all means try, but remember to keep turning the plants for even growth. In natural light, you will pot your tuber in March, and get flowers in late spring and summer, only.

Under fluorescents, keep the tops of the plants within 4″ of your tubes—you'll have to move the plants down or the tubes up as the leaves grow.

Water thoroughly when the soil surface begins to go dry.

Feed with a very dilute solution of plant food (say, ⅛ strength) with every watering, as long as the plant is in active growth.

The leaves will grow rapidly.

Humidity. Well, it is time to do our humidity number again. Yes, gloxes need humidity: more of it than African violets, a minimum of 50%, and as much as 80% if you can manage that. Without the humidity, the growth will not be as thrifty as otherwise and, most important, the buds will not open. A daily misting helps, but it isn't enough, by far. See Chapter 5, RAISING HUMIDITY.

Buds. Buds form in the axils of leaves ("axil" means armpit). They are often a contrasting color to the foliage, so they are not hard to see, even though they begin so small. They, too, will grow rather rapidly, and within a few more weeks your buds will be of a size to open. If your light is good but your humidity low, buds will form, but they will *blast*.

While the plant is in bud, it must continue to be fed well

[274]

and never allowed to dry out at all. Buds will also blast if the plant goes dry.

And that's all there is to getting flowers in your living room from the most spectacular houseplant we grow.

PROPAGATION

For these gloxinias, or for their miniature sinningia brothers, propagate from any part of the plant (see Chapter 17), or from the fine seed (see Chapter 16). All fertile sinningias are super from seed. (Unfortunately, some of the most delightful miniature sinningias are sterile.) The seed ripens rather quickly on the plant (say, 2 months on a full-sized glox), and comes up within a few days or a week, if fresh. You'll get a flowering plant from seed within 5 months.

PROBLEMS

Once you've licked humidity, gloxes are really quite resistant to most problems.

GROOMING

Be sure you remove from the plant all spent blooms and bad leaves. Since you grow gloxes in high humidity, poor sanitation could promote fungus.

Break off all but a single stem. Gloxes are better grown with a *single crown*; otherwise the leaves crowd each other. Of course, put the extra top in your prop box.

DORMANCY

After flowering, your gloxinia may go dormant. And, then, it may not. You *can* get more than one blooming cycle from your tuber: when you are certain the plant is making no new buds, cut it right back to the tuber, leaving only about ¼ " of stem. The tuber should then resprout, and by treating it as you have been, you should get more buds and bloom. Your tuber may even give you a *third* cycle.

But, after one cycle or three, your tuber will go dormant; that is, it will refuse to make new growth and will go into rest.

Tubers can be rested in the pot or out. In the pot, just put

[275]

in a cool place, and tickle occasionally with water; enough to keep the tuber from drying up. Out of the pot, fill a small bag with vermiculite, moistened with a very few drops of water. Remove the tuber from the pot and put it into the plastic bag and seal it off with a twist tie. Put into a drawer until you want to start it up again, or until the tuber shows a bit of growth on its own.

JOYS

We cannot catalog the joys of growing gloxinias: they are too many. But above all, the incredible flowers.

MINIATURE SINNINGIAS

These are the baby brothers of the large gloxinias, and their leaves, though tiny, are usually velvety. The flowers are similarly lobed, and sometimes more interesting, and even larger—in proportion to the tiny foliage, that is.

There are two delightful advantages to the miniatures: they take up very little space and they don't go dormant; the plants we describe here will give you virtually continuous flowering over months and months.

What follows isn't by any means supposed to be an exhaustive listing: there are so many of these little tuberous wonders, and more being hybridized all the time, by professionals and amateurs. These minis are just the ones we've grown successfully.

You will notice that we do grow more of the miniatures than most apartment gardeners: after all, we're active in plant societies and that's a great way to get plants that are new introductions.

Or you might want to try to hybridize your own. Many are fertile, and the offspring will sometimes give you some new plant. Remember, the discoverer or crosser of a new cross gets to name it: after spouse or self or any way you please. Tempting?

SINNINGIA PUSILLA

This is the tiniest of the lot, with purple flowers that can be 1″ long over leaves less than a ¼″ across and a crown of foliage less than 1″ in diameter. The flowers come at least two at a time, usually more, and are lobed, long-lasting, and borne high above the foliage.

It self-seeds very freely, and you can have hundreds of plants from a single seed pod.

S. pusilla 'White Sprite.' This is a pure white sport of *S. pusilla* and quite startling against dark soil in a terrarium. It is exactly the same as *S. pusilla*, except that it's white. Also an easy self-seeder; you wake up one day and your jarred *S.* 'White Sprite' is surrounded by a green carpet of baby plants.

S. 'Snowflake.' This is a hybrid of *S.* 'White Sprite.' The lip of the flower is rippled and the flower itself is a little smaller. A little harder to grow.

CULTURE

Within a protected environment the culture is ridiculously simple. Plant the tiny tubers in our basic soil mix and keep evenly moist. Feed once a month with dilute plant food.

Keep these plants toward the dimmer ends of the tubes (save the centers for your saintpaulias or larger sinningias, they need it), and they will flower freely for you. We've never done well with them under natural light, though you can try with a brilliant northern exposure or a good eastern one.

They shouldn't really go dormant, though they may slow down. If they do, or if they get a bit straggly, pinch off the top growth for propagation, and the tuber should start up quite quickly, coming to flower perhaps within a month.

SINNINGIA CONCINNA

About the same size and form as *S. pusilla*, the leaves are a little larger and veined with red, and the flowers have purple lobes and a white throat which is speckled in purple. This speckling can be found in larger-flowered hybrids which have *S. concinna* as one parent.

We have found this mini slightly shyer of bloom than *S. pusilla*, but the flowers are quite lovely. Though it is fertile, it does not self-seed as readily as *S. pusilla*. You may have luck setting seed if you keep it warm. Or better yet pollinate it by hand. Culture is the same as for *S. pusilla*.

SINNINGIA 'BRIGHT EYES'

This is a hybrid, about the same size plant as *S. concinna*, and with purple flowers larger than *S. pusilla*'s. We keep cutting *S.* 'Bright Eyes' back to the tuber after its first heavy flowering and get heavy flowering after heavy flowering!

In an apartment, this is another container plant, with the culture the same as *S. pusilla*.

SINNINGIA 'LITTLE IMP'

(Formerly called *X-Gloxinera* 'Little Imp.')

Slightly larger-leaved and with fewer leaves, this hybrid will flower when about 1″ across. The flowers are trumpet-shaped, with a long tube in proportion to the width of the lobed lip, and of a purplish pink.

Culture is the same as for *S. pusilla*. It will form lovely flowers, one or two at a time, over many months before going a bit leggy. Then, cut it back to the tuber and start all over again. These leggy tops propagate very easily.

Just the perfect size for a small brandy snifter.

SINNINGIA 'PINK IMP'

(Formerly called *X-Gloxinera* Pink Imp.')

Same as *S.* 'Little Imp,' but with pink flowers.

SINNINGIA 'PINK FLARE'

(Formerly called *X-Gloxinera* 'Pink Flare.')

Similar to the 'Imps,' but with clear-pink flowers, and a tendency to go leggy in reduced light. But the tuber resprouts very quickly if you cut it back. A free flowerer, and charming in containers—as are all we've mentioned so far.

Aside from slightly higher light requirements, culture is the same as for *S. pusilla*.

SINNINGIA 'TINKERBELLS'

(Formerly *X-Gloxinera* 'Tinkerbells.')

If we grew only three gesneriads, the 'Tink' would surely

be one of them. It flowers extremely freely and *doesn't need the protection of a container*. If you can flower African violets, you can certainly flower this delight. In fact, it prefers the slightly drier air outside a container. In a high-humidity protected environment it will go leggy and sprawly, while in the open, on a pebble tray, it can be kept in relatively thrifty habit by frequent pruning.

Its flowers are a reddish pink and can be had a dozen at a time on a plant 4″ high.

Propagates readily from tip or petiole cuttings (see Chapter 17), though you might not think it from the small size of the leaves. Don't look for seeds: it's sterile.

SINNINGIA 'RAMADEVA'

(Formerly *X-Gloxinera* 'Ramadeva.')
This is one of Frances Batcheller's marvelous hybrids. It is a medium-small plant with clear-pink flowers, borne continuously on the plant. It can be in constant bloom because it doesn't self-seed.

Give it a bit more light, but otherwise the culture is the same as for *S. pusilla.*

SINNINGIA 'MODESTA'

(Formerly *X-Gloxinera* 'Modesta.')
In size and form like *S.* 'Ramadeva,' above, and of the same culture. The flowers are a salmon-pink, and slightly smaller. What a marvelous new color!

By the time you read this, though, it may be replaced by one of the larger-flowered and easier salmon-colored minis that Mike Kartuz is working on.

SINNINGIA 'FRECKLES'

We're moving up a bit in size with this plant, but we still are in the miniature class. *S.* 'Freckles' will form stems almost 6″ long and make a very handsome and bushy plant, outside of a container, if you can provide *some* moderate extra humidity.

The flowers are most handsome: large (for a miniature plant), purple-and-white with purple spots on the white throat, and a swelling underside.

However, culture is basically the same: keep evenly moist and feed moderately, and even this one doesn't require strong light.

SINNINGIA 'CINDY'

The flowers of S. 'Cindy' are quite similar to S. 'Freckles,' but they will be a bit larger and have *streaks* in the throat instead of spots.

This miniature requires a protected environment and high humidity for best growth, where it can make a plant about 8″ across, with many heart-shaped leaves.

S. 'Cindy' is sterile, but there is available a fertile and larger-flowered version of it (tetraploid, for you genetics freaks), which should make the plant much more available as seed gets around: *Sinningia* 'Cindy-ella.'

SINNINGIA 'DOLLBABY'

This is a real doll and the largest of the miniatures in general circulation. Its flowers are large and held quite high above the foliage. The leaves should lie close to the soil, rather than growing upright as with S. 'Tinkerbells' and S. 'Freckles.' The flowers are purple with a white throat, and most often you'll see them borne in pairs, though prize plants are sometimes more floriferous.

The leaves are dark green, and sometimes crinkled—so don't think you're doing something wrong. When the plant goes leggy, cut back and propagate. It will propagate from petiole cuttings or tip cuttings (see Chapter 17) or from the seeds, which set very easily (see Chapter 16).

We prefer the plant in a container, though many growers grow it successfully in the open. It will make larger and lusher foliage if protected.

Incidentally, both this great plant and S. 'Tinkerbells' were hybridized by amateur growers.

These are all incredibly rewarding and satisfying plants; an apartment garden isn't complete without several of them, blooming their crowns off for you, either in or out of containers.

The "slipper" type gloxinia flower grows at right angles to its peduncle.

OTHER FULL-SIZE SINNINGIAS

If you have the space, these slipper-flowered beauties are well worth the effort.

SINNINGIA EUMORPHA

This is not an easy plant: it is more difficult to bring into good habit and heavy bloom than the gloxinias. Its flowers, while attractive, are smaller than the gloxes, too. The slipper-shaped blooms are almost pure white, with a blush of yellow down the throat and some faint purple streaks.

When grown well, this is a marvelous plant, with very large glossy leaves (not velvety), a most handsome compact habit, and ample clusters of flowers. To reach this desirable state requires more light and humidity than the full-sized gloxes, a large pot—and *room*. You've got to give this one space, or you'll damage the leaves.

But aside from its attractiveness, what makes this plant desirable is that it makes a great parent for several excellent hybrids. For example, tiny *Sinningia pusilla* crossed with large *S. eumorpha* gives us the hybrid, *S.* 'Dollbaby,' which has the same size flowers as *S. eumorpha* on a much smaller plant.

Propagates easily from seed or from leaves or leaf wedges (see Chapters 16 and 17).

SINNINGIA REGINA

This plant is indeed a "queen" among sinningias: the flowers are the richest royal purple, and the leaves are beautifully purple-backed. Altogether, a raving beauty, requiring the same culture as gloxinias. And as easy to propagate from seed (Chapter 16) or from leaves, wedges, or tip cuttings (Chapter 17).

Crossed with gloxes, you get some extremely beautiful, large-slipper-flowered plants.

SINNINGIA CARDINALIS

(Formerly called *Rechsteineria cardinalis*.)

The tuber of this plant should sit *half out* of the soil, rather than buried beneath it, and should be allowed to go rather dry between waterings. Its flowers look quite different from other sinningias, being much more tubular, and bright red (the reason why they were long thought to be another genus). Another difference: allow two or more crowns (stems) to grow from the tuber, rather than pinching out the extras. The crowns tend to grow *out*, and so do not crowd each other.

COLUMNEAS

An epiphyte in nature, this is a varied genus. The leaf size of available species and hybrids can range from the tiny *Columnea microphylla* (less than ½″ across) to the very large *C.* 'Campus Favorite' (with smooth leaves 6″ across). Flowers may range from smooth 3″ giants to 1½″ hairy and striped oddities and usually appear all along the stems at every node.

They are fibrous-rooted, like saintpaulias and episcias, and no more difficult to flower than either. They are mostly trailers, making handsome hanging baskets; but there are some large-growing upright types, not really suited to an apartment.

Unlike many of the gesneriads in apartment culture, some columneas are seasonal bloomers; but the winter and early-spring bloomers will only come into flower with good bright autumn and early-winter sun. If you can't give them that, stick to the everbloomers or the spring and summer bloomers. *C.* 'Yellow Dragon' (yellow flowers and dark foliage) and *C.* 'Early Bird' (red-and-yellow flowers and small pale leaves) are both everbloomers, and will flower freely for you under lights as well as in a bright window, coming into flower quite young: you can have a 6″ plant of either, covered with blooms.

C. 'Ithican' (red flowers and medium-green leaves) and *C.* 'Cornellian' (orange-red flowers and large leaves with red undersides) are both everbloomers of the "Cornell hybrids" series. These hybrids are quite strong growers and free flowerers.

CULTURE

Columneas do best for us if somewhat *underpotted*, so don't be too quick to move them to large pots.

Use our basic soil mix and an azalea pot; allow to dry slightly between waterings; and give either your brightest fluorescent light space or a sunny window—with protection through the hottest and brightest of the summer days. (They can take more sun than African violets.)

Feed every 2 weeks with ½-strength food.

PROBLEMS

Columneas are rather susceptible to mealy bug and aphids, and since the bugs get deep into the leaf axils, it may be a job to get them out. (See Chapter 13.)

A paling of the leaves may mean too much heat, or that the plant is living too close to your fluorescent light tubes.

It is natural for columneas to lose leaves along the stems after a season of growth. However, it is also natural for new young growth to start from near the soil; so, keep those bare stems cut back. Prune, prune, prune. The new growth will come in vigorously and you'll have in essence a new and bushier plant.

PROPAGATION

Columneas are so quick from stem cuttings and so slow to come to flowering size from seed that cuttings are obviously the way to propagate them (see Chapter 16); you can get dozens of cuttings from a mature plant. Pot half a dozen rooted cuttings together to make a hanging basket.

If the flowers are pollinated you get handsome berries— white or various pastel shades, depending on the kind—and the seeds inside are usually ready to plant when the calyx curls back (the berry will not change its color). Spread the berry on a piece of paper and you'll see the shiny yellow-brownish seed inside. Plant them on milled sphagnum moss, as described in Chapter 17.

JOYS

Lots of flowers, lovely berries, and handsome shapes. Even as foliage plants, hanging baskets are especially desirable in apartment windows—if only to block out your neighbors.

HYPOCYRTAS

Some hypocyrtas are called "candy-corn plant" and it's easy to see why. Or the flowers may resemble, to you, little gaping fish, and so the other common name, "gold fish plant." Whichever, the flowers are most handsome and the foliage is the glossiest green.

At a recent flower show, viewers kept asking of a *Hypocyrta* 'Tropicana,' "Is it real?" or "What do you put on the leaves to make them so shiny?" The grower of the plant didn't do anything special—except to give the plant good cultural conditions. Hypocyrtas just have those shiny, waxy, bright-green leaves that look too good to be true.

We've always found hypocyrtas shyer to bloom than columneas, and when they do bloom, their flowers are sometimes hidden under the leaves. (They look great viewed from below—which makes them marvelous for hanging high, from that loft or duplex railing). However, the display of bloom goes on longer than with columneas, because the hypocyrtas also have colorful calyces (the calyx is the little "cup" at the base of the flower) which often stay on the plant long after the flower has gone.

H. wettsteinii, H. radicans, H. 'Rio,' *H.* 'Tropicana,' and the gorgeous *H. perianthomega* (with large waxy leaves and striped flowers) are all worth trying, and available from gesneriad specialists.

CULTURE

Basically the same as for columneas; they do seem somewhat more sun-resistant, so give them a bright sunny place. They also do very well under strong fluorescent light.

PROPAGATION

From tip cuttings (see Chapter 17) or seed (see Chapter 16).

AESCHYNANTHUS

This was the first hanging gesneriad that flowered for us, and it is still among our favorites. The flowers are borne, in season, in clusters at the ends of the long, trailing stems. The colorful flower tubes push out of the dark calyces, which are sometimes an inch long themselves. To see a red flower pushing out of the dark calyx tells you immediately why this is called "lipstick vine."

The flowers are not long-lasting, but they are quite spectacular. *Aeschynanthus marmoratus* has an interesting variegated foliage and is easy to flower on a windowsill, but the green flowers are almost invisible, and hardly worth the having. A hybrid of this plant, *A.* 'Black Pagoda,' keeps the handsome markings on the leaves (in fact, they are more visible in the hybrid), and puts it together with very handsome red flowers and the easy-flowering habit. *A.* 'Black Pagoda,' in fact, flowers under very little light indeed, blooming for us on our windowsill, in spite of being shoved behind other plants. Free-flowering in that kind of light, and undemanding otherwise, as long as you don't let it go really dry, it makes an ideal apartment plant.

NEMATANTHUS

Another trailer of habit and culture similar to columneas, this genus bears its colorful flowers on long hanging "strings." Very striking. There aren't many of these in cultivation, but look for *Nematanthus* 'Stoplight' which has red flowers and a dark-red patch on the underside of its leaves. Those "magic" brothers, *N.* 'Black Magic' and *N.* 'Green Magic' (formerly *X-Hypotanthus* 'Black Magic' and *X-Hypotanthus* 'Green Magic') are interesting. The former has very-dark-green glossy leaves but tends to go straggly; the latter's leaves are paler, and it has a more compact habit.

CULTURE

Similar to columnea, except that for us it requires more frequent watering.

PROPAGATION

Tip cuttings (see Chapter 17). With all of the preceding trailers, try this; instead of just sticking the end of your cutting in the medium, lay the whole length of the cutting *on* the medium (hairpins or broken paperclips will help to secure it). It will root from every node. You can then either cut it into separate plants or pot the whole thing up and expect to get a stem from every rooted node. You can start a hanging basket from one 4″ cutting this way.

Columnea, hypocyrta, aeschynanthus, and nemathanthus: difficult names, but not difficult plants. They all make lovely hanging baskets, in or out of bloom. Sure, Swedish ivy also makes a lovely hanging basket—but this quartet will flower for you with no more sun than saintpaulias.

And you needn't spend a lot of money for a large basket of these beauties: a small plant will give you cuttings enough to make a basket (see "Propagation," above).

STREPTOCARPUS

This is an extremely varied genus, African in origin, with tiny miniatures and giants, upright growers, trailers, and rosette forms. Some of them are perennials, some die off after flowering.

In general, you don't find the single-leaved giants offered for sale in catalogs. They are strictly greenhouse plants in North America.

The very tiny *Streptocarpus rimicola* is an excellent terrarium plant, self-seeding often and spreading that way; even though it is monocarpic (dies after it flowers and fruits).

The rexi hybrids are rosette forms with large flowers of handsome shape and various colors. Several of the long leaves are formed on a plant, and it may take a dormant period when it can look like hell.

"Nymph" hybrids bear smaller flowers than the rexi but more of them. They are mostly in the purples and blues, though a white has recently become available. Lots of growers like S. 'Constant Nymph' (purplish) and S. 'Blue Nymph.'

S. holstii and S. kirkii are upright growers and bear their small flowers well above the top leaves.

S. saxorum is a small-leaved and easily grown trailer that you wouldn't recognize as a strep except for the "twisted fruit" (that's what "streptocarpus" means) left on after the many small, pale blue flowers.

CULTURE

That varies, too.

S. rimicola is strictly a terrarium plant, flowering very freely in high humidity and moderate light. We grow this one in brandy snifters at the ends of our fluorescent tubes.

The rexi hybrids, the similar Weismoor hybrids, and the "nymphs" need *room*, good humidity, and a *soil without peat moss* in it, so be sure you drop that from the mix. We've seen one very successful professional growing his streps in long-hair sphagnum moss. Allow to go surface-dry before re-watering. Their light requirements are not great: a good, bright east window should flower them.

We have found S. holstii and S. kirkii more demanding of humidity than the rosette streps, and try to keep them in an open or semi-open terrarium, with the brightest fluorescent light we can manage.

S. saxorum will do well in any soil and at lower humidity than most of the others, but it needs *sun* to flower, so let it hang in your brightest window and let it go rather dry between waterings.

PROPAGATION

S. rimicola, from seeds, which set readily and germinate well (see Chapter 16).

The "nymphs," rexis, and weismoors, from petiole cuttings or leaf wedges (see Chapter 17), or from seeds.

The uprights and S. saxorum, from tip cuttings, or from seed.

All streps seem to set seed quite easily. The seed is ripe when the long, twisted seedpods split open.

PROBLEMS

●With the rosette types, the tips of the leaves will brown if they touch something. Do cut that brown off with a scissors or it will likely die all the way back and cost you the whole leaf.

●Peat moss in the soil can lead to rot, so don't use it in your mix.

●The rosettes also may take a dormant spell, at which time they will look rather ratty. Reduce watering and just mist the foliage occasionally.

JOYS

Not everyone can grow the rosette forms of strep, but if you can, they are simply spectacular flowering plants. And anyone *can* grow *S. rimicola* in a protected environment, and *S. saxorum* in a bright window. You can find a strep to suit your conditions.

NAUTILOCALYX

This is a genus of upright plants, some of them quite large growing (too tall for many situations), grown for their handsomely colored or quilted foliage. The flowers are generally quite insignificant, half hidden down in the axils, and short-lived when you do get them. But they are still handsome plants to grow.

We have grown three species quite happily: *Nautilocalyx bullatus*, with dark-green pebbled foliage; *N. forgetii*, whose foliage is deep reddish; and *N. lynchii* whose dark-green leaves veined with wine-red are purple underneath.

CULTURE

Moderate humidity and good fluorescent light will insure you excellent vegetative growth and even some flowering. Pot into our standard soil mix, in pots just a little bigger than you think the plant needs. They like root room. They will tumble over if they get too tall for the pot, so you may want to stake it when you repot.

Keep well watered.

PROPAGATION

Propagate from tip cuttings or separate out the offsets that form at the base of the plants. (See Chapter 17.)

PROBLEMS

Their main problem can be the height that a plant like *N. bullatus* can reach. It is quite fast growing. Prune for better shape.

GESNERIA

This is a genus of, generally, small terrarium plants, making many bright yellow to red flowers. It grows in a rosette shape which will eventually extend into woody stems. There are several forms of *Gesneria cunneifolia*, with orange or reddish flowers, and this is the most widely grown. *G. citrina* has lovely lemon-yellow flowers and a tendency to be more upright. *G.* 'Lemon-drop,' a new hybrid by Mike Kartuz, is similar to *G. citrina*, but slightly larger, with larger yellow flowers. *G. christii* has a crinkled leaf and red flowers.

CULTURE

For apartment growers, these are plants strictly for a protected environment, and constant moisture. They will flower for you, however, with less light than, say, saintpaulias, so they needn't get the center of your light set-up, or your brightest window.

We flowered *G.* 'Lemon Drop' in moderate natural light, using an abandoned fish tank.

Use our standard potting mix, and feed whenever you water the container.

PROPAGATION

Usually from seed (see Chapter 16). You can get stem cuttings if the woody stems form—though they tend to be slow to root.

PROBLEMS

We've had only two real problems with gesnerias: we have let them dry and killed them that way, and we have put a new, large-growing hybrid into a bottle (not knowing it was a large-grower), and it grew right out the neck of the bottle—in bloom.

JOYS

With good light and humidity, and kept constantly moist and fed, these little jewels will bloom their heads off for you.

RHIZOMATOUS GESNERIADS

See Chapter 27, BULBS, TUBERS . . . for a description of a scaly rhizome.

ACHIMENES

Sometimes called "magic flowers" in catalogs, achimenes are beautiful plants. They are small trailers that make exquisite hanging baskets—on your aunt's sunporch in Nebraska. In a window in a city, they don't do quite as well. They are pollution-sensitive and will refuse to flower in even moderately polluted air.

So. If your apartment is fully air-conditioned, or if you live where the pollution is below the achimenes' tolerance, great, because these plants are definitely worth having.

They are miniatures, really, and their stems seldom grow longer than a foot. Their flower colors cover much of the spectrum: white, yellow, purple, pink, blue. Beautiful.

Achimenes 'Ambroise Verschaffelt' has white flowers with purple streaks; *A.* 'Wetterlow's Triumph' is a very large-flowered pink; *A.* 'Tarantella, another handsome pink and a new hybrid, is a very early bloomer; *A. flava* has tiny flowers, but they are yellow, an uncommon color among gesneriads; *A.* 'Paul Arnold,' named for the Registrar of the American Gloxinia and Gesneriad Society, is deep purple. There are so many lovely achimenes hybrids! Since we can't grow them well, we sometimes send one to a New Hampshire mother-in-law where the air is still pure.

CULTURE

Wait until your rhizomes show the first signs of growth—about March. Using our basic soil mix (see Chapter 7), plant about 8 rhizomes to an 8″ hanging pot. Don't bury them: rather, press them horizontally into the soil so that they are about half-exposed. We then like to cover the rhizomes with a thin layer of vermiculite, to hold the moisture. Water well, and put in a bright window. A south window will likely burn the foliage unless there is some protection against the sun.

Keep well watered and feed every 2 weeks with ½-strength plant food when growth shows itself well started.

Don't ever let them run really dry while in growth, or they'll go into dormancy and your growing season will be over.

In the fall, after flowering, allow to go gradually dry; when the soil is completely dry, go through the soil carefully to harvest the new rhizomes. Depending on the variety, you should harvest about 4 for every rhizome you planted—granting good culture.

Store the rhizomes in a bag of dry vermiculite (with perhaps a few drops of water added), until the spring.

PROPAGATION

As soon as the stems are 4–6″ long, propagate from 2–3″ cuttings (see Chapter 17), which strike roots very quickly and form new rhizomes.

Rhizomes can be divided, with each individual scale having the potential of growing a new flowering plant.

PROBLEMS

Pollution, as we said. Also, if you don't keep the achimenes well watered, they may think it's fall, and go into dormancy.

JOYS

When conditions are right, these plants flower heavily; a basket of them makes a gorgeous display.

KOHLERIA

This is a plant not really much suited to apartment culture: it tends to grow too large. There is a series of New England hybrids which will flower when small, as will *Kohleria* 'Rongo,' but even they tend to outgrow your light stand or windowsill. They tend to get sprawly and lanky, too, so if you're going to try them, keep them pruned. Their flowers are most spectacularly colored and spotted, and their velvety foliage is quite handsome, but they can be trouble.

CULTURE

Set the rhizome about ½″ below the soil in our basic mix. Keep well watered and fed, and give a bright and sunny location, misting the leaves to provide a bit of extra humidity. Store the rhizomes in the fall, as with achimenes.

PROPAGATION

Tip cuttings or petiole cuttings (see Chapter 17) shoot roots very quickly; or divide the large rhizomes; or try it from seed (see Chapter 16).

PROBLEMS

Size and ungainly shape. You'll probably need to stake yours.

JOYS

Lovely leaves and flowers and a real sense of accomplishment if you can grow one that is shapely.

SMITHIANTHA

An autumn bloomer, this plant also tends to be pollution-sensitive; but, given moderately high humidity, it will flourish for you as a foliage plant, and its foliage can be spectacular. Extremely velvety and wine-colored or streaked, or plain green, its leaves are a real eye-catcher.

We've seen it do well in a large terrarium.

Look for *Smithiantha cinnabarina*, *S. zebrina*, *S.* 'Little Wonder,' and *S.* 'Little one.' Flowers range from cream to red and are usually held high above the plant. They are bell-shaped, and so the common name, "temple bells."

CULTURE

As for kohleria, but instead of a windowsill, give it a good, humid place under lights or in a large terrarium. Store the rhizomes in the fall, as with achimenes.

PROPAGATION

Propagate as kohleria.

JOYS

It's hard to pass this plant without touching it, the leaves are that velvety.

KOELLIKERIA

Only one species of this small gem is generally grown: *Koellikeria erinoides*. It also comes from a scaly rhizome, but it does not take a dormancy period. Its foliage is like a designer's dream: heart-shaped green leaves with reddish veins and silver spots. Its cream-and-maroon flowers are small, but quite effective and produced profusely on groups of flower stalks held high above the silver-speckled foliage. A mature plant should reach no more than 6″ across. (See drawing page 348.)

CULTURE

A terrarium for this miniature, as it requires high humidity and constant moisture. It should flower under moderate fluorescent light, but if you find it losing its flat shape and going leggy, put it into a brighter location. Our basic soil mix does quite well.

PROPAGATION

Propagate by seed (see Chapter 16) or by tip cuttings (Chapter 17) or by digging up the rhizome and dividing it.

A prize-winner among miniatures.

DIASTEMA

Diastema vexans (white tubular flowers with purple spots) has soft hairy leaves and should grow no taller than 6″. *D. quinquevulnerum* (pink spots on the flowers) has stiffer and brighter foliage, and will make a compact basket.

CULTURE AND PROPAGATION

Same as for koellikeria, terrarium and all.

PHINEA

We love this tiny (3″ tall) plant because it flowers so freely, making perhaps dozens of its white flowers, setting seed, and being altogether very busy. *Phinea multiflora* is the only species in cultivation.

CULTURE

Strictly for terrariums; even an hour outside a very-high-humidity environment can have this plant drying and dying.

Use our basic soil mix and keep evenly moist, feeding whenever you water the terrarium. Modest fluorescent light will keep this one in constant flower until dormancy.

Self-seeds quite easily.

If the plant goes dormant, allow it to dry out and harvest the tiny rhizomes. These are difficult to store because they are so small, and not easy to get started again (a little bottom heat may help). Or you can leave the rhizomes in the container and water it very lightly.

PROPAGATION

Very easy from seed (see Chapter 16); not so easy from the rhizomes.

PROBLEMS

In a terrarium, there should be no problems, except for grooming off the deadheads.

JOYS

They stay small in a terrarium, forming plenty of white flowers.

This is just a bare survey of the gesneriads in cultivation. We've tried to give you hints on the ones you'll see commonly in catalogs. There is no family of plants so rewarding as this one, and so readily available to you for so little extra trouble. Just a bit of humidity—is that asking too much?

23. In Praise of Bromeliads

Gesneriads are plants you bring into flower yourself; bromeliads are plants you often buy in "flower," with the expectation that they will stay in "flower" for months.

Bromels are the only plants we'll buy from a stranger, with confidence. They are the only plant for which we'll spend in two figures.

Of the hundreds of telephone questions we've received about symptoms which could be traced to trauma, not one of them was about a bromeliad. Bring them into an apartment and they just don't suffer from what we've described as trauma. They will survive poor culture, dim light, too little water, low humidity and downright neglect. They really are marvels of adaptability.

Aechmea chantinii in spike.

BUYING A BROMEL

Nowadays, you see bromeliads in the windows of every florist and plant store. They'll range in price from about $8 to $50, depending on the variety, size of plant, and the shop.

Most often you see them with the flower-spike well advanced, sticking up out of the vase shape formed by the leaves.

THE SPIKE

Let's assume we're buying an *Aechmea fasciata* (an attractive plant, widely available).

Most bromeliad *flowers* last only a day: but that spike on which they grow will last for months, keeping color and form quite well. The flowers pop out, open, and then shrivel within the day; the spike, when it is fully emerged from the vase, tends to stay the same for several months, until it begins to brown and die.

Ideally, a bromel should be bought when the spike is still well down inside the vase. Look down the center of the plant. If there is *no* visible spike coming out of the center, don't take the florist's assurance that one will come. (Or, if you do take that assurance, don't take it for a lot of money.)

If you can see the spike coming, great; it takes a while to come out, and that will just add to the length of time you enjoy the beauty of it.

If the spike is out but the tip hasn't opened fully, also very good, because then, too, you'll have the spike for that much longer.

If the spike is fully out and open, look at the flowers. *Ae. fasciata* flowers start out blue and turn red, later forming berries. More red flowers, or berries, will mean that it is just that much more mature. If you see berries, don't buy it, except at a reduced price. It has been around the shop for a long time, and you may have the beauty of it for only a few weeks.

But remember, even out of spike, bromels can be lovely foliage plants.

SCURF

"Scurf" is neither a disease nor an obscenity. It is the white stuff that makes the designs on the aechmea and other bromels (or that completely covers some bromels). It absorbs water and holds it against the leaves. If you mist your plant at home, the scurf absorbs it, holding it against the time when the air is drier.

So, when you get the plant home, do *not* wash off the scurf: the plant needs it.

PUPS

Often you'll see a "pup" on the plant. That's a bonus. A pup is an offset, connected by stem to the parent plant. The plant propagates itself vegetatively that way.

You see, that aechmea you buy will never bloom again.

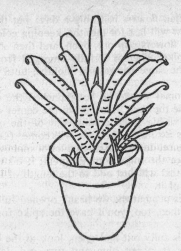

Neoregelia with pups.

The plant will hold that spike for a good long time, then, slowly, begin to die. But it forms offsets while going downhill. These can be cut off and potted up separately, encouraging more pups to come.

But you can also leave the offset right in the pot. Eventually, when the parent plant dies back, after months perhaps, the pup (or pups) will be left, off-center in the pot, to become the main plant. The offsets are then watered and fed just as you did the original plant.

Later on we'll give directions for potting up pups, if you want to try that.

POTTING

Your bought bromeliad will live all its life in its original pot. It won't need to be transplanted.

If you wish to pot up the pup, use our bromeliad mix in Chapter 7, SOILS AND SOIL MIXES.

TERRESTRIAL—EPIPHYTIC

The pineapples (ananas) and cryptanthus are terrestrial bromeliads. Most of the others we recommend are epiphytic.

Terrestrial plants live with their roots in the earth. For bromeliads this earth is usually very light, high in organic material, and with excellent drainage.

Epiphytic plants live off the ground, in trees, on telephone wires, etc. You don't believe that about telephone wires, eh? Then you've never been in the South and seen Spanish moss (*Tillandsia usneoides*), which is not Spanish and not a moss, but a bromeliad. This is a real epiphyte. As a mature plant it has no roots at all; it takes all its nutrition and water out of the moist air, dew, and rainfall. As Hamlet says, they "eat the air promise-crammed—you cannot feed capons so."

Similarly, many bromels live with their roots in the detritus that gathers in the crotches of trees. They take little water or nutrition from their roots—the roots just hold on like hell. Collectors who go up trees after these bromels have to hack them out.

The soil mix (or, rather, soil-*less* mix) we use for bromels could be used for any epiphytic plant. And it requires the addition of only a very little soil to make it suitable for the terrestrial bromels.

SOME GOOD APARTMENT BROMELIADS

Aechmea fasciata is the commonest in spike in the stores, and it is of a good size for apartments—not too wide. However, *Ae. chantinii* is also available, and worth looking for. It is a taller plant and requires bright sun, but the inflorescence is quite complex and beautiful. *Ae.* 'Foster's Favorite' and *Ae. fulgens discolor* are ideal plants for that modestly lit location; the latter's foliage is purple-backed, and both are bicolored.

Ananas comosus is the commercial pineapple. Later on we'll describe how to pot your own pineapple top. If you want the variegated kind (very handsome but spiny), you'll have to buy it. *A. nanus* is a miniature, making a 2" pineapple. They require a good deal of sun, but will burn if left unprotected in midsummer. Ananas are terrestrial bromels.

There are several billbergias suited to apartment culture. *Billbergia nutans* spreads like crazy in very modest light and is an excellent apartment plant. *B.* 'Fantasia' and *B. macrocalyx* have been doing quite well on our balcony all summer unprotected. They are both tall growers, about 2', but not wide. *B.* 'Fantasia' has beautifully mottled foliage. There are smaller-growing types available.

Cryptanthus are among our favorite bromeliads. They do well in the shade, though some varieties will blush red in brighter light. *Cryptanthus bivattatus* usually won't grow more than 6″ across. The flowers are white and easy to have on your windowsill, but rather inconspicuous ("cryptanthus" means hidden flower). *C.* 'It' is a startling new sport with shades of pink, and large-growing. The price was very high on *C.* 'It' but it is coming down. *C. zonatus* has striped leaves with wavy margins. Cryptanthus are also terrestrial bromels, and very well suited to warm apartment culture.

Guzmania lingulata minor is a small grower with an inflorescence that doesn't last as long as some, but its size makes it ideal for windowsills.

Neoregelia carolinae tricolor is one of the most desirable bromels in terms of color, and resistant to drought, but its rosette shape does take up a lot of windowsill room. And without brighter light than most we've mentioned, it will lose that rosette shape and grow upright. Still, it needs protection against full summer sun. If you can give it proper lighting, this plant may stay in color for several months.

You will sometimes find *Quesnellia testudo* available in spike: skip it. It is a killer, with spines that seem to reach out and grab you. Besides, they need too much light.

We love tillandsias—especially the miniatures (and these are *real* minis, some only a few inches across). We mount them on cork bark and hang them on the windowframe where they'll get all the sun we have to offer. (See below for "Mounting.") *Tillandsia schiedeana, T. ionantha,* and *T. streptocarper* work especially well in an apartment. *T. xerographica* is much larger, trailing to almost a foot, but they all get the same treatment from us: a weekly soaking in a bucket of very dilute plant food, and an occasional spraying when the air is dry.

Vriesea splendens is especially fine for a dull windowsill, and *V.* 'Mariae' for one with a little more light. They both have splendid inflorescences, which will last as long as 3 months. These vrieseas don't usually make outside pups (or offsets) as do most of the others, but rather a single new plant *inside* the center of the old one.

CULTURE

Bromeliads are marvelous because they will take almost any culture you give them and survive—as long as you don't leave the base of the plant sopping wet all the time. That will lead to rot.

LIGHT

Light needs vary. See the list of desirable "Apartment Bromels" above. However, even some of those bromels which have high light requirements may need some shading in summer afternoons. But several, like *Aechmea fulgens discolor* and some of the small billbergias, can be very happy under fluorescent light.

For the general run of bromeliads, you'll need a light set-up with 4 to 6 tubes.

HUMIDITY

Most of the bromels offered for houseplant culture prefer a high humidity. They will, however, get along very well during the warm months with only an occasional misting. In the winter, however, when the humidity is so low indoors, a daily misting is a must.

WATERING

The vases should be filled occasionally, and never allowed to go dry. The soil at the roots should be watered only about once a week, unless the air is quite dry, in which case you will want to soak the bottom more often: they shouldn't be allowed to go bone dry.

FEEDING

Bromels are light feeders—unlike most houseplants. Add a tiny bit of plant food in very dilute solution to the vases once a month.

For tillandsias (which get soaked weekly), make a very dilute solution of food for every weekly soaking.

FOLIAR FEEDING

Bromels can absorb food in liquid form through their leaves. You can feed them by dissolving plant food into a very dilute solution and misting the leaves with that solution. However, this is an inefficient way of feeding, and one you don't want to use exclusively, as the fertilizer salts can build up on the leaves.

If you do foliar feed routinely, then make sure you gently flush off your leaves with plain water at least once a month.

FREE BROMELIADS

You can have large and lovely foliage plants from the tops of the pineapples you get from your greengrocer. They are easy to have, and make desirable plants—as long as you chose varieties that are not spined.

Pick a ripe pineapple whose leaves are mostly in good condition. Grasp the top firmly in one hand and twist it off the fruit. It should come off easily, with a cone-shaped section of the meat.

With a sharp, clean knife, scrape away any loose meat: the meat is softer than the center, and it's that center you want.

Peel off the lowest, small leaves, or any low brown leaves, baring the lowest part of the stem.

Put it aside while you prepare a pot and soil and tape.

Bromeliads will not grow well unless they sit firmly. In fact, the chief function of bromel roots is to hold on. Your pineapple will not strike roots if it is wobbly in its pot and

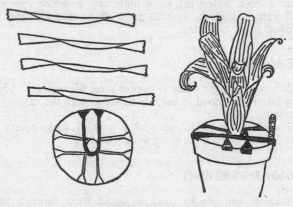

Taping a bromeliad.

must be held firmly while its roots are forming. We do this with 4 strips of cloth tape looped around our pineapple top, near the bottom.

POTTING THE PINEAPPLE TOP

A 4″ azalea pot should do for growing the plant on to a quite respectable size. Crock it with something heavy, and fill it to within about ½″ of the rim with our terrestrial bromeliad mix (see Chapter 7). Dampen the mix.

Now, don't say "ridiculous" until after you've tried this, it works, no matter how damn silly it seems:

Tear off 4 strips of sticky tape ¼″ wide (1½″ tape can be torn in half lengthwise), each about 7″ long.

Leaving about 1″ at either end, fold the tape lengthwise so that for most of its length the stickum is stuck to itself. You're going to wrap the tape around the pineapple top and you don't want it to stick to the plant—just to the pot. Fold each of the 4 pieces, leaving the same inch at either end unfolded.

We do this work in the bathroom, and stick the bits of tape to a towel rack, near to hand, where they won't gum up anything else.

Center the top in the pot, and hold it erect. The bottom should be *on* the soil, or just a bit under. (If you have a third hand, get ready to use it.)

Stick one end of one piece of tape over the lip of the pot, bring the tape around over the lowest leaves of the top, and loosely stick the free end next to the stuck end.

Take another piece of tape and attack the opposite side of the pot. Stick one end over the rim, bring the tape around, over more low leaves, a little tighter this time, and stick the free end near the stuck end. With two loops, the top may stand on its own.

Halfway between the two tapes, put on a third in the same way.

Stick the fourth tape on opposite the third. Now, tighten the tapes so that the top is held firmly (but not strangled).

Mist the top with tepid water and put under lights or into a no-sun location. Don't shove it into the sun immediately, though it will want some sun after it begins to root. (We must add here that although the pineapple is well known to be a full-sun plant, we have one that has been growing like crazy for 4 months under a combination of bright fluorescents and a bit of daylight.)

OFFSETS

Sometimes, several small offsets are formed around the top of a pineapple. Just pull these off and put them into an open propagation box (see Chapter 15).

Cryptanthus also make offsets like this. They are propagated very simply. Just break them off and sit them in an open prop box, or pot right onto some damp terrestrial bromeliad mix.

TAKING A PUP

There is nothing simpler than taking the pup of a mature bromel.

Wait until it is about ⅓–½ the height of the parent plant (there is a lot of leeway), then take a sterile knife and cut the pup off, close to the original plant. Even if there is a long stem, cut it off near the original.

Then tape it into a pot as you did the pineapple top, and set under lights.

Pour some clear water into the vase. It may require daily filling for a while—sometimes the vases of these pups don't hold water as well as those of mature plants. Don't feed for the first few weeks.

PUPS (AND OTHERS) BY MAIL

Bromeliad pups are tough young things and you can usually trust them to the mails. And mail order is a fine way of increasing your bromeliad collection at very little cost.

Our chapter of the Bromeliad Society orders wholesale from Florida and other places. We then divvy up the order. We can get desirable plants for as little as 50¢ that way.

You'll find addresses for mail order in the back of the book.

Just tape up the pups as we've already described, and they will usually grow into handsome plants.

You can also buy through the mail rather mature bromeliads that come bare-rooted. They survive the hazards of the post quite well that way (as do orchids, also). Either pot

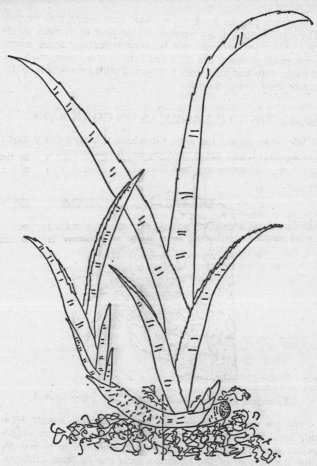

Cut or break off pup close to parent plant. (Notice the start of a new pup near the old cut of the rhizome.)

them up in the appropriate mix, immobilizing them with tape as we did the pineapple top, or mount as we describe below.

MOUNTING

Some bromeliads in apartments go through their entire life

cycle from pup to flowering without ever seeing a flowerpot. They get mounted, by various means and to various mediums. Mounted bromels can be very attractive. Some active apartment growers use driftwood trees (or trees made of chicken wire and cork bark) mounted with bromeliads to decorate their living rooms.

MOUNTING TILLANDSIAS ON CORK BARK

We often mount the little tillandsias this way (they make great gifts); it only takes minutes, and it really works.

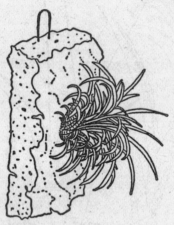

Tillandsia ionantha *glued onto a 2"x3" piece of cork.*

We use real cork bark (not cork paneling), bought from our local Bromeliad Society chapter, cutting it to an appropriate size. The bark has nooks and crannies in it and we glue the bottom of the tillandsia onto one of these crannies. We use ordinary airplane glue (any waterproof glue will do), applying it to the bottom of the plant (after taking off any dead or dying leaves) and to the cork bark.

If the plant has an end thin enough, we take a hairpin, cut the pin to about a ¾" U, and press it into the bark to hold the plant in place. (See drawing above.)

Cut the ends off another hairpin and press the pin into the *top* of the piece of bark, to make a hanger for the plant. Don't soak all this until the next day, to make sure the glue is really set.

MOUNTING LARGER, ROOTED PLANTS

Dampen some sheet sphagnum moss and squeeze it out well. Wrap the roots of the bromel with the moss, covering all the roots in a cup of moss about 1″ thick, and bringing the moss up over the bottom of the leaves.

Tie this moss into place with some very light fishing line or very thin wire (don't use copper wire).

Mounting a mature aechmea. (Fill the vase as usual.)

Now you can hang the bromel as is, or mount it farther on a large piece of cork bark or driftwood, or onto a "bromeliad tree," or any way you please. Just remember that these mounted bromels must be watered by submerging and soaking the entire plant, including the moss, in a bucket of water. So, if you are mounting to a tree, make your mountings removable.

All your mounted plants need more frequent misting than

Cement in a box will anchor a "bromeliad tree."

your potted plants: daily when the air is dry, every few days in the summer.

Bromeliads have such tough leaves that they are seldom prone to fungus, so you can mist them in the evening if you wish.

FLOWERING YOUR BROMELS

There are some bromeliads that will not flower for an apartment gardener. In fact, sometimes they won't even flower for the Brooklyn Botanic Garden. We have an *Aechmea distichantha schlumbergata* which has made lovely and long foliage for 8 years now, but never a flower. We asked the taxonomist of the Brooklyn Botanic what we were doing wrong. His answer was that the plant has never flowered for the Garden either.

There are some plants quite easy of flower: cryptanthus will flower on your windowsill, and tillandsia minis on your windowframes.

But for the bulk of the bromels we grow, apartment conditions are not conducive to "natural" flowering. However, they can be forced into bloom chemically.

Other members of the Bromeliad Society have told us of using apples. Ripe apples give off ethylene gas, which *inhibits* bloom on some plants but will stimulate bloom on a mature bromeliad. By mature, we mean at least 3 years old. Don't try to force a bromel younger than that: it's a waste of time.

Get a plastic bag large enough to hold your plant. Put the plant and a *ripe* apple inside the bag and seal it off, then set in a bright place for *5 days*. Within a couple of months you may see the start of a spike.

For those of you who are more science-minded, there is a product called Brombloom (BOH), available through some bromel suppliers, which will bring mature bromeliads into spike. The appropriate amount of the liquid is dripped into the vase, and, if it works, you'll get a spike a month or so later.

Or, if you're prepared to take a chance on killing a small percentage of your plants, try this. Turn the plant upside down to empty out the vase. Make a solution of ¼ ounce calcium carbide and 1 quart tepid water, and pour it into the vase. Most healthy, mature plants will come to spike in from 1 to 3 months. We've never done it ourselves, but we've had it highly recommended to us.

NATURE'S WAY

For the bulk of bromels, give them good, diffuse light, not enough direct sun to burn their leaves but enough to keep their habit thrifty; keep their humidity high; keep them lightly fed and well watered; and you may, when the plant is mature enough, get bloom.

But one of the great things about bromeliads is that you needn't provide these greenhouse conditions to get an enormous amount of pleasure from them, and even bloom, perhaps.

PROBLEMS

Practically none!

These really are desirable houseplants, virtually whatever your conditions. You can even go on vacation for 3 weeks, if you'll fill their vases, soak their bottoms, and leave them out of bright sun. For thriving on sheer neglect, the only thing to beat bromeliads is cacti.

24. Cacti
and Cactuslike Plants

This chapter and the next are divided according to *culture*, not according to *name*: you'll find some true cacti in both chapters, and some other succulents in both.

Here we'll deal briefly with those cacti that are more difficult to grow in an apartment, and in the next chapter with the easier ones.

Any of the following more common cacti should be treated as described in this chapter: opuntia, cereus, cephalocereus, oreocereus, cleistocactus, lemaireocereus, aporocactus, echinocereus, echinopsis, chamaecereus, lobivia, rebutia, ariocarpus, astrophytum, echinocactus, ferocactus, gymnocalycium, frailea, notocactus, melocactus, coryphantha, mammillaria.

And so should these succulents from other families—lithops (and other living stones), certain crassulas, certain gasterias, certain euphorbias, stapelias, certain aloes, and certain agaves—which we consider "cactuslike."

(You'll notice we saved the many jungle cacti for the next chapter.)

CACTI IN THE APARTMENT

With all the talking we've been doing about how dry apartments are and how much you must work to raise your humidity, you may wonder whether cacti and succulents are the solution to a problem apartment. Perhaps.

It all depends upon how much *sun* you get. Not how much light, but how much sun. You see, most cacti and many succulents require a good deal of sun just to do well—let alone flower and thrive for you.

WHAT'S THE DIFFERENCE BETWEEN CACTI AND SUCCULENTS?

All cacti are succulents, but not all succulents are cacti.

There are succulents you are familiar with in families you wouldn't suspect (aloes and gasterias are in the lily family; hoyas are in the milkweed family; agaves are in the amaryllis family), and families you wouldn't suspect that have succulents (there are succulent gesneriads, begonias, geraniums—there are even succulent mints and peppers: plectranthus and peperomia).

Any plant can be considered a succulent if it has thickened leaves and/or stems to hold additional water for a dry spell.

For some cacti, these dry spells may last for years.

PLANTS AND DRYING

Plants react to the loss of water in different ways. Some shrivel (and then come back if you water them quickly enough: we've seen basil plants that looked already through death's door come back after a watering); some drop leaves, like gardenias; some curl their leaves to expose less leaf surface to evaporation, like certain gesneriads.

In a sense, cacti (at least the spined ones) have curled their leaves so tightly that they have evolved into spines. Yes, those spines are the cactus' leaves. Can you imagine any leaf that would evaporate less water? Remember, a deciduous tree can give up hundreds of gallons of water daily through its leaves.

Also, cacti have evolved a further survival device in terms of shriveling. If we had let that basil go dry for a few more hours, it would have died. The cell walls would have collapsed, and the plant's circulatory system would have been destroyed. In cacti, the collapsing of the cell from lack of water doesn't destroy it. Cacti can be visibly shrunken, and still, with water, come back to their original size, and then grow on into healthy plants.

CAN YOU TELL A CACTUS BY ITS SPINES?

Not really.

Most true cacti do have spines, but there are several non-cacti succulents with spines; and there are many plants with spines that are neither cacti nor succulents. And just to make the confusion complete, there are many cacti without spines.

But most of the cacti we will be talking about in this chapter are spined. In fact, as a rule of thumb, you can say that the more heavily spined a cactus is (or "hairy" like "old-man cactus," *Cephalocereus senilis*) the more sun it needs—and the more sun it needs, the more difficult it can be in an apartment.

THE OLD LIGHT CART

We have friends who keep a collection of cacti under a 2-tube light stand. We really ought to talk to them because that stand looks like a terminal ward. There are some very uncommon plants there, but they are dying a lingering death. They are etiolated. Not only do they never flower—they are no longer even handsome plants. A 2-tube fluorescent fixture just doesn't provide enough light for desert cacti. A 4-tube fixture wouldn't either. Those cacti need sun.

If you have a bright sunny window you can look forward to a great (if prickly) time flowering and flourishing cacti and sun-loving succulents. But, if your apartment has little sun, you may as well skip over this chapter and go on to the next.

WHAT DO YOU BUY, AND WHERE?

Frank Bowman, the best cactus grower we know (he was television's "Green Thumb"), says he buys small cacti in Woolworth's. We buy our cacti from Frank.

However, you can be sure that most of the commercial growers in your city are buying their cacti from a very few sources (in Arizona, Texas, Florida, and California). And, since cacti are easy for professionals with the facilities, the cacti that your local dealers have for sale are probably pretty healthy.

If we had a sunnier apartment we would join the The Cactus and Succulent Society and buy our plants from the local chapter.

Whoever you buy from, buy small plants—they require more water, and more frequent watering than the giants, but if they don't survive they are a small investment. A $50 monster can die on you very quickly if it gets rot.

Try to buy named varieties. With many plants you can search them out by photos or drawings in various books, but cacti are often so similar to one another that it's quite hard to identify them even from the pictures in *Exotica* (see page 356). Of course, you can buy named varieties and then find that they've been mislabeled, too.

If you've got good cactus conditions, don't be afraid to try varieties that are described as difficult—especially if you find them as small plants, when they are cheap. It's a great thrill to take something few others can grow and do well by it.

What are "good cactus conditions"? Simply: bright sun, warm days, cool nights; cool winter days.

REPOTTING?

Don't be in a hurry to repot the cacti you buy (or the cacti you own), because it can be dangerous. Repotting almost always damages the roots, and damaged cactus roots rot easily. In fact, cacti will generally survive longer bare-rooted than they will if potted into wet soil.

We potted a lovely stapelia into a piece of lava rock and thoughtlessly watered it immediately only to watch it rot and die.

If your soil is depleted, fertilize rather than repot; it's a lot safer.

A mature cactus should be repotted no more often than every 2 years.

When you do decide to repot, move up one size only. At maximum, cacti only want about an inch between the body of the cactus and the rim of the pot. And since they are shallow-rooted, stick to shallow pots. We recommend clay pots for large cacti: clay allows the soil to dry out more quickly.

To handle a cactus for repotting, you may want to use leather gloves or a few thicknesses of newspaper. There are some dragons you just can't handle in an apartment without getting stuck. We avoid these; we're horticulturists, not heroes, and we've gathered our share of scars already.

Before potting, your medium should be mostly dry (barely damp is another way to put it). And then after repotting, *don't water for 2 weeks, at least*. The plant won't at all mind sitting without water for 2 weeks.

And make sure your plant keeps the same neckline. Leave too much neck exposed and the plant may wobble and break; bury the plant too deep and your plant will rot.

A good grower we know pots his cacti so that the neckline sits a bit out of the soil, and then puts down a layer of gravel up to the neckline. He says he never gets neckline rot.

And contrary to what you learned in Chapter 11, you'll want to put your sun-lover right into sun as soon as you repot it.

SOIL MIX

In nature, cactus are used to sitting in a very well-drained soil, a soil which doesn't hold the water to the roots. To provide that extra drainage, we just add an additional measure of perlite to our standard mix (see Chapter 7) and we also add an extra helping of bone meal—the breakfast of champions for cacti.

If you are using coarse sand for your soil mix, add an extra measure of that—but we'd like to know where you got it. We can't find it in the city. We could use bird gravel, available in pet shops in 1-pound boxes, but that's an awfully expensive way to pot, and the extra helping of perlite seems to work well.

WATERING

There is more junk written and spoken about watering cacti than any other plant. First of all, it is not true that cacti need virtually no water. If you give them a teaspoonful of water every two weeks, they will slowly but certainly die.

Understand the desert. When it rains in the desert, it *rains*. Because the soil is so well drained the water doesn't sit around the roots, but a great deal of water passes over those roots. The roots absorb what they can and the rest drains off.

Your cacti at home should be watered on the same principle. When you water, give plenty of water. And then allow the plant to drain. If your soil mix is light and drains well, there will be no excess water to cause problems.

Several very good cactus growers we know water their plants only from the bottom, allowing them to sit in a bowl or bucket of water for half an hour, and then letting them drain off well.

It's been said that you can't kill a cactus with neglect. That shows how plant advice has swung full circle. It used to be that people killed their plants with overwatering; nowadays, they kill them (perhaps more slowly) with underwatering.

You *can* kill a cactus with neglect. Especially a young cactus. In fact, *cactus seedlings need as much water* as any other seedlings: constant moisture.

Of course, your cactus will want more or less water depending on the season and on its growth. A large cactus in a small pot, in full growth, in a well-drained soil, in a hot midsummer, may well require watering every other day. In the winter, in dormancy, in a cool window, that same cactus may not need watering for a month at a time.

DISH GARDENS AND TERRARIUMS

We couldn't let this moment go by without heaping a little scorn on cacti in terrariums. Aside from the jungle cacti we'll discuss in the next chapter, cacti do well in the arid (meaning low-humidity) deserts. In high humidity they are subject to fungous diseases and rots. A terrarium, or any kind of enclosed environment, where the aim is to maintain high humidity, is the worst place to grow cacti.

In a dish garden, where there are usually no drainage holes, a plant can sit in sour water and just rot. Most dish gardens are sold with baby plants, not with miniatures, and these babies, as we said, need more water than adult cacti. If you must make yourself a cactus dish garden, use a planter with drainage (then place it on something to keep your table from staining), and stick to miniatures, rather than babies.

DORMANCY

Some cacti require a dormant period to flower, others require only plenty of sun.

Dormancy can be a problem in a hot city apartment. We've solved it by turning the heat off in a small storage room and sitting the cacti on the window ledge and window-sill with the window partly open. This way, they get the best light we can give them, which in the winter is very little—equivalent to "semi-shade"—and the coolness they must have to slow down their growth processes. (A cooler night temperature is, in fact, desirable all year round.)

This doesn't mean you can allow your cacti to freeze. We lost 23 plants one winter by leaving that window wide open while we were away and the temperature dropped to 17°. Dormant cacti do best at a temperature in the low 40's. We listen to the weather forecast and raise or lower the window accordingly.

(There are hardy succulents and we'll deal with them in the next chapter.)

As soon as the days begin to warm up and some sun begins to come up past the building across the way, we water once a week, and watch our cacti come back into growth.

FLOWERING

Some cacti will show signs of bud development immediately after they start spring growth. Gymnocalyciums (chin cacti), for example, are easy of flowering immediately after dormancy and will form buds and flowers (very large for the size of the plant) over a period of 3 months (though the flowers are not long-lasting when fully developed). *Euphorbia obesa* too (called golf-ball cactus, though it's not a cactus: cacti are all from the New World; euphorbias are their equivalents from the Old World), begin showing signs of bud development within a month of dormancy.

All the cacti we've listed want to winter in dormancy even if, like *Astrophytum myriostigma* (bishop's cap), they have no spines. So do the spiny aloes, the thick-leaved agaves, stapelias, living stones, and gasterias.

(Mammalarias, which will take dormancy, will grow well all season if given a bright spot, and will flower at almost any time and stay in flower for weeks.)

CACTI FROM SEED

We spoke of cactus cuttings back in VEGETATIVE PROPAGATION, Chapter 17, but cacti can be so quick and easy from seed it's worth an added mention.

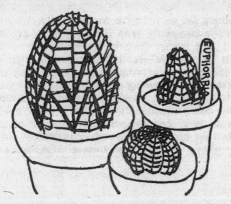

Three Euphorbia obesa. *The plant on the right shows etiolation.*

Cactus seed stays viable for a long, long time: years in fact (a carry-over from the fact that it may be years between rains heavy enough to germinate the seed). But the fresher you can plant it, the faster it will come up.

Use the techniques described in Chapter 16, milled sphagnum moss and plastic cover and all. Cactus seedlings need lots of water, just like any seedlings. Cactus seed also need light to germinate, so don't cover them with the moss. As do other seedlings, cactus seedlings thrive under fluorescent lights.

Keep the clear plastic on until the seedlings push it off, and then keep them in those pots for as long as 6 *months*, or until they can be handled easily. Transplant in the spring, preferably, but never in late fall.

We planted some frailea and gymnocalycium seed recently, and the stuff germinated in a week, and grew very strongly. This is really a fine way to propagate cacti, if you can get seed from a reliable source.

WHY GROW CACTI?

This question is often asked from behind a curtain of African violet blooms. After all, many cacti have wicked spines; they seldom have great beauty, and most of them are quite slow growing. But as Koko says, "There is beauty in the bellow of the blast . . ."

Where is the excitement?

Perhaps it's a matter of "to know them is to love them." Certainly, their beauty is not for every eye—except that when they do flower they are often so spectacular as to rank with orchids and bromeliads. The blooms are often almost the size of the entire plant—though they seldom last and are unscented (the night-blooming cereus is a notable exception, as is pereskia, but we'll talk about them in the next chapter).

Also, their very slowness is a plus for an apartment grower. It's really a pleasure to have a group of plants that don't require repotting every few months, which can sit, a dozen or more to a windowsill, and make no demands over a whole winter.

25. Easier Succulents

Succulents can be extremely rewarding plants. They will, for the most part, tolerate reduced watering and can be left alone if you're on vacation. Mostly they require only moderate sun (sanseveria will thrive without any sun at all) and are indifferent to humidity. Succulent foliage can be quite interestingly variegated, even when the plant is not in flower. And many of them will flower with little trouble in good light.

CULTURE

For the most part, they like a well-drained soil, so include an extra measure of perlite in our basic soil mix (see Chapter 7).

They like to go well dry between waterings (we'll note a couple of exceptions as we get to them), but in the summer, as with cacti, we water them often.

They feed a bit more than do cacti, and we water them occasionally with a ¼-strength solution of a 15-30-15 food or fish emulsion.

They are mostly very easy of propagation: the leaves or stem sections of most will strike roots quite quickly. In some cases it's even easier than that, as with the two plants below.

THE GIFT THAT GOES ON GIVING

Aside from a female cat, there's nothing that lives up to that promise better than *Kalanchoe diagremontiana.* We've had it for years. It was one of our first succulents and it has been—as one of its common names says—mother-of-thousands.

The way this delightful and unusual plant propagates is to form tiny plantlets in the zigzaggings of its leaves. Come spring and summer, these plantlets grow tiny roots, two pair of leaves, then fall to the soil, to root in whatever pot they happen to land, whether they are wanted there or not.

Their culture is extremely simple. We've always given the plant a moderately bright location, and fed it when we thought of it.

It tends to grow leggy after a year or so (especially in our crowded window), then we chop off the top and root it in an open propagation box (see Chapters 15 and 17).

The "kittens" we gather and plant by laying them on damp potting soil where they root quickly and grow quickly. When they are an inch or so tall, we'll transplant them to small pots where they can grow on.

Smaller-growing for us, but of the same culture is *Kalanchoe tubiflora,* which bears its plantlets only on the ends of its small cylindrical leaves.

Both also propagate very easily from leaves laid flat on damp rooting medium (see Chapter 17).

SMALL TRAILERS

Some of the very nicest succulents are trailers. That is, small plants, too small for large hanging baskets, really, but grand to drape from a window top.

The ceropegias are among our favorite trailers. We grow three kinds, *Ceropegia woodii, C. barkleyi,* and *C. debilis. C. woodii* is called rosary vine or string-of-hearts—very appropriate, as the leaves look like flat little green hearts on a thin string.

These plants grow from tubers which should lie on the surface of the soil (any potting mix will do). Propagules (little tubers—see Chapter 27) will form at the leaf axils, and these can be cut off and pinned to the soil to root. They look quite

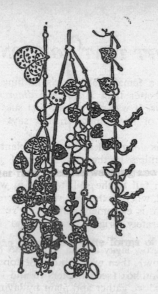

Ceropegia woodii. *The round and bumpy things at some nodes are propagules. The tubular things on the right are flowers.*

odd hanging there; when we first saw them, we went diving into our *Exotica,* to find what was wrong.

Impatiens repens is a small-leaved impatiens which makes large yellow flowers. It grows quite well under lights (close to the tubes), and if cut back and the cuttings rooted, can make a good-sized basket. Don't allow it to get as dry as most other succulents.

We've been told that the common name of *Tradescantia navicularis* (you know other tradescantias: they are among the wandering Jews) is "pussy ears". It could come from the fuzzy, alternate, very close-set leaves. At any rate, even in moderate light this plant makes beautiful trailing stems which propagate readily.

Senecio herreianus and smaller-leafed *S. rowleyanus* are both known as green-marble plant or string-of-beads. It forms trailing stems with little gooseberrylike beads on them. These are the plant's leaves, and the stripes are tiny "windows" which adjust to the light. Be careful not to overwater this succulent. Given good culture, it can make stems 2' long in an apartment window.

Sedum morganianum has made us happy and sad. It is the

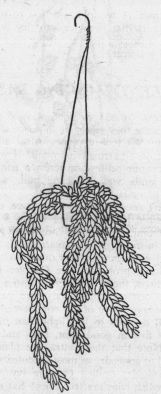

Sedum morganianum *makes an excellent small hanging-basket plant.*

burro's-tail sedum, and makes a terribly impressive hanging plant—though large baskets of it take years to develop. It requires more sun than we can give it in the winter, and then tends to get a bit etiolated on us. Come spring, though, its growth gets compact again and it is a beauty. Its leaves are light green and covered (as are the leaves of many succulents) with a blue-gray blush that helps to protect it against the strong sun it was born for. Each small leaf can form roots and make a plant. In fact, if a leaf gets injured, you may find a small plant forming right there on the wound, while it is still on the stem.

One thing to remember about plants that you hang without

saucers (in Chapter 11 we told you how to make your own hanging baskets) is that they tend to dry out sooner than plants sitting on a saucer, or even sitting on a pebble tray or balcony without a saucer.

SUCCULENT HANGING BASKETS

Hanging baskets are a very good way of growing apartment plants, because they can sometimes be allowed to grow bigger than many windowsill plants. After all, how large a plant can you fit on a narrow windowsill? If you can screw a hook safely into your ceiling, or screw a hanger safely into your window's jamb, you can hang quite a large plant—something in an 8" or 10" or 12" basket.

Also, you don't need to start with a huge, expensive plant to have a nice-sized hanging basket within a few or several months. The several varieties of Swedish ivy (*Plectranthus oertendahlii, P. australis, P. marginatus*—this last one variegated) are rapid growers, and root quite easily in any sterile medium in a closed prop box (see Chapter 15). Take and root several cuttings, then put them all into a larger hanging basket with the original plant, and there you've got a big plant. That's the way many of the commercial growers do it. Swedish ivy will do well in less light than many succulents (though it does fine in good light, too) and is a relatively quick grower. Note that these attractive plants will not be happy if allowed to go as dry as most succulents.

Senecio mikanioides (called German ivy, though neither this nor the Swedish ivies are true ivies) has most handsome ivylike leaves that are stiffly succulent. Propagate it like Swedish ivy and make yourself a very handsome hanging basket.

HOYAS

We find hoyas very interesting and grow several: *Hoya carnosa, Hoya carnosa variegata* which will have some reddish leaves in good sun, though it is a slow grower (there are several hybrids with names like 'Krimson Princess' and 'Krimson Queen' which have redder, more pointed leaves), *H. bella* (rather more compact and small-leafed), *H. mostekei, H. australis*, and a large-leafed variety we've come by only recently, *H. bandaensis.*

We've never flowered a hoya, but we know someone on

Manhattan Island who has flowered *H. bella* under lights and *H. lacunosa* in natural light: she has an incredibly bright eastern exposure and an air-conditioned apartment (though even her buds will blast on an especially polluted day if she opens a window). Flowers or no, we love the foliage, variegated or solid.

The leaves, if put into a sterile medium in a closed prop box, will form plantlets at their base. Don't be fooled into treating hoyas like anything other than succulents: they prefer going quite dry between waterings, especially in the winter.

RHIPSALIS

Many rhipsalis resemble thin rods of coral, hence the common name, coral cactus.

Rhipsalis is a genus that should be better known. It has many handsome (and some rather ugly) species. It is a designer's dream, growing in lines, angles, waves, rods, and segmented shapes. *Rhipsalis coriacea*, which stays small, flowers in our window: small star-shaped flowers give way to small white berries. Charming. *R. lindbergiana* is a coral cactus with pink flowers; *R. burchellii* has pink berries.

Rhipsalids are jungle cacti, as are zygocactus and schlumbergera (Christmas and Easter cacti) and epiphyllum (orchid cactus), all of which can do well in cultivation. All of these jungle cacti require more water and less sun to thrive than do desert cacti. We give pereskia, a viney cactus with *thorns and leaves*, the same treatment.

Though they need ample watering to do their best, rhipsalis can stay alive for long periods without water. They propagate easily from sections of stem.

OTHER JUNGLE CACTI

Epiphyllum are the so-called orchid cacti, and there are several forms of this handsome plant, many of which will hang well when mature. (There are also upright varieties.)

Water them well in growing season and propagate by cutting the flat "leaves" across at their thickest. Our first epiphyllum came from a large blade that was given to us. We cut it into 3 pieces, and all 3 rooted by being staked upright on some damp vermiculite.

The top piece grew additional segments in the shape of the

top piece—that is, rather thick. The bottom piece, which was rod-shaped, grew additional segments in rod shapes. The middle piece rooted, but has to this day, after 6 years or so, not made a single bit of additional growth except to swell very slightly fatter. We infer from this that the best part of the plant to root is a cutting with about 4–6″ of a growing tip.

UP THE LADDER FOR A NIGHT-BLOOMING CEREUS

We flowered an epiphyllum—one winter's night. The plant hung for the whole winter with one branch sticking out the top of our window, that branch freezing and dying. And one night the plant made a white flower of such surpassing beauty and scent that we spent the night until 3:00 A.M. taking turns climbing a ladder to peek down into the blossom and smell it. It had folded in the morning when we awoke, and never reopened.

One night only. Sigh.

Water yours well, and give it plenty of sun and lots of fresh air, and good humidity, and you may get your own night to remember.

Christmas cactus and Easter cactus (*Zygocactus truncatus* and *Schlumbergera bridgesii*) make beautiful flowers at their respective seasons, but in this latitude the Christmas cactus must be given special treatment to flower. It is a long-night plant, which means that it must have 12–14 hours of uninterrupted darkness (even the too-often turning on of a light switch will disturb its cycle). Starting in September (and we're not kidding), put the plant into a closet at 6:00 P.M. and don't take it out until 8:00 A.M. At the same time, reduce watering to a minimum. In December, buds should form.

We prefer the Easter cactus, for which no special treatment is required. We simply keep it on our windowsill and, come spring, it flowers.

Both plants propagate quite readily from two-segment pieces of stem, and can be turned into quite respectable plants if you're ready to break off these pieces. We've found they will root right in the same pot, with no special medium.

Closely related is a very handsome genus, rhipsalidopsis. These usually have fleshier stems than the zygocactus and are, at least for us, freer flowering, with the same treatment as schlumbergera.

A BALCONY ROCK GARDEN

You don't believe you can have a rock garden on your balcony? Heed and believe.

There are hardy succulents which will survive the winter either with no protection or with the minimum protection that the building itself gives, radiating heat into the world.

Hardy sempervivums (hens-and-chicks) and sedums (watch out: there *are* some tender sedums) can make a beautiful small balcony rock garden. These subjects will survive the winter, looking good all winter because they are evergreens. They start into spring growth quite early, giving a delightful early showing, flowering in spring or summer, depending on the variety. And watch those sempervivums spread.

BEGINNINGS

First of all, pick a sunny spot—a *small* sunny spot.

Check your balcony for sun at various times of day before you go into a hardy rock garden: it needs sun, preferably in the afternoon. If you don't get any sun, either because of exposure, or high balcony walls, or overhang from the balconies above, forget it.

Also forget it if the rock garden will wind up being a sandpile for kids or an animal litterbox.

An irregular area 2' by 3' is, believe it or not, quite ample (even 1½' by 2' is more than you think). After all, once you set up this rock garden, you can't walk on it, so you don't want to eliminate a big part of your balcony.

BUYING HARDY PLANTS

Do not go to your usual houseplant sources for these hardy plants. For rock-garden plants you have to go to a perennial nursery. In our area, we would cadge a lift out to Viette Nurseries on Long Island. Or order by mail from Oakhill Gardens in Dallas, Oregon. Both are specialists in this kind of hardy plant. It's good to buy hardy plants from a grower in your own area—*or farther north*.

At a nursery, your plants will often come in small flats or

large composition pots. One of these will amply plant more than a square foot.

DOING IT

Lay down some heavy plastic to protect your balcony. Make certain that the plastic doesn't curl up: you have to allow for free drainage. Or you can curl the plastic up deliberately and punch holes in particular spots to force drainage—off the back of your balcony, say.

Outline the area with bricks or blocks of wood (it should not be a symmetrical area, remember).

A rock garden has to have levels—and rocks. Gather some large rocks or buy some feather rock (feather rock is very light lava rock, very cheap at quarries), and place them in the marked-off area to create levels.

Mix up a large amount of moderately-light just-damp soil and lay it down a few inches thick. Build it up against the rocks to make their placement look natural. Put some *between* the rocks, too. It may take a rain or two to smooth off the rough edges.

Unpot your plants from their flats and break up the clumps. Plant them about, rather sparingly. They will spread.

Don't water for a week or so. (If it rains, it rains, but you don't water.)

The sedums go nicely in the places between the rocks and the sempervivums we prefer on the open areas, but you can decide for yourself.

You may want to rake (that is, tilt) the whole thing, making it highest near the wall and lowest away from the wall. At any rate, don't leave large areas of flat soil. That is dull.

Put an inconspicuous label near each plant, so that you'll know the varieties.

By the fall, you should have a lovely show.

Sempervivum arachnoideum is covered with weblike white hairs, and *S. tectorum* has several good hybrids. All the sempervivum are low and hardy.

We use *Sedum reflexum* and *S. Hispanicum*, but all the following sedums are hardy and low-growing: *Sedum acre, S. album murale nigra, S. cauticolum, S. dasyphyllum, S. ewersii, S. kamtschaticum, S. lidokense, S. oreganium, S. pluricoule, S. sexangulare, S. spathufolium purpureum, S. spurium.*

WATERING YOUR ROCK GARDEN

Preferably, God will do that for you, but if you find that the area of balcony of fire escape you've chosen is too protected from the rain, you'll have to do some watering. Over the winter, however, don't bother. The small amount the garden gets (if it gets any at all) will keep it green.

ALTERNATIVES

Don't have a balcony? You can still winter these hardy succulents outside.

For a standard windowsill, get a large bulb pan (see Chapter 10), crock the bottom, put in a couple of inches of soil, and set in only one or two varieties of sempervivum. Winter it on the *outside* of your windowsill. You won't even have to water it.

If you have a bit more room than that, get a galvanized iron tub, punch several holes in the bottom, pour in a few inches of perlite, then cover with a few inches of soil, and plant up sparsely with handsome varieties. And then winter it outdoors. You'll love it.

Don't winter your sempervivums or hardy sedums indoors. We had a difference of opinion about that one year, and we put a 10″ bulb pan outside and a few small pots inside, on a cool windowsill. The bulb pan thrived; the inside pots died.

MINIATURES THAT FLOWER READILY

Crassula cooperi is a little gem that forms tiny white flowers at the ends of its branches, even in modest windowsill light. The flowering stems get leggy as the buds form.

Anacampseros rufescens has a name bigger than it is. It's true: the plant flowers at about 3″, and that in a 1½″ pot. As many succulents do, the foliage takes on a reddish cast in the sun: a suntan.

Haworthias will flower for you, and the fleshier sorts are especially interesting and attractive (if you like that sort of thing). *Haworthia truncata* looks as if it had been cut off. *H. turgida* is quite readily available. These are "window" plants.

The upper surfaces of the leaves have little "windows" which open and close, adjusting to the amount of sun: which permits them to survive well on a moderately bright windowsill.

Euphorbia splendens (crown of thorns) is hardly a miniature, as it can grow to a bushel-basket size in an apartment (though this is rare). However, it will bloom while quite young. We've had 6″ pieces flowering for us. There is a more miniature form available recently, *E. splendens prostrata;* it is free-flowering and quite charming. Keep these euphorbias watered or they will lose their leaves.

ETIOLATION

Plants have their own normal growth patterns. There is variation, but a plant is recognizable from specimen to specimen because it has inherited its "normal" appearance from its ancestors. In poor growing conditions, that appearance changes. Just as people get tanned in the sun or grow thin with lack of food, or their complexion gets bad from poor diet, so a plant will change its appearance with changes in its diet or environment.

If any plant gets too little sun or too little food, it will make weak, thin growth, compared to its normal growth. This weaker, thinner growth is called "etiolation." Any plant can become etiolated. But the history of its hard times are written on a succulent because it has *survived* them rather than succumbed.

When you don't put your cacti into winter dormancy, but rather water them and keep them warm, the winter sun, in most apartments at these latitudes, is not strong enough to keep their growth going along at the same healthy, *normal* rate. At the end of a year of growth, you can "read" these winter periods by the thinner etiolated growth. The waves on a cryptocereus will flatten out if it doesn't get enough sun. If you later put it in a sunnier location the beautiful pattern will resume on the younger growth, but the etiolated sections remain as reminders of its hard times.

SOME FOLIAGE SUCCULENTS

Except for ferns, there is no such thing as a strictly foliage plant; not in this book. Everything flowers, given the proper conditions; even that sanseveria will flower, if it gets enough

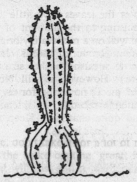

This lophocereus had good culture, then bad (shown by etiolation), then good again.

light and gets to be about 10 years old. Still, there are some plants that are difficult to flower, which have lovely lovely leaves.

We like pedilanthus, perhaps because we learned a lesson from our first.

A friend, leaving New York, brought us a *Pedilanthus tithymaloides* (devil's backbone), a zigzaggy plant which she called a ribbon cactus and which she had treated like a cactus—keeping it very dry between waterings. This is a plant with variegated foliage, but there were very few leaves on the stems. We weren't surprised. We knew it was in the euphorbia family, and we knew that crown of thorns (*Euphorbia splendens*) will lose its leaves if allowed to run too dry—as this plant obviously had.

We watered it very well—soaked it, in fact—and within a few days, under fluorescent lights, the plant had started into leaf. Within a couple of weeks, the stems were *covered with leaves*.

We now keep it on our windowsill (the red of the leaves won't come out for us under lights), and it is still in very full leaf. So, don't treat your leafed succulents like desert cacti.

Peperomia is a jungle plant with very fleshy leaves of many different forms. If you don't like the variety you've bought, look around; there are scores of other handsome kinds. It, too, resents going dry and will drop a perfectly healthy leaf to show its resentment. You can propagate peperomias either from stem cuttings or by setting a leaf into sterile medium. Their flower stalks look like very elongated mushrooms—but they serve the purpose.

Hoya carnosa (mentioned earlier, in the section on hanging baskets) has mutated into curly-leaf varieties, too. Now, we have absolutely no success with these odd looking creatures, but they are very slow-growing, and you might want to try them for yourselves. There are certainly many plants we can't grow which other people do.

A LOW-LIGHT SUCCULENT

Not all succulents demand your sunniest place: sanseverias (snake plant) don't need any direct sun at all. In a way, they are the perfect gift plant. You can give a sanseveria to anyone without fear of their killing it (unless they are an habitual drowner). And there are so many forms of this tough plant that growing them can be quite interesting. One of our fellow folk-dancers is now raising 36 kinds, which he has collected within the last 18 months.

Propagate by division (see Chapter 17, VEGETATIVE PROPAGATION), or from horizontal sections of the leaves.

Leaf sections don't come true to color: they all make plain green plants, whatever the variegation of the parent leaf. For the color, you have to have a bit of the thick rootstock.

Keep in a small pot and feed very seldom.

SOME MISCELLANEOUS SUCCULENTS

Crassulas are in general excellent plants if you have sun. The jade tree (*Crassula argentea*) has lovely dark foliage and will grow into quite a shrub if you can keep it cool during the winter months. (Difficult to flower without a greenhouse.) *C. argentea variegata* has pale-green-and-white leaves which will blush red in the sun. *C. lactea* seems to want more sun than the others to maintain a compact habit. They all propagate from leaves or stems.

Aloe vera (burn plant) will do well on a windowsill. Keep a plant handy when you play with fire: it's said to contain an excellent unguent. Our *Aloe eru*, which we've had for years, is currently 3 feet tall and almost 2 feet wide. There are several aloes available, but don't try them if you don't have good sun.

The same is true for agaves and gasterias. We grew an *Agave americana* (century plant) from one of the offsets formed on the flower stalk. In Bermuda, where we picked up our offset, the flower stalks run about 20 feet tall. And they do not take a century to bloom; but they won't flower as apartment plants. The plant did well as a baby, but we killed it with too much water. Other agaves we've given away because they were so spiny.

As for gasterias, they do stay small (not an inconsiderable virtue in an apartment), but their sun requirements are usually rather high, so be warned. We've done well with *Gasteria lingua* on our windowsill.

If you can manage gasterias, you should do well with kleinias. There aren't many species in cultivation, but they are quite varied. *Kleinia stapeliaeformis* has the squared-off stems of stapelia; *K. tomentosa* is very handsomely fuzzy.

Senecios aren't quite as demanding of light as are kleinias, but *Senecio cuneatus* is most unusual and desirable (it is called spearhead senecio), with leaves that end in little spearheads.

You might try the widely-available *Kalanchoe blossfeldiana* hybrids. Their flowers come in several shades of oranges and reds. They are smallish plants, but only the *K. b.* 'Tom Thumb' can really be considered a dwarf. Leaf cuttings root readily. *K. tomentosa* is beautifully fuzzy and brown-edged.

26. Orchids

This will be a short chapter because we just don't know a great deal about growing orchids in an apartment (we could tell you a little about how to *kill* orchids in an apartment).

To flower orchids in a city apartment you have to be lucky, or very good, or rich.

We have been lucky; we have a rich near-neighbor; and we have a friend who is definitely very good.

THE RICH

Who says money can't buy happiness? If you have the

money you can have orchids in bloom all the time, whatever your growing conditions, just by *buying them in bud*. Orchid buds don't blast when you bring them home, they make a marvelous production of opening, and a flowering may last for months.

We have a friend who lives in a house on Long Island who always has a few orchids blooming in her window greenhouse. (If you have a house, *do* consider a window greenhouse, because nothing beats that overhead sunlight.)

But we have a neighbor who does a lot better than that, right in the middle of Manhattan. He lives on the first floor of a two-story brownstone. His large front window faces west, across the avenue from an elementary school only three stories high.

He has orchids in flower every time we walk past that window. It's great: let us tell you what his set-up is like.

He has built a plastic greenhouse inside that window, with wooden boards as the uprights. One side opens as a door. The overall dimensions are about 8′ high by 3′ deep by 8′ wide.

Inside there is a very small fan which keeps the air circulating, a small humidifier which works only occasionally, 2-tube fluorescents for supplementary lighting across the ceiling, and a roller window shade to block the hot summer afternoon sun.

The cost of this interior greenhouse is really quite low: the expense lies in being able to afford the old brownstone with large windows where you can do construction of this sort. You just can't do it in a rented apartment.

WHAT DO ORCHIDS NEED?

Orchids are classified by several means. Some are sympodial (spreading), some are monopodial (upright); some are terrestrial, some are epiphytic (defined on pages 298–299 when we were praising BROMELIADS); but the most practical classification for amateur growers is cool, intermediate, and warm.

COOL ORCHIDS

Cymbidiums, odontoglossoms (some species), and oncidiums (some species), are the most popular of the cool orchids, and they are not for an apartment. Cool culture is very difficult to maintain outside of a greenhouse. Even those who have orchid greenhouses have separate cool and warm greenhouses.

You see, cool for an orchid means that the winter evenings should drop to about 50°, and that the summer temperatures should not go above about 70°. Put this together with the need for a great deal of sun, and you have a plant that's just not an apartment plant.

WARM ORCHIDS

These can be grown in an apartment most successfully. They require night temperatures between 60° and 65° which is where people can be comfortable, too, and many of them are quite undemanding of light, which means they can be great on a windowsill or under lights.

INTERMEDIATE ORCHIDS

You shouldn't eliminate the intermediates from your apartments entirely, because the warm-intermediates, like miltonias, are possible. Cattleyas are intermediate orchids, but most of them require just too much light.

FRESH AIR

Most plants need some air circulation: but you can grow gesneriads, ferns, begonias in bottles with barely a breath of fresh air and they will thrive. A terrarium can do marvelously without any fresh air beyond what comes in when you open it occasionally to water or groom.

But orchids demand fresh air. Freely circulating air is a must. If you can't provide fresh air for your orchids, you can't provide for your orchids.

A New Jersey homeowner we know successfully grows *Ludisia discolor* (a warm, terrestrial orchid formerly called *Haemaria discolor*) in her basement, on a plant cart: she keep a fan going all day to keep that air circulating.

LIGHT

Light demands vary from genus to genus, and even within the genus.

As mentioned, cymbidiums and cattleyas require, generally,

too much light for apartments. But if you have 4-tube fluorescent fixtures, you can grow epidendreaums and brassavolas in an apartment set-up; and even with only a 2-tube fixture you can flower cyprepidiums, phalaenopsis, and miltonias.

If you can provide some supplementary daylight with the fluorescents, you will find it even easier.

We have flowered phalaenopsis hybrids and a cyprepidium hybrid on our windowsill, and it was very exciting.

(Speaking of light, the very best amateur orchid grower we know, a man who wins all the blue ribbons, reverses day and night. He grows only under lights, and he has painted his basement windows black and set his timers to come on at 6:00 P.M.—*when he comes home from the office.* He has the lights on when he can work on his plants, not when nature has decreed.)

THE LUCKY

We had all but given up the idea of flowering orchids in our home. In the early days we bought cattleyas on the assurance that they were the easiest for an apartment: they are *not* easy in an apartment—they are hardly even possible. We kept them around as foliage plants.

But we are stubborn; and finding a 15-year-old magazine article on how phalaenopsis (moth orchids) are easy in an apartment, we bought some unnamed hybrids, put them on our windowsill, and wished ourselves luck.

They worked and we'll tell you how.

The plants sat on our radiator pebble tray, where they were watered with a very dilute plant food at every watering (either fish emulsion or 15-30-15), given as much light as our obstructed eastern exposure could afford (which during the winter months isn't much), and *dripped on almost daily.*

If you'd like an explanation of that last bit of culture, it goes like this. We *hang* a lot of plants around our window and over our windowsill, and since we water well, they all drip on the plants beneath. So, apart from watering and feeding at their roots, the orchids also got a good deal of haphazard foliar feeding, as well as the extra moisture on the leaves. And we fully believe that's what did it.

Let us tell you what it's like to flower a phalaenopsis. First, a flower stalk forms from between two leaves. As it grows, buds begin to come out. After about a month, the first flower begins to open—swelling and swelling, then parting, then opening flat. Then the next bud begins to open, and so on 11 times! From the formation of the flower stalk to the dropping of the eleventh flower was a full 3 months. Now *that* is a production number.

THE GOOD

But we have a friend* who flowers her orchids in a less haphazard style, and who knows the names of the hybrids she grows. And she has flowering all year round.

She especially recommends the warm growing cypripediums as easy to flower in an apartment and of long-lasting flower. *Cypripedium spicerianum* has been in flower for her for almost a year and is still making new buds; *C. harrisinium* blooms several times a year; *C. bellatulum* will bloom every time it makes new growth (and doesn't want as much water as most cyps); *C. glaucophyllum* is long-flowering; *C. godefoyae* and *C. concolor* are also recommended.

Miltonia regnellii flowers very easily and doesn't need much light; in fact, it will turn yellow with too much light.

(One very good grower tells us that you should give an orchid as much sunlight as it will take without scorching. If you're growing in natural light, that's a good rule of thumb. Under fluorescents your plant may respond by *yellowing* rather than burning. Among orchids, yellowing is a sign of too much light).

Brassavolas also have a good chance in your apartment. *Brassavola nodosa* is fragrant at night.

Our *good* grower agrees with us *"lucky"* growers that phalaenopsis and epidendrums are easy in an apartment.

HUMIDITY

For her, a room humidifier points directly onto the light set-up, providing a humidity constantly between 50 and 60%.

AIR

Her humidifier has a small fan which is also directed onto the plants and which keeps the air moving. (She's convinced

*Our thanks to Jane Maurice for her specific recommendations.

that this freely circulating air and humidity are the key to her success.)

LIGHT

Her fluorescent lights are kept on 14 hours a day. Epidendrums and brassavolas are kept under 4-tube fixtures and cypripediums, phalaenopsis, and miltonias are kept under 2-tube fixtures.

SPACE

The major difference between our light set-ups and that of our friend is the space. She leaves room between her plants, and between plants and her tubes. With us, growing so many gesneriads and begonias and other exotics that like to be right close to the tubes—well, we just don't have the kind of space she has. So we flower what we can on our windowsills. Orchids need space.

WATERING

In general, orchids with pseudobulbs (those swellings out of which come the leaves) like to go quite dry between waterings. Orchids without this storage device prefer more frequent watering (every few days in our apartment) but still need to dry a bit between waterings.

Soak the orchids with pseudobulbs really well when you water them. When these roots dry out, a simple watering won't wet them.

DRAINAGE

Just as orchids need more fresh air around their heads than do most other plants, they also need more air around their roots than most other plants. Orchids must have perfect drainage—which is why most of their potting mediums are so light.

Orchid roots are spongy—for both air and water.

Orchid pots often have chunks cut out of their bottom edges to allow in more air. And many epiphytic orchids are grown on "rafts" (very open redwood baskets) or on slabs of tree fern or cork bark, as are bromeliads.

MEDIUMS

See Chapter 7, SOILS AND SOIL MIXES, for a list of orchid mediums. Recent investigations have put down osmunda fiber as a preferred medium and moved toward fir bark.

FEEDING

Orchid feeding depends largely on the medium they're growing in.

Terrestrial orchids will want a 10-10-10 food.

If you're growing in bark, start off feeding 30-10-10, then switch to our old friend 15-30-15 for flowering.

Feed your orchids at *full* label strength (but no stronger) with every other watering.

PROPAGATION

While we don't flower many orchids, we certainly can propagate them.

SEED

Orchid seed are among the smallest in the world, and not really for the apartment hobbyist. (The seeds don't include any food, and they, in nature, require the presence of a fungus to break down food to the point where they can assimilate it. Commercial growers and the racier hobbyists plant the seed in sterile flasks on a bed of agar-agar—a nutritive medium.)

BUDDING

This interesting new development may, in the near future, make young orchid plants no more expensive than gloxinias.

A microscopic bit of meristematic tissue is cut off the growing tip of the plant, and it is made to multiply—and the end product is a plant *exactly* like the parent, genetically. Strictly a laboratory procedure, but fascinating.

VEGETATIVE PROPAGATION

Here's something we can all do.

Orchids with pseudobulbs can propagate from division of the "backbulbs." Backbulbs are the pseudobulbs from previous years' flowering. They are no longer capable of flowering, and if left alone they sit there looking totally dead. But if they are separated they can make you a new plant.

Cymbidium backbulb in sphagnum moss, making a new plant.

Our propagation course was given a large cymbidium plant with about 35 backbulbs (cymbidiums are poor apartment plants, but the technique is the same for, say, epidendrums). We turned the plant out of its pot, then took a sterile knife and cut the backbulbs into one-bulb sections (that is, we cut the plant so that each division had one backbulb). We now have a lovely juvenile plant from *one* backbulb, but experts recommend at least *three* per division.

The pieces can be potted directly into medium, but we prefer to start these divisions in some long-hair sphagnum moss.

We packed the moss tightly into a pot, around the backbulb and any roots: orchids must have their mediums packed tightly around their roots.

It took two months for our backbulb to sprout, though

some of our students got theirs sooner. So, until it rots or shrivels, keep watering.

Phalaenopsis may be divided, if more than one crown is well developed. Just cut down between the crowns with a sterile knife, and pot them up.

Cane-type orchids, such as dendrobiums, may propagate from stem cuttings. Make cuttings about 6″ long and lay horizontally in sterile medium in a closed propagation box. (See Chapters 15 and 17.) Pot up when roots are about an inch long. We have found only a small percentage of success with this kind of cutting.

Dendrobium keiki in sphagnum moss, making new growth.

Keikis are a kick. They are small plants which form on the stems of some orchids (such as epidendrums and dendrobiums). They form their own root systems, have their own leaves: they really are small plants. Remove them gently from the plant by twisting them off or by cutting with a clean knife. Just pot them up and put them where you wish. They are plants and ready to go.

HARDY NATIVE ORCHIDS

All of the hardy native orchids are protected by law (and by good sense). They require much-too-cool culture for an apartment, or a basement, or a window greenhouse. Leave them where they are.

PROBLEMS

Not many. Orchids are very tough plants. They can be shipped bare-rooted around the world and then go through the high-heat fumigation process that the United States Department of Agriculture requires of all plant material entering the United States—and still come up growing.

They are disease- and insect-resistant, and even without flowers they make vigorous and enthusiastic foliage plants.

If you don't give them fresh air, they will be subject to fungus, but if you don't give them fresh air, you can't really grow them.

Orchids are subject to viruses. These diseases are incurable and may kill the plant off quickly, or not for years. Protect yourself by buying only from reputable, recommended growers; and avoid plants with unhealthy spots on their leaves.

JOYS

Orchid plants live a very long time in nature, and longer than most plants in your apartment. Their flowers are terribly interesting and beautiful, most of them scented (the scent goes after you cut the bloom off), and mostly quite long-lasting.

27. Bulbs, Tubers, Corm, Rhizomes, Cha-Cha-Cha

Bulbs, tubers, corms, scaly rhizomes are storage units; they are means of getting a plant over hard times; of storing up food and water until the weather warms or the rains come.

TRUE BULBS

True bulbs last from year to year, and they have a "basal plate" at their bottom, from which come roots and offsets.

Onions and garlic are true bulbs. The onion stores its food in layers, the garlic stores it in scales (each garlic clove is a scale). If kept out of the fridge (which tends to hold bulbs dormant—that is, still alive but not in active growth), both will sprout, and make considerable top growth—without any water or food, except what the bulb has stored within itself. (See Chapter 21 for sprouting onions and garlic.)

AMARYLLIS

We don't have much luck with spring-flowering bulbs, apartment temperatures are too warm; but there is one true bulb we do just fine with: amaryllis (hippeastrum)—a tender bulb.

We have had our amaryllis for years now, and it blooms for us winter after winter—just as if we had a contract with it.

Of course, in an overheated city apartment, the flowers don't last as long as they would in a thermostat-controlled home or greenhouse, but we enjoy it while it lasts—and even the growth and development of the flower stalk and bud are a show (as it is with orchids).

Here's how we did it. First of all, we bought a mature bulb. Probably you can't get a flowering size amaryllis bulb for less than $3, and $5 is likely closer to the current market, but you're buying for the future as well as for the present. Usually, the bulbs are ready to flower if you buy them in the fall or winter.

(We visited a friend's office to survey his outside space for planting—a large set of balconies on a downtown office building—and saw something that blew our collective mind: he'd bought several amaryllis bulbs and had left them in a paper bag. One of the bulbs had made—from inside the bag, without soil, without water or light—a flower stalk large enough to push open the bag and stick its head into the world, *and flower*. Yes, there the flowers were, growing out of a paper bag. Now, that's a bulb!)

Pot up an amaryllis bulb with only about half of it under the soil, and firm the soil well around the base. Use our standard potting soil (see Chapter 7) with an extra helping of bone meal and cow manure (both are rather slow and are more for next season than this).

Keep the potted bulb on a windowsill, where it can be both bright and cool. The flower stalk will develop before any foliage, grow a foot or two (depending on the variety and maturity of the bulb). Water the bulb when the soil begins to dry out.

Enjoy.

After the flower dies, allow the flower stalk to dry up and then cut it off. Foliage—long straps—should begin into growth (if it hasn't already). Give the plant a top-dressing of bone meal and put in the brightest spot you have—outside, if the weather permits.

We do not find the floppy long straps particularly lovely, so we put the bulb in a spot where we don't have to watch it all the time—a corner of our tiny balcony. But this strap period is terribly important to next year's flowering.

You see, the bulb now stores up the food and energy which will make next year's flowers. So it must be fed and watered and given as much sun as you have (which in most apartments is little enough), if it is to flower for you again.

We have a friend with a friend with a greenhouse. And every spring she gives her greenhouse friend two spent amaryllis plants, and every fall, he gives her the bulbs back, ready to flower in the winter. We're not that lucky. So we water and feed, and make sure the foliage gets sun all through the spring, summer, and into the fall, right up to the first frost.

What we've been doing is to allow the foliage to freeze (if the frost is light the bulb is safe, and the flower stalk starts soon after). But you might want to bring in your plant just before frost. Allow it to dry enough to kill off the foliage, then keep it just barely watered, and set in a coolish place.

When flower stalk growth starts up once more, water, and there you are, all over again.

SPRING BULBS

If you insist on knowing how to force spring bulbs, here's how we've done it:

First of all, buy only bulbs that are grown for forcing—usually the largest size. Some will be "prepared"—that is, they will have been kept in a quite cool place for a period of time, so that they will be ready to start into rapid growth as soon as you plant them. It is characteristic of hardy bulbs that their growth is stimulated by a period of cold. These pre-cooled bulbs should be potted up, watered, and then covered with a dark paper cap. Put into a cool place and keep an eye on the top growth. Don't let them dry out completely. When the top growth is a few inches along, bring them out into a cool, dim location, then into a brighter location as the sprout greens up with the light.

Bulbs for forcing cannot be pre-cooled ("prepared") in your home refrigerator: it's much too damp for that kind of work, and fungus is likely to set in.

If you must force unprepared bulbs, we would say that hyacinths are your best bet.

Bury the bulbs about halfway under the soil, 3 large bulbs to a 6″ pot (clay or plastic—it doesn't matter). Water well, and then allow to drain thoroughly.

Now, tie a cardboard (or aluminum foil) collar around the pot so that it sticks up about 4″ above the tops of the bulbs. The pot will look like a soufflé dish ready for baking.

Planting hyacinths on October 18 for our late-winter pleasure. First, 3 bulbs go in each 6″ pot, then are covered with mulch held on by an aluminum-foil collar.

Fill the enclosed area with some mulching material: peat moss, fine wood chips, broken-up peanut shells, etc. When it's filled, pack down very slightly, and refill.

Place the pot in a location where it can be cold without freezing hard. (Though these bulbs are hardy to hard frost in the ground, they are not hardy to the freezing and thawing that occurs in a pot. Mulching like this will help to keep the soil from freezing hard.) An outside window that you keep open, even a crack, makes a good place; the warm air from the room keeps the air immediately outside the window in a good temperature range.

Starting in January, or late December, you can begin checking every few weeks to see if there has been any moderate top growth started. If so, bring the bulbs indoors, keeping them still cool, and remove the mulching stuff and the collar; water, and allow top growth to get on.

Eventually, you'll get flowers—and now that we remind ourselves, the scent of those home-forced hyacinths is really lovely enough to make it all worthwhile.

By the way, if you don't want to go the route of the collar-and-mulch business, you can get a wooden box (provided you have room outside your windowsill), fill it well with clinkers or dead leaves or peat moss or broken-up peanut shells, or other mulching material, and set the pots in the box, covered by a few inches of mulch. The timetable should be about the same.

Hyacinth Jars. These are vases, usually about 10″ high, with a pinched "throat," somewhat like a bottom-heavy hourglass. You fill the jar with water up to this throat, then set a forcing-size hyacinth bulb in the top section, so that the basal plate sits just over (not in) the water.

Put the vase in a cold and dark place (a cool cellar with a temperature below 50° is best) until the root system fills the jar. Then bring the bulb into a cool part of the house proper, hardening the top growth against sunlight as you did above.

Keep the vase filled with water up to the neckline, but never allow the basal plate to sit in water.

These were very popular in grandma's time because houses were just cooler, and often did have a cold cellar. Where are you going to put yours? In a warm place they make weak growth and may not flower at all.

A word about the expense of forcing bulbs. With the amaryllis, no matter how much you pay for the bulb, you're getting something that, with reasonable care, will last and last. With these spring bulbs, you cannot reasonably expect to keep them over until next year in an apartment. If you have a garden, you can stick them there after flowering, and they will survive, very likely, but they are unlikely, even in a garden, to flower next year.

FORCING PAPERWHITES

Among the named varieties, Chinese sacred lily (white) and Soleil D'or (yellow) are the favorite forcing narcissi. But we're happy with the large unnamed bulbs we buy simply as "forcing paperwhite."

For these, you'll want a decorative container; one that is glazed and will not leak out its water, one that you won't mind looking at while the narcissi are flowering, and one that is about twice as wide as it is high.

Once again, don't stint on the bulbs. "Bargain" bulbs will often disappoint you.

You won't be able to save these tender bulbs for flowering next year, either.

Fill the container almost to the top with a material to support the bulbs: aquarium gravel is popular and clean; peat moss will do; anything that will give the roots something to hold onto while at the same time not giving them a hard time. (Soil will not do.)

Set as many bulbs as will fit, into the medium, so that half of the bulb or less is covered. Now, pour in water until the water level reaches the bottom of the bulbs.

Put the container into a cool, dark place (about 50–60°— but certainly no warmer). The water will stimulate root growth and the cool darkness should inhibit top growth.

Keep the water level at the same height: the base of the bulb. You can tell the water level by sticking your finger into the pot.

After weeks (the number varies according to your temperature and bulbs), when the top growth is a few inches tall, bring the container out into a not-too-bright-but-still-cool location. (It's all this "cool" stuff that makes it so hard for us apartment dwellers.) Keep for a few days in this location, then move into a sunny location. The warmer the spot, the faster your bulbs will flower—and die.

Throw the bulbs away when they're finished flowering. (Yes, it hurts us to say it and you to do it. Perhaps we should all move to Bermuda where these tazetta narcissi now grow wild.)

RHIZOMES

Rhizomes are adapted stems, which grow either above or under the ground, depending on the plant.

RHIZOMATOUS BEGONIAS

A good example of a rhizome is the so-called beefsteak begonia (*Begonia erythrophylla*). Chunks of this hairy creeping stem will root and make new plants, even if the leaves of the plant have all dropped off for lack of water (and it's happened to us).

Rhizomatous begonias make terrific plants, either on windowsills or under lights. If you grow them on a windowsill, make certain you turn them frequently or they will grow one-sided.

Under lights, you may have trouble bringing them into bloom, because they are "long-night" plants: that is, they need an uninterrupted night of at least 12 hours to flower. But rhizomatous begonias have, as a rule, such undistinguished flowers that they are best grown for their foliage any way.

These are among the easiest houseplants, and very rewarding. We grow dozens of varieties, and except for a few which require the higher humidity of a protected environment in an apartment (*Begonia versicolor*, *B. gogoensis*, *B.* 'Rajah,' *B.* 'Exotica,' for example), they require a minimum of care.

We give them bright light, but not much direct sun, permit them to got a bit dry between waterings, and we get excellent results.

Rex begonias, which are also rhizomatous, are a different matter entirely. They require high humidity, they resent going dry, and their lighting must be a compromise between the intense light they need to bring out good color and the direct sun that will burn their leaves. We grow a couple, but have killed several, convincing ourselves that our life is too casual to grow rexes outside of a protected environment.

Rhizomatous begonias don't go fully dormant (except rex begonias; see below), but they do slow down their growth and can look straggly after flowering, especially in natural light. This slowing down can be scary, because when some houseplants do it it can be a sign that something is quite wrong. If your rhizomatous begonia gets this slow and ragged look, examine it for pests. If everything looks all right otherwise, just water it a bit less and stop feeding until new growth starts in again.

Rexes *can* go dormant—especially when they first come into your apartment—dying right back to the rhizome, or losing a few leaves and looking like hell. Water less and stop feeding until leaf growth comes back, but don't allow it to go fully dry.

There are literally hundreds of rhizomatous begonias in cultivation and available through various growers, but a few of the ones we grow successfully are: *Begonia ricinifolia* (quite large-growing, it can get to be a yard across in an apartment), *B.* 'Cleopatra' (or *B.* 'Maphil'), *B. sunderbruchii*, *B.* 'Persian Brocade,' *B.* 'Joe Hayden,' *B. boweri* (and the *B. boweri* and *B.* 'Joe Hayden' hybrids), *B. erythrophylla*, *B. heracleifolia*, *B.* 'Texas Star,' *B.* 'Cool Waters,' *B. fuscomaculata*, and *B. masoniana* (the Iron Cross begonia).

While there are named rex hybrids—*B.* 'Merry Christmas,' *B.* 'Duarte,' *B.* 'Vesuvius,' etc.—the rexes hybridize so readily that most of them you see will not be named, or lumped under the general name of *Begonia rex culturum*.

Besides being easy to propagate from rhizome cuttings, these rhizomatous begonias will also propagate from a leaf, or even from a part of a single leaf. (See Chapter 17.)

SCALY RHIZOMES

These storage devices look something like elongated little pine cones. They are made up of tiny fleshy "scales" strung

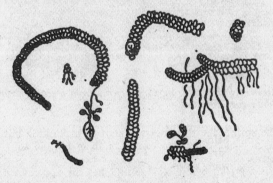

Scaly rhizomes.

on a thin central stem. Each scale is capable of making a plant; just lay them on sterile medium in a closed prop box. However, for flowering-sized plants, keep several scales to a piece, at a minimum.

Most of the scaly rhizomes plants we grow are GESNERIADS: phinea, koellikeria, diastema, achimenes, smithiantha, kohleria. Turn to Chapter 22 for their culture.

Scaly rhizomes are very interesting things. Like corms, they do not live from year to year. Rather, the rhizome you set in the soil gives rise to a plant and then dries up. After a season of growth, when the plant goes into dormancy, you can let the soil go dry and dig up several new rhizomes, which can be stored as described in Chapter 22.

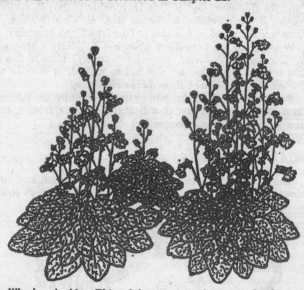

Koellikeria erinoides. *This miniature grows from a scaly rhizome, but seldom goes dormant.*

In the spring, the rhizomes will start to make little bits of growth, at which time you can plant them up and start all over again.

Oxalis regrellii, whose storage unit has the appearance of a scaly rhizome, is the best houseplant oxalis we've seen, with white flowers in constant bloom, either on a modestly sunlit windowsill or under lights. As of this writing, we have a pot of it which has been in bloom constantly since January 1— more than 11 months. We understand that it doesn't really go dormant at all. We'll have to see about that, but at any rate, 11 months of flowering isn't bad.

MORE RHIZOMES

More rhizomes? Well, this is just terminology. In most general catalogs, you will find all storage units referred to as "bulbs," be they tuber, rhizome, corm, scaly rhizome, or tuberous root.

Cannas and lily-of-the-valley are the most common of this group, probably, and they are poor houseplants. In fact, lily-of-the-valley always does terribly for us (and in most warm apartments).

We've had some small success with cannas, with the rhizomes buried under 3″ of soil in 8″ pots, out on our tiny balcony, in as much sun as we can give them. They should do fine in tubs on a full-sun penthouse terrace.

CORMS

Corms are different from true bulbs, though they are called bulbs commercially and do look quite similar. However, a bulb stays intact, growing from year to year. Corms die off every year and new corms grow over the dying parent. The

A corm of Oxalis lasiandra, *with a cormel at its base. (The leaves are folded for the night.)*

new corm forms within a couple of months, but you have to give the cormous plant a season of growth if you expect to dig up a mature new corm or corms and a lot of small "cormels" at the end of the season. Shallow planting will tend to produce more cormels.

There are corms and there are corms.

Crocuses are corms, and they make rather poor houseplants, because they need that cold winter dormancy.

Many oxalis are corms, and *some* of them make great houseplants.

O. deppei does well for us on a windowsill, though it also flowers under lights. The flowers are a coppery pink.

O. lasiandra has redder flowers and quite unusual green-splotched-with-red foliage. The flowers, which have highlights of other colors in them, too, refused to open at all under lights, and only for the brightest part of the day on our windowsill.

It is in the nature of oxalis that the flowers and foliage open and close—open when the light is bright, close at night or on very dull days.

Other popular garden or greenhouse corms, like gladiolus and freesias, are just not appropriate for the apartment.

TUBERS

A potato is a tuber. The eyes are potential growth points, out of which will come stems and a new plant, if given the chance. If you leave a mature potato on a shelf, without water, without soil, the eyes will even then sprout and make considerable viney growth, feeding off the body of the potato to make the growth. Eventually, the body of the potato will shrivel up to practically nothing, and, without further food, the stalks will die. In this way, you can see how a tuber stores what a plant needs to make growth, even when the growing plant is out of contact with either soil or water.

Tubers grow from year to year: a tuber can burst its pot (so can a bulb).

SINNINGIAS

Without a doubt the greatest tuberous houseplants are GESNERIADS: the gloxinias and miniature sinningias. For details of their culture, turn back to Chapter 22.

This 4-year-old gloxinia tuber is 2½" across.

The full-size sinningias will have a complete dormancy. If you find them staying too long in dormancy, you can urge them out of it by putting them where they will get some gentle bottom heat—such as over the ballast of your fluorescent lights. This gentle heat most often stimulates the tuber into growth, though you have to water it a bit so that it won't dry out. And watering a dormant tuber *can* lead to rot and loss of the tuber—though the tuber wasn't doing you any good just sitting there, was it?

The miniatures don't take a real dormancy period.

CALADIUM

Caladium is a tuberous member of the arum family, which makes a good foliage plant.

When buying caladium tubers, make sure you're buying fancy-leaved caladium, not the elephant-ear type. The latter is just green, while the former is available in many shades, including white and red—fancy indeed. The foliage size of the caladium depends largely on the tuber size, so you can expect larger foliage from year to year as the tuber grows.

The tubers will go dormant if allowed to go dry, or if they get cold, or simply because it is autumn. When the plant goes into dormancy, allow it to dry out. Remove the tuber and store it in a bag of vermiculite until early spring. Put up a good-sized tuber into a 6″ pot.

TUBEROUS BEGONIAS

These magnificently flowered plants are difficult in an apartment because they like cool evenings and high humidity. The best tuberous begonias we've ever seen were grown on Nantucket Island—the damp cool weather and intense sun (which can be shaded to conform to the plant's preference) seem to give it the extra boost it needs. The next-best tuberous begonias we ever saw were growing in the hills (cultivated, of course) of Luxembourg. Again, cool damp spring weather. It's hard to give your tuberous begonia a cool damp environment in an apartment.

If you do want to try them, after flowering they will begin to look ragged. Allow to go dry, then dig up the tuber and store it as we do the other tubers: in a plastic bag of vermiculite. Pot up in the spring when you see the start of new growth.

Tuberous begonias are acid-lovers.

TUBEROUS ROOTS

This is a kind of catch-all phrase for plants that don't fit into the other categories, but which have fleshy underground storage units. Dahlias and sweet potatoes are good examples of tuberous roots.

CHA-CHA-CHA

There are a few plants we grow which are not true bulbs or tubers, which have thickened stems or propagules which look like bulbs or tubers.

CEROPEGIA

We've discussed this charming genus in EASIER SUCCULENTS, Chapter 25, and it is indeed an easy plant. The tuberlike propagules that form at the leaf axils root readily and send out new stems.

Additionally, stem cuttings, rooted and potted up, soon form these tuberlike swellings at the soil line.

BEAUCARNEA RECURVATA

Also called ponytail plant, this is a real beauty for the apartment. It soon adapts to lower humidity if you give it any help at all—like putting one in a grouping of other plants.

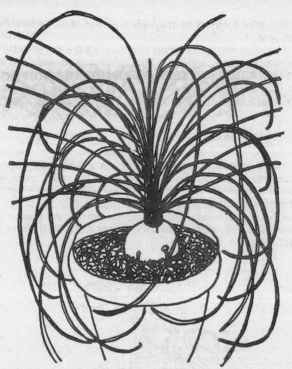

Do not bury the bulb of Beaucarnea recurvata.

The foliage comes from a very much thickened swelling at the base of the plant that looks just like a large bulb. But it's not; it's a thickened stem. The "bulb" should sit mostly out of the soil.

The leaves have a fountain habit which is most attractive.

Offsets form on the "bulb" and these can be rooted in a closed propagation box.

BOWIEA VOLUBILIS

Also called sea onion.

A real curiosity, this plant makes a quite large bulb-like swelling (which should be potted mostly out of the soil), from which comes a stem, a few feet long, which has lacy foliage.

If you're lucky, you may get a flower stalk (white flowers), too.

The plant will go dormant and drop all the top growth, after which reduce watering, stop feeding, and wait for new growth. Water lightly, now and then: don't allow the pot to go bone dry, but the soil must never be soaking wet, either. It's great fun, if a bit of a bother.

BERTOLONIA

This is a most unusual genus. It has a thick, hairy upright stem which sits on the soil (none of this thick stem gets buried in potting). It is a tropical plant which needs a protected environment for apartment growing. But its lovely quilted and hairy leaves are well worth the effort. Its flowers are pink and small, and are held on flower stalks well above the dark foliage.

Our bertolonia, coming out of dormancy. The small leaves allow us to see the fleshy hairy stem.

We allowed our *Bertolonia marmorata* to get too dry, and it dropped all its leaves and stood with that fleshy, hair stem staring at us reproachfully. We watered lightly, and, sure enough, within 2 months we got new leaf growth as the plant came out of dormancy.

PART VII

———————◆———————

SOURCES AND
RESOURCES

28. Exotica

If you have the money to buy it (or a horticultural library in your neighborhood to refer to) there is no book like *Exotica* for reference on houseplants. It is written by A. B. Graf and published by the Roehrs Company, Rutherford, N.J. It costs an arm—over $60—but it's actually worth it.

It is a big book, weighing over 12 pounds and with nearly 2,000 pages.

About ¾ of the book is black-and-white (and a few color) photos of exotic plants, the balance given over mostly to descriptions and culture of the plants. Its main index is of Latin names, but it also includes a common-name index, and some plant geography. The plants are shown according to families. There is also a good illustrated propagation section.

We feel personally grateful to Alfred Byrd Graf for the contribution he has made to horticulture in compiling this massive volume.

HOW TO USE IT

If you have a plant for identification, you have a few options.

If you know the Latin name of the plant, look it up in the general index, which will refer you to a photo; for culture, check the alphabetical descriptive list toward the back of the book. There will be letters and numbers after the genus name (first name) of the plant. These refer to the culture code, which is located just before the descriptive list.

If you know a common name for the plant, look into the common-name index, which will give you a Latin name and then proceed as above. But you can't be certain with common names. They vary from region to region, and sometimes growers just make up common names.

If you have no name at all, start browsing through the photos. There are only 12,000 photos to go through—but we've done it, and so can you.

EXOTIC PLANT MANUAL

From the same author and publisher comes the *Exotic Plant Manual*, which has overcome some of the shortcomings of *Exotica*.

It is much smaller and lighter, and easier to handle. It costs about $32, and it has an expanded common-name index. It has, of course, fewer pictures, many of them reduced versions of the pictures in *Exotica*.

This smaller book is organized differently, the plants being grouped together by use (for example: colorful foliage plants).

The culture code is much more extensive, and there are symbols with each photo.

However, the general index is poor in our opinion. Instead of indexing all plants by genus and species, as in the larger book, only generic names are indexed. That makes it much harder to look up a specific plant.

Despite this small drawback, we like the book and use it gratefully.

29. Where and How to Get Houseplant Information

So, you've read this book from cover to cover and you still don't know why your leaves are turning yellow. And you've searched through *Exotica* and you can't really tell just which mamillaria you've got. What do you do?

You take some of those yellowing leaves, or you pick up that mamillaria, and you go looking for a live body to help—a living and breathing horticulturist.

Further on in this chapter, we'll give the results of a survey we made, asking various horticultural centers in the United States and Canada just what horticultural information services they offer. But first let us make a few general comments on getting information to solve your plant problems.

COUNTY AGENTS

County agents can be found in the seat of almost every county in this country. Their primary job is to solve agricultural problems, but they can often help in horticultural and houseplant problems, both from personal experience and from the large amount of literature available to them from federal and state governments. Yes, there are county agents servicing even the largest metropolitan centers, though they tend to be more visible in surburban and rural areas. Often, services through county agents (including literature and soil analysis) are free or available at little cost.

Write your state capital for the one nearest you.

BOTANIC GARDENS

Botanic gardens are usually goldmines of information. Many publish bulletins, at some charge, but most will diagnose plant problems free. At the same time, you can see there what your plant would look like under very good conditions. Don't be discouraged by how good a plant looks in a botanic garden's greenhouse compared to how it looks for you. With money and generations of knowledge, you could get the same result. But, all kidding aside, remember that botanic gardens have plants die or refuse to flower for them, too. But these plants aren't kept out front where the public can see them.

Most botanic gardens also offer courses at more or less nominal cost; these courses often give you invaluable practical experience.

Check by phone with your local botanic garden for their plant clinic hours (even if we've given you the hours—they change), or to see if they offer the service at all.

ARBORETUMS

An arboretum is a tree garden, and, unless they have other horticultural exhibits or greenhouses attached to them, seldom seem to offer houseplant information services (at least, that's what our survey told us). However, check by phone with any we don't list. Our letter may have given them a good idea, or perhaps we just have missed them.

HORTICULTURAL SOCIETIES

We have a soft spot for horticultural societies because a great deal of our horticultural growth comes from information provided by the Horticultural Society of New York. The Massachusetts and the Pennsylvania Horticultural Societies are the greatest, but often *state* horticultural societies are oriented toward the orchard grower or farmer. So, don't suppose that ever horticultural society has a library for you or courses and plant clinics. Check by phone.

PLANT SOCIETIES

Ten of thousands of people in the United States and Canada belong to various houseplant societies, and these societies can be among the best places to get specific solutions for specific problems. The older members are often very free with information and plant material.

Also, most plant societies provide programs (often, to the nonmember as well as to the member) that can be quite informative.

We have provided addresses for as many plant societies as responded to our survey—and for some that didn't.

LIBRARIES

Libraries are your good, true friend, whether for circulating books or for research. And being able to read several books on a particular subject can help to make it quite clear. But experts disagree. It's the nature of the beast.

If we didn't disagree with much of what we've read about houseplants, we would never have written this book. And the same holds true for other authors. When you see something written in a book, that doesn't mean that that is the perfect solution, or even a *possible* solution for your plant—in your circumstances. After all, the author is, we hope, writing from his or her experiences, although sometimes an author is merely copying from another writer. What he or she says may be perfectly true for that writer, under those conditions, in that part of the country, and so forth. A local expert, looking directly at your plant, and knowing what's "making the rounds" of your area, is a much sounder bet for diagnosing what's ailing it.

WHERE TO GO

The following listings are the result of more than 200 questionnaires we sent out to horticultural centers, societies, libraries, plant societies, etc. We were surprised at the number of negative responses we got, and pleased at the positive. We will not print information we don't have, so we can only include here what was sent to us (except for the plant society addresses).

If *you* are a horticultural center and we've left you out, please send us the information you would like included, and in any future edition, we'll be happy to include you.

The following list is by state, with the Canadian listings following the states. Sometimes the words are theirs, sometimes ours.

We suggest you call or write any of the centers before bringing a plant over: policies change even as we look at them.

UNITED STATES

ALABAMA

BIRMINGHAM BOTANICAL GARDENS
2612 Lane Park Road
Birmingham, Alabama 35223
(205) 879-1227

The director and a horticulturist answer houseplant questions by phone from 9:00 A.M. to 3:30 P.M., Monday through Thursday. "The Horace Hammond Memorial Library (a horticultural library) is open to the public and anyone may check out books. Free courses on various plants and methods of gardening are given at different times during the year. ..." In the spring the Garden holds an Annual Garden Fiesta and plant sale.

ARIZONA

DESERT BOTANICAL GARDEN in Papago Park
P.O. Box 5415
Phoenix, Arizona 85010
(602) 947-2800

"We answer daily inquiries on plants ... in our desert area. ... We give slide lectures and talks to many groups in the southwest and also to civic clubs and retirement groups.
..."

The director is on call for consultation work; books, pamphlets, and plants are available by mail order and at the Garden.

ARKANSAS

UNIVERSITY OF ARKANSAS
Division of Agriculture
College of Agriculture and Home Economics
Agricultural Experimental Station
Department of Horticulture and Forestry
Fayetteville, Arkansas 72701
(501) 575-2000

"We handle inquiries on house plants through the Ornamental Extension personnel with the University of Arkansas. As in many other states, citizens of Arkansas having questions regarding house plants should call their local county extension agent. If the agent is unable to answer the questions, he will seek the assistance of the State Ornamental Specialist located in Little Rock. All of the facilities and resources of the University of Arkansas are available to anyone in the state by going through the Extension Service. Our Extension Ornamental Horticulturist and area ornamental specialist conduct short courses or workshops which may include information on houseplants when requested to so by any county agent. A significant program which includes education on houseplants is the Adult Education courses that are offered by many of the school districts in Arkansas. These courses generally last 10 weeks and meet one night a week. A nominal admission fee is usually charged for enrollment, and resource persons are often supplied from the colleges and universities in the state."

CALIFORNIA

COUNTY OF LOS ANGELES ARBORETA AND BOTANIC GARDENS
301 North Baldwin Avenue
Arcadia, California 91006
(213) 446-8251 or 681-7718

"The Los Angeles State and County Arboretum provides a daily consultation service, either by phone, mail, or in person, during the regular five-day work week, Monday through Friday. Hours are 9-11 and 2-4. This service is not available on weekends or legal holidays. However, plant material can be left at the information window on weekends for Monday replies. This service includes plant identification, information on sources of plants and materials, and general information on all phases of horticulture. Any problems which the Botanical Information Consultant cannot solve are referred to staff specialists and we maintain active liaison with all other government agencies in this area.

"The Arboretum also maintains a special library for staff reference. It is also available to the public for reference, but books are not loaned.

"A very active educational program is presented during the fall, winter, and spring which includes classes in house plants and container culture."

DESCANSO GARDENS
(Same address and phone as above, but, apparently, a different facility.)

"We are happy to give information on the care and growing of houseplants to our visitors or over the phone. Our hours for both are 8:00 A.M. to 4:30 P.M. from Monday to Friday inclusive.

"Our library is open to the public every Thursday from 1:00 P.M. to 3:30 P.M. While our horticultural classes stress all phases of gardening, the subject of houseplants is taken up. Classes are given to children on the care and growing of houseplants on Saturday mornings."

UNIVERSITY OF CALIFORNIA, LOS ANGELES BOTANICAL GARDENS—HERBARIUM
Los Angeles, California 90024
(213) 825-4321 (UCLA information)

"The Botanical Garden here provides information on an *ad hoc* basis by telephone or for people who bring plants in."

LAKESIDE PARK GARDEN CENTER LIBRARY
666 Bellevue Avenue
Oakland, California 94610
832-9329

"The Lakeside Park Garden Center Library is open Monday, Wednesday and Friday afternoons from 1:00 to 3:45. Membership is $2 a year, permitting circulation of some of our books. . . . Our library is located in a lovely garden, maintained by the Oakland East Bay Garden Center, Inc., the address is given above."

STRYBING ARBORETUM AND BOTANIC GARDENS
9th Avenue and Lincoln Way
San Francisco, California, 94122
(415) 558-3622

"Strybing Arboretum and Botanic Gardens provide the following:

"Gardening information including houseplants from 9 A.M. to 4 P.M. daily, phone number (415) 558-3622.

"Courses in practical horticulture, under the sponsorship of the Strybing Arboretum Society . . . are given in spring and fall. The lectures and demonstrations include clinics on houseplants.

"The Helen Crocker Russel Library of Horticulture at the Strybing Arboretum is open daily from 10 A.M. to 4 P.M. Reference library only, it has an outstanding collection of books including many on the care and culture of houseplants. Telephone # (415) 661-0822."

SANTA BARBARA BOTANIC GARDEN
1212 Mission Canyon Road
Santa Barbara, California 93105
(805) 963-1886

". . . Our offices are open from 8 A.M. to 5 P.M., Monday through Friday, during which time we answer all types of questions relative to plants. . . . Our horticultural and botanical reference library is open during our office hours. Plants and more often bits and pieces are brought in for identification also."

COLORADO

DENVER BOTANIC GARDENS
909 York Street
Denver, Colorado 80206
(303) 297-2547

Plants may be brought to the greenhouses for consultation with the horticultural staff, 9:00 A.M. to 5:00 P.M., Monday through Friday. Houseplant courses have been given, though none are scheduled as of this writing. Library reference is available to the public by telephone, 9:00 to 5:00, Monday through Saturday, 1:00 to 5:00 on Sunday.

Garden membership is $7.50, which includes a quarterly publication, *The Green Thumb*, that features frequent houseplant articles. Members may take books out of the library.

DISTRICT OF COLUMBIA

U.S. NATIONAL ARBORETUM
28th and M Street
Washington, D.C. 20002
(202) 399-5400

"Horticultural questions are answered by phone on weekdays from 2:00 to 4:00 P.M., plant specimens (leaves or plants) may be sent or brought to the Visitors Center for identification or a determination of insect or disease problems.

"The library in the Administration Building is open to the public from 8:00 A.M. to 4:30 P.M., daily, though only staff members may check out the books."

FLORIDA

HORTICULTURE STUDY SOCIETY OF FLORIDA, INC.
3280 South Miami Avenue
Miami, Florida 33129

"Most plants ordinarily thought of as 'house' plants are equally at home and happy outside in Dade County's climate. Therefore, the main thrust of our interest and activities does not center on this phase of horticulture.

"Our membership is largely derived from a yearly six-week course which we sponsor cooperatively with our local county agriculture agents. It is a general course which furnishes background for further group and individual study. We meet as a club once a month with programs provided by specialists and our own 'share and tell' exhibits. We maintain a library for our members only but the public is invited to attend any of our regular meetings. These meetings are held every second Wednesday at the Science Museum.

"There is a fee both for our course and for membership in the Society. Our library is open only during the regular monthly meetings."

FAIRCHILD TROPICAL GARDEN
10901 Old Cutler Road
Miami, Florida 33156

"The display area of the garden contains hundreds of species of plants growing outdoors which are grown as houseplants in the north as well as in Florida. The public can thus visit this Garden to see what mature specimens of many palms, aroids, dracaenas, etc., that they grow in their houses look like.

"The Garden is open from 10 to 5 daily and the admission fee is $1. There is a good horticultural library which can be used by the public but books may be checked out only by members.

"Adult education classes and workshops are held at the Garden throughout the winter season."

Individual memberships start at $15. In addition to library circulation privileges, members get free admission to the Garden and invitations to lectures, as well as a quarterly bulletin.

USDA
Agricultural Research Station
Plant Science Research
U.S. Plant Introduction Station
13601 Old Cutler Road
Miami, Florida 33159

"If an occasional individual comes in with a problem houseplant one of our horticulturists would more than likely make a diagnosis, but by and large we would not list among our services 'houseplant clinic.' "

MIAMI BEACH GARDEN CENTER
2000 Garden Center Drive
Miami Beach, Florida 33139
(305) 534-7511 (Ext. 587)

"The Miami Beach Garden Center and Conservatory, a facility of the Parks Division, Parks and Recreation Department, has a nurseryman on duty daily and weekends for consultation with the public, if required.

"A small library is maintained at the Garden Center; hours are 8:30 A.M. to 5:00 P.M.

"The Miami Beach Garden Center and Conservatory Committee, representing the four major garden clubs of Miami Beach, sponsors weekly Wednesday morning Workshop Sessions from November through March of each year. While the topics may vary from year to year, there are usually several in the series devoted to houseplant information.

"Tours of the Miami Beach Garden Center by school groups, garden clubs from nearby communities, when arranged in advance, are provided with a 'briefing' by a horticulturist. This service is scheduled through our office.

". . . The facility is open seven days a week, year-round (except Christmas Day), from 10:00 A.M. to 3:30 P.M."

GEORGIA

FERNBANK SCIENCE CENTER
156 Heaton Park Drive, N.E.
Atlanta, Georgia 30307
(404) 378-4311

"Our horticultural program for the adult general public consists of five-week lecture courses on various garden subjects throughout the year at a minimal cost per person. Horticultural questions will be answered by phone from 8:30 to 5:00 daily. The science library is a reference library only, but may be used by the general public. We also have courses for children during the year after school hours and during summer vacation."

CALLAWAY GARDENS
Pine Mountain, Georgia 31822
663-2281

"At the Garden, we do conduct various workshops and

symposiums on various botanical subjects. Our most recent symposium was on Indoor Gardening.

"Also, we have the plants in our conservatory and greenhouses labeled and we do offer service through correspondence on plant problems and answer general horticultural questions."

HAWAII

FOSTER BOTANIC GARDEN
180 N. Vineyard Boulevard
Honolulu, Hawaii 96817
(808) 531-1939

"... Foster Garden provides telephone inquiry service daily from 7:30 to 4:00 except on Saturdays and Sundays relative to any horticultural questions, including houseplants. In addition, Foster Garden sponsors occasional classes (unfortunately, these are not on a regular schedule) dealing with general horticultural skills which touch upon the care and feeding of houseplants. In the near future a program dealing with the culture of potted materials for indoors and for lanais will probably be instituted due to the fact that more of our population is now beginning to move into apartments and high rises. Heretofore, there was little interest in houseplants. People normally grew their plants outside where they belong, and had little need other than an occasional indoor ornamental. This picture is beginning to change."

IDAHO

COOPERATIVE EXTENSION SERVICE
University of Idaho
College of Agriculture in cooperation with the USDA
Box 300
Boise, Idaho 83701
(208) 384-3486

"... The University of Idaho Cooperative Extension Service provides houseplant information through the county agent offices. USDA bulletins and mimeos, etc., are available from county agent offices, generally located in the courthouse in each county. Garden schools are held periodically, and there is nearly always a talk on houseplants. Questions are also answered by phone and home visits."

ILLINOIS

LINCOLN PARK CONSERVATORY
2400 North Stockton Drive
Chicago, Illinois 60614
(312) 549-3006

"Here at the Lincoln Park Conservatory, we answer horticultural questions by phone daily from 9 to 4; conduct free guided tours and lectures by appointment; classes are given to schoolchildren especially in the propagation and care of plants; free lectures are given by staff members in the various Park fieldhouses; free houseplants are made available to schools and clubs if the request is for educational purposes; our library is open to the public daily from 9 to 4, but no books may be taken out."

INDIANA

BALL STATE UNIVERSITY
Christy Woods Field Area
Muncie, Indiana 47306
(317) 289-1241 (Ball State information)

"Christy Woods, one of four field areas of Ball State University and operated by the Biology Department, is located on the campus adjacent to the Life Science Building. It is an 18-acre area and was set aside in 1918 for outdoor laboratory work.

"Located in Christy Woods are two sets of greenhouses, a teaching-research greenhouse and an Orchid house. The teaching-research house is used primarily for growing plants for Biology laboratory classwork. A very large collection of houseplants is grown for use by the students and viewing by the visitors. Some research is conducted in the greenhouses.

"The other greenhouse contains the W. O. Wheeler Orchid Collection, a gift to the University two years ago. The Orchid Collection is not always open to the public but is used for research.

"Christy Woods and the teaching-research houses are open to the public 8:00 A.M. to 4:30 P.M. Monday-Friday for viewing and answering questions either by phone or calling in person. The area is open on weekend's during spring, summer and fall if weather is good. Closed all holidays.

"The greenhouses and Christy Woods are open for tours by school groups, garden clubs, and civic groups located in the east central Indiana area.

"By special request, personnel of the greenhouses or members of the Biology faculty will make available programs to interested groups during the evening."

MARYLAND

UNITED STATES DEPARTMENT OF AGRICULTURE
NATIONAL AGRICULTURAL LIBRARY
Baltimore Boulevard
Beltsville, Maryland 20705
(202) 655-4000 (the address is Maryland, but the phone is the District of Columbia)

"The Library is open to the public 8:00 A.M.-4:30 P.M., Monday-Saturday, although only USDA employees may take out books. Requests for information may be submitted by letter, telephone or teletype (TWX 710-828-0506). The Library also provides xerographic copy of materials from its collection at 10¢ per page.

"The horticultural collection of books and journals is extensive. A particularly important aspect is the Horticultural Trade Catalogs Collection, established in 1904 with gifts from the Massachusetts Horticultural Society. It is comprised of some 125,000 catalogs, price lists, and broadsides, containing descriptions, illustrations, and prices of plant materials offered for sale by nurserymen and seedsmen throughout the world. In addition to its historical significance (some items date back to 1845), the collection constitutes a national center for information on the introduction and sources of new species, particularly in regard to ornamental plants, fruits, nuts, vegetables, and field seeds."

MASSACHUSETTS

UNIVERSITY OF MASSACHUSETTS
Amherst, Massachusetts 01002
(413) 545-2674

Basically a reference collection, this "Biological Sciences"

Library is open to the public during regular terms, Monday-Thursday 8:30 A.M.-11:00 P.M., Friday and Saturday 8:30 A.M.-5:00 P.M., Sunday 2:00-11:00 P.M. Copies of material can be made for home use.

Horticultural questions are answered by phone—but try to call during the week.

MASSACHUSETTS HORTICULTURAL SOCIETY
300 Massachusetts Avenue
Boston, Massachusetts 02115
(617) 536-9280

The Horticultural Hot-Line answers houseplant questions from 9:00-4:30 daily (these are the Society's hours).

"The Library and Garden Information Services are open to the public. Members only may borrow books . . . and this is no matter where they live in continental U.S.A. or Canada. Hawaii and Alaska are excluded because of the time it takes to mail books to those distant areas."

Membership is $15 for an individual and $20 for a family. Even out of the area you get your subscription to *Horticulture*—and that's worth having. There is a major spring flower show.

MICHIGAN

BELLE ISLE GREENHOUSE
Bell Isle Park
Detroit, Michigan 8207
(313) 224-1100

Houseplant questions will be answered by telephone from 7:30 A.M. to 4:00 P.M. daily. Plants may be brought to the Greenhouse for diagnosis or identification during the same hours. (Check by phone before going in at 7:30 A.M.)

"We do not conduct houseplant courses or classes but we do send our staff members to address groups on request."

FERNWOOD, INCORPORATED
1720 Range Line Road
Niles, Michigan 49120
(616) 695-6491

A nature preserve which offers some courses in houseplant culture. Membership begins at $5 for individuals ($10 for families).

"We do not have an answering service as such, at designated hours, but we do welcome members to bring in plants for identification or diagnosis, and call in questions if they wish."

Courses prices seem nominal. There is a small reference library. Fernwood is open 8:00 A.M. to 4:30 P.M., Tuesday-Sunday, April 1 to November 1.

MINNESOTA

COMO PARK CONSERVATORY
1224 North Lexington Parkway
Saint Paul, Minnesota 55103
(612) 489-1740

"We answer gardening questions every day of the year, from 10:00 A.M. to 4 P.M. in the summer. By this winter, we hope to have weekend workshops for the indoor gardener in terrariums, hanging baskets, orchid growing, aquarium landscape, tropical ethnobotany and more."

NEW HAMPSHIRE

NEW HAMPSHIRE COOPERATIVE EXTENSION SERVICE
University of New Hampshire
College of Life Sciences and Agriculture
Durham, New Hampshire 03824
(603) 862-1520

"The University of New Hampshire maintains a conservatory greenhouse where a collection of economic and botanical plant specimens are on display for students and the general public 8:00 A.M. to 4:00 P.M. Monday through Friday. Additions of contemporary foliage plants are being constantly made. Plans are underway to construct and maintain additional lighting demonstrations for houseplant display and culture.

"Extension specialists and some members of the county agent field staff are in a position to answer commercial and consumer questions on houseplant care. Occasional lectures, field days, and demonstrations are conducted on the selection, care, and culture of houseplants. Several leaflets and bulletins are available on the topic of houseplants from this university."

NEW JERSEY

RUTGERS—THE STATE UNIVERSITY OF NEW JERSEY
Cooperative Extension Service
College of Agriculture and Environmental Service
P.O. Box 231
New Brunswick, New Jersey 08903
(201) 247-1766

"Rutgers University, through the Cooperative Extension Service, makes available considerable information on indoor plants. The best source is the local County Cooperative Extension Offices. . . . All of these offices have bulletins and most have knowledgeable people who can answer indoor plant questions. Many counties arrange meetings and courses of various types related to indoor plants. A 35 mm. color, sound film is also available."

Rutgers will supply a list of all the County Extension Offices in New Jersey, upon request.

DUKE GARDENS FOUNDATION, INC.
Route 206 South
Somerville, New Jersey 08876
(201) 722-3700

"The Duke Gardens horticultural staff are always happy to answer questions by telephone or from visitors on houseplants. Correspondence on horticultural topics is also maintained with the general public."

There is an admission charge to the Gardens. If you're there, don't miss the orchid house.

NEW YORK

STATE UNIVERSITY OF NEW YORK
Agricultural and Technical College
Alfred, New York 14802
(607) 871-6111 (University information)

"We do answer questions about houseplants on an individual basis. Faculty are available on a daily basis Monday through Friday between the hours of 9:00 A.M. and 4:00

P.M. We have given houseplant courses in our Evening School and probably will continue to do so about every three years.

"Our library is open to the public, but only students may borrow materials."

THE NEW YORK BOTANICAL GARDEN
Bronx, New York 10458
(212) 933-9400

"Members of our staff are usually available to answer horticultural inquiries from 9:00 A.M. through 5:00 P.M., Mondays through Fridays."

The Garden also offers some excellent horticultural courses, and has a magnificent reference library open Monday-Friday, 10:00-5:00 (11:00-4:00 during the summer).

BROOKLYN BOTANIC GARDEN
1000 Washington Avenue
Brooklyn, New York 11225
(212) 622-4440

The Brooklyn Botanic answers 60,000 questions a year through its various departments, and they are not anxious to increase that number. However, they do answer questions by phone through their Plant Information Service, Monday through Friday, 1:00 P.M.-2:30 P.M.

They have a large research library, open from about 10:00 to 4:00 (depending on the New York subway system), and offer some first-rate courses in houseplant culture and other stuff. The Garden also publishes very good horticultural handbooks.

In Westchester, the Garden offers courses at the KITCHAWAN FIELD STATION, on Route 134, 2 miles east of Taconic State Parkway. On Long Island, they offer courses at the CLARK MEMORIAL GARDEN, 193 I.U. Willets Road, Albertson, Long Island.

WAVE HILL CENTER FOR ENVIRONMENTAL STUDIES
675 West 252nd Street
Bronx, New York 10471
(212) 549-2055

Houseplant questions are answered at the greenhouses or by phone (548-4833) seven days a week, 10:00-5:00. The

Center has two excellent plant sales a year, in the spring and fall.

QUEENS BOTANICAL GARDEN
4350 Main Street
Flushing, New York 11355
(212) TU6-3800

This newest of the New York City Botanic Gardens has a reference library open Monday-Friday, 9:00-4:30. They will answer questions by phone or at the Garden during the same hours. They offer several courses a year of interest to the apartment gardener.

THE HORICULTURAL SOCIETY OF NEW YORK
128 West 58th Street
New York, New York 10019
(212) 757-0915

The extensive library is open from 10:00 A.M. to 4:00 P.M. on Mondays, Wednesdays, and Fridays. Only members may take out books, but it is open to the public for reference.

The Society offers houseplants courses, lectures, trips, and flower shows, and is home for the annual Houseplant Societies Show.

Membership starts at $15 for individuals.

THE GARDEN CENTER OF ROCHESTER
5 Castle Park
Rochester, New York 14620
(716) 473-5130

"The garden center is open on Tuesday and Wednesday from 9:30 A.M. to 3:30 P.M. We do answer questions by phone. Plant material may be brought to us for question or identification. We have volunteer consultants. We have a very adequate horticultural library but only members may take books out."

STERLING FOREST GARDENS
Tuxedo, New York 10987
(914) 351-2163

"We are very much service-oriented, although commercial, and offer much free advice to anyone asking. We have printed 'How to Care for' handouts for many of the plants we sell and reprints from Extension Service Bulletins just for the asking.

". . . Our locations are as follows: (1) The Plant Sales Tent located at Sterling Forest Gardens open April to November. (2) Sterling Forest Garden Center, Route 17, Tuxedo. (3) Sterling Forest Garden Center Inc., 820 Morris Turnpike, Short Hills, N.J."

There is an admission charge to the Garden.

NORTH DAKOTA

COOPERATIVE EXTENSION SERVICE
NORTH DAKOTA STATE UNIVERSITY OF AGRI-
CULTURE AND APPLIED SCIENCE
USDA
State University Station
Fargo, North Dakota 58102
(701) 237-8944

"The only organized agency for dissemination of this type of information is the State Extension service. Publications on houseplants are available to the public at all county extension offices—52 (county agents and home agents).

"Questions are answered by phone at county offices from 8:00-5:00 daily where agents are familiar with the subject, otherwise inquiries are referred to my office at North Dakota State University for reply.

"The public may also call the Department of Horticulture 8:00-5:00 for horticulture information also."

For the Department of Horticulture, call the University, (701) 237-8011. For the county agents, check your county seat.

OHIO

EDEN PARK
950 Eden Park Drive
Cincinnati, Ohio 45202
(513) 352-4080

"We provide answers to the public with their problems on an informal basis. Persons may call the Cincinnati Park Board at 352-4080 during our normal hours, 8:00 to 4:30, Monday through Friday, and an on-duty horticulturist will answer their questions. Oftentimes we also invite callers to come in with their plants so we may better judge the problem and give advice.

"We prefer that this be handled through our Park Board office in Eden Park, 950 Eden Park Drive. The florists at the Irwin M. Krohn Conservatory, also located in Eden Park, are always quite willing to discuss plant problems with visitors and will take a look at plants and give advice, although no formal clinic is set up."

THE GARDEN CENTER OF GREATER CLEVELAND
11030 East Boulevard
Cleveland, Ohio 44106
(216) 721-1600

"The services of the Garden Center might be summarized as follows: Open 9:00-5:00 daily and 2:00-5:00 Sunday, closed Saturday; 10,000-volume horticultural library open same hours, only members may borrow books; plants identified or diagnosed and gardening questions answered 9:00-4:00 daily; classes and lectures on houseplants, many plants on display."

An individual or family membership is $10.

KINGWOOD CENTER
900 Park Avenue West
P.O. Box 966
Mansfield, Ohio 44901
(419) 522-0211

"Horticultural questions are answered from 8:00 A.M.-12:00 A.M. and 1:00 P.M.-4:30 P.M., Monday through Friday and 8:00 A.M. to noon on Saturday. Plants may be brought in during those hours, but it would be best for the individual to make an appointment beforehand. Lectures and short courses are given throughout the year. Some of these programs are open to the public, while others are presented for garden clubs and other organizations at their request. The Kingwood Library has a comprehensive collection of reference material on houseplants. The library is open from 8:00 A.M. to 5:00 P.M., Tuesday through Saturday. Books may be taken out by the public."

OHIO AGRICULTURAL RESEARCH AND DEVELOPMENT CENTER

Wooster, Ohio 44691
(216) 264-1021

"Our Center is open Monday-Friday from 8:00 A.M.-5:00 P.M. for all visitors. The floriculturist is available at any time for phone calls, letters, or personal visitation. If the floriculturist were unavailable, then a message could be left with the Secretaries of the Horticultural Department.

"Publications ... are available through the Extension Service."

THE GARDEN FORUM OF THE GREATER YOUNGS-
    TOWN AREA, INC.
123 McKinley Avenue
Youngstown, Ohio 44509
(216) 792-7961

"We offer classes in horticulture all during the year, many of our classes pertain to houseplants. All classes are open to the public and are listed in the area newspapers.

"Our library is open to the public Monday through Friday, 10:00 A.M. to 5:00 P.M., though only members may take out books."

Membership starts at $3 for an individual.

PENNSYLVANIA

AMBLER CAMPUS LIBRARY
TEMPLE UNIVERSITY
Ambler, Pennsylvania 19002
(215) 643-1200 (the university number)

"Hours.   Mon-Thurs. 8:30 A.M.-12:00 midnight
            Friday   8:30 A.M.- 5:00 P.M.
                         7:00 P.M.-10:00 P.M.
            Saturday   2:00 P.M.- 5:00 P.M.
            Sunday   2:00 P.M.- 5:00 P.M.
                         7:00 P.M.-12:00 midnight

"Service   Public is welcome to use materials in library. Reference service given. Circulation to Temple community only.

"There are five acres of gardens and greenhouses. Visitors welcome."

LONGWOOD GARDENS
Kennet Square, Pennsylvania 19348
388-6741

"Horticultural information pertaining to plants grown at Longwood Gardens is given to visitors, either in person, by telephone or letter.

"Short courses are available for the serious amateur interested in increasing horticultural expertise."

There is a nominal charge for courses. Admission to the Gardens is 50¢ weekdays, $1 weekends; 50¢ to lectures.

THE PENNSYLVANIA HORTICULTURAL SOCIETY
325 Walnut Street
Philadelphia, Pennsylvania 19106
WA 2-4801

"Horticultural questions are answered by mail, as well as on the telephone Monday through Friday from nine until five. The PHS library consisting of more than 12,000 volumes is one of the most complete horticultural libraries in the area. It is open to the public from nine until five Monday through Friday and members may borrow either in person or by mail.

"A free plant clinic which is open to the public is held one Sunday each month from September through May except during the month of March. This clinic is open from one until 5:00 P.M. and it is suggested that anyone interested call the PHS headquarters to find out the particular date for that month.

"Members of PHS may take advantage of the many clinics and lectures which are offered throughout the year, several of these which apply directly to indoor gardening are concerned with such topics as terrariums, houseplants and bulb forcing."

One thing not mentioned in their letter is a huge annual flower show, with first-rate competitive classes in many houseplant areas.

HUNT BOTANICAL LIBRARY
Carnegie-Mellon University
Pittsburgh, Pennsylvania 15213
(412) 621-2600

The library is open from 8:30 A.M. to 5:00 P.M.; anyone may do research, but no books can circulate. The collection is mainly historical.

[378]

They answer houseplant questions insofar as their director is able to, on an informal basis.

TENNESSEE

UNIVERSITY OF TENNESSEE
Institute of Agriculture
Department of Ornamental Horticulture and Landscape Design
P.O. Box 1071
Knoxville, Tennessee 37901
(615) 974-7324

"Our services are similar to other state agricultural extension services in the United States. We are open from 8:00 A.M. to 5:00 P.M., 5 days per week, except holidays, giving services to all that call on any problem. Tennessee has 95 county extension offices rendering the same type of services. In event there are problems that can't be answered on a local level, then they are referred to our department at the University of Tennessee at Knoxville.

"We have an agricultural library of over 50,000 books, magazines, etc., which ... are not generally open to the public but can be obtained through our local city-county library system."

THE TENNESSEE BOTANICAL GARDENS
AND FINE ARTS CENTER, INCORPORATED
Cheekwood, Cheek Road
Nashville, Tennessee 37206
(615) 356-3306

The Garden offers 3- to 5-meeting courses on horticultural subjects at a modest fee ($6-15).

There is a research library available to those who pay the Garden entrance fee, including more than 8,000 color slides and 1,200 seed and flower catalogs, open Tuesday-Friday, 9:00 A.M.-4:00 P.M.

TEXAS

SAN ANTONIO GARDEN CENTER, INC.
3310 North New Braunfels Avenue at Funston
San Antonio, Texas 78209
(512) 824-9981

"The San Antonio Garden Center maintains a library of more than 1,300 books on horticultural subjects, open to the public from 9:00 A.M. to 3:00 P.M., Monday through Friday. There is always someone there during these hours to answer questions via telephone or in person. The Garden Center's regular meetings are held the first and third Wednesdays of each month, September through May.

"Also, in San Antonio we have a County Extension Horti-culturist; 203 West Nueva, Room 310, 78207, tele: 220-2774; hours: 8:00-12:00 and 1:00-5:00, Monday through Friday.

VIRGINIA

THE AMERICAN HORTICULTURAL SOCIETY
7931 East Boulevard Drive
Alexandria, Virginia 22314
(703) 768-5700

". . . library and information services are available to members of AHS. Membership is $15 annually, which includes subscription to the quarterly magazine, *American Horticul-turist*, and the periodic newsletter, *News and Views*."

WASHINGTON

THE UNIVERSITY OF WASHINGTON ARBORETUM
Seattle, Washington 98105
(206) 543-8800

The Arboretum will attempt to answer houseplant questions, "if the problem is relatively simple." They occasionally have people bring their plant to the Arboretum nurserymen for examination. "We do not encourage this practice, however." Make sure you call first.

WISCONSIN

HORTICULTURAL CONSERVATORY
Mitchel Park
Milwaukee County Park Commission
524 South Layto Boulevard at West Pierce Street
Milwaukee, Wisconsin 53215
(414) 278-4383

"Phone requests are answered by return call only when the

floriculturist's duties permit, usually afternoons, 1:00-3:00, Monday through Friday. Information and/or cultural brochures are returned promptly when letters are accompanied by a self-addressed, stamped envelope, business size. We hold two annual open houses at our growing greenhouses where the staff answers questions and sets up houseplant displays. Informational displays are held in the conservatory lobby throughout the year."

CANADA

MANITOBA

PROVINCE OF MANITOBA
Department of Agriculture
Marketing and Production Division
Sales and Crops Branch
Horticulture Section
702 Norquay Building
Winnipeg, Manitoba
R3C OP8

"In Manitoba we have some 45 Horticultural Societies scattered around the province with about 6 or 7 of them located in the City of Winnipeg. Members of these Societies . . . are always willing to pass information out at any time.

"The City of Winnipeg operates the Assiniboine Park and the Conservatory in connection with this park. There is a full-time florist supervisor on hand each day from 8:30 A.M. to 5:00 P.M. and he has a staff who are always anxious and willing to receive calls on houseplant problems and who are able to answer them. The supervising florist is Mr. W. H. Gray, Assiniboine Park Conservatory, S.O. 25, St. James, Manitoba.

"During the summer months the University of Manitoba has a 'Hort-line' and has a student on hand who accepts telephone calls and keeps in touch with one of the staff at the University when these problems cannot be answered over the telephone immediately.

"The Department of Agriculture (Soils and Crops Branch, Horticulture Section), also has a student on for the summer months. . . . In addition we opened up early in the year a new Plant Pathology Laboratory which is located at the University of Manitoba although it comes under the Horticulture Section of the Department of Agriculture. There is a plant pathologist in charge of this laboratory and he has a technician with him."

NEWFOUNDLAND

GARDEN INFORMATION CENTRE
c/o Pippy Park Commission
Nagle's Hill
St. John's, Newfoundland
P.O. Box 12
(709) 726-4000

"Phone consultations are available from 9:00 A.M. to 5:30 P.M. daily, Monday through Friday.

"There is also a small reference library.

"In addition, the Newfoundland Horticultural Society holds informal clinics at the regular monthly meetings on the second Tuesday of each month in the basement level of the Arts and Culture Centre in St. John's."

ONTARIO

THE NIAGARA PARKS COMMISSION
School of Horticulture
Box 150
Niagara Falls, Ontario
L2E 6T2

"The School of Horticulture does not have an extension service, however, we do try and assist the general public when they visit or telephone the school office for assistance in horticultural plant materials, houseplants included."

ONTARIO DEPARTMENT OF AGRICULTURE AND
    FOOD
Horticultural Research Institute of Ontario
Vineland Station, Ontario
(416) 562-4141

"The Horticultural Research Institute at Vineland Station maintains a staff for extension purposes, and in the field of ornamentals and houseplants we are equipped to answer questions on any facet of houseplant growing.

"Our staff consists of pathologists, entomologists, and specialists in other fields of horticulture. The Institute is open from 8:30 until 5:00, Monday through Friday. We have a library which is open daily and can be used for reference by anyone, though only members of staff may take books from the library."

ONTARIO MINISTRY OF AGRICULTURE AND
   FOOD
Agricultural and Horticultural Societies Branch
Parliament Building
Queen's Park
Toronto, Ontario
(416) 965-1091

The Assistant Director of the Agricultural and Horticultural Societies Branch says there are 240 local horticultural societies in Ontario. Write and ask him for one in your area.

INFORMATION DIVISION
Canada Department of Agriculture
Ottawa, Canada
K1A OC7

Canadian residents may write the above address for a list of free horticultural pamphlets.

30. Houseplant Societies

If you are interested in a particular plant or plant family, a houseplant society is a must. Even if you can't go to meetings, the national magazine and/or local newsletters are often full of good cultural information.

Write to the addresses below either to join or to inquire about a local branch in your neighborhood.

AFRICAN VIOLET SOCIETY OF AMERICA
P.O. Box 1326
Knoxville, Tennessee 37901
  Many local branches.

AMERICAN BEGONIA SOCIETY
10331 South Colima Road
Whittier, California 90604
  Over 40 local branches.

AMERICAN FERN SOCIETY
Department of Botany
University of Tennessee
Knoxville, Tennessee 37916

AMERICAN GESNERIA SOCIETY
Information
Box 91192
Worldway Postal Center
Los Angeles, California 90009
  Enclose a self-addressed and stamped envelope if you want
a reply.

AMERICAN GLOXINIA AND GESNERIAD SOCIETY
Membership Secretary, Mrs. Charlotte Rowe
P.O. Box 174
New Milford, Conn. 06776
  Several local branches. (Our love.)

AMERICAN ORCHID SOCIETY
Botanical Museum of Harvard University
Cambridge, Mass. 02138
  Nearly 275 affiliated local societies throughout the world.

BONSAI SOCIETY OF GREATER NEW YORK
Box "E"
Bronx, New York 10466
  Chapters and affiliates also in Brooklyn, New Jersey, and
Long Island.

THE BROMELIAD SOCIETY
Office of the Secretary
6153 Hayter Avenue
Lakewood, California 90712
  Twenty-one local branches.

CACTUS AND SUCCULENT SOCIETY OF AMERICA
Box 167
Reseda, California 91335

INDOOR LIGHT GARDENING SOCIETY OF AMERICA
1316 Warren Road
Lakewood, Ohio 44107

INTERNATIONAL GERANIUM SOCIETY
Arthur Thiede
11960 Pascal Avenue
Colton, California 92324

THE PALM SOCIETY
Mrs. T. C. Buhler
1320 S. Venetian Way
Miami, Florida 33139
   Only a few local branches.

SAINTPAULIA INTERNATIONAL
P.O. Box 549
Knoxville, Tennessee 37901
   Many local branches.

31. *Plants, Seeds,*
and Supplies

The following suppliers come highly recommended. Most of them have catalogs, which they will send you either free or for a small fee. Ask for the catalog; if they charge, they'll let you know.

In case you didn't know, it is a federal offense to use the mails to defraud, so you can order from these suppliers with assurance.

Alberts & Merkel Bros., Inc.
2210 South Federal Highway
Boynton Beach, Florida 33435
bromeliads, orchids, other exotics

Antonelli Brothers
2545 Capitola Road
Santa Cruz, California 95060
tuberous begonias, gesneriads; catalog 25¢

Arndt's Floral Garden
20454 N.E. Sandy Boulevard
Troutdale, Oregon 97060
gesneriads, African violets, irradiated seed

Frank Bowman
771 Williams Avenue
Brooklyn, New York 11207
cacti, succulents, and great cultural information

Buell's Greenhouses
Weeks Road
Eastford, Connecticut 06242
African violets, gesneriads; catalog and culture book $1 (includes $1 discount coupon)

California Jungle Gardens
11977 San Vicente Boulevard
West Los Angeles, California 90049
bromeliads and other exotics

Caprilands Herb Farm
Silver Street
Coventry, Connecticut 06238

Channelview Nurseries
16501 Market Street Road
Channelview, Texas 77530
bromeliads, exotics; stamped, self-addressed envelope for list

Victor Constantinov
3321 Twenty-first Street
Apartment 7
San Francisco, California 94110
African violets

Cornelison Bromeliad Nursery
225 San Bernardino Street
North Fort Myers, Florida 33903

Davis Cactus Garden
Kerrville, Texas 78028

Fenell Orchid Co.
26715 S.W. 157th Avenue
Homestead, Florida 33030

Henry Field Seed & Nursery Co.
Shenandoah, Iowa 51601
seedsmen

Fischer Greenhouses
Box GL
Linwood, New Jersey 08221
African violets, gesneriads; catalog 15¢

Arthur Freed Orchids, Inc.
5731 South Bonsall Drive
Malibu, California 90265

Granger Gardens
1060 Wilbur Road
Medina, Ohio 44256
African violets; wholesale only

Green Hills Nursery
2131 Vallejo Street
St. Helena, California 94574
ferns

Bernard D. Greeson
3548 North Cramer
Milwaukee, Wisconsin 53211
labels, pots, other supplies; list 25¢

Gurney Seed & Nursery Co.
Yankton, South Dakota 57078
seedsman, onion sets

Herb Hager, Orchids
Box 544
Santa Cruz, California 95060

Orchids by Hauserman, Inc.
P.O. Box 363
Elmhurst, Illinois 60126

Henrietta's Nursery
1345 N. Brawley Avenue
Fresno, California 93705
cacti, exotics

J and L Orchids
20 Sherwood Road
Easton, Connecticut 06612

Johnson Cactus Gardens
2735 Olive Hill Road
Fallbrook, California 92028

Jones and Scully, Inc.
2200 N.W. 33rd Avenue
Miami, Florida 33142
orchids

Michael J. Kartuz
92 Chestnut Street
Wilmington, Massachusetts 01887
*gesneriads, begonias, succulents, miniature geraniums, exotics;
catalog 50¢*

Lager and Hurrell
426 Morris Avenue
Summit, New Jersey 07901
orchids

Lauray of Salisbury
Undermountain Road (Route 41)
Salisbury, Connecticut 06068
*gesneriads, succulents, begonias, bromeliads, exotics; catalog
35¢*

Logee's Greenhouses
55 North Street
Danielson, Connecticut 06239
begonias, geraniums, ferns, cacti, oxalis, herbs

Lyndon Lyon
14 Mutchler Street
Dolgeville, New York 13329
African violets, gesneriads

Rod McClellan Co.
1450 El Camino Real
South San Francisco, California 94080
orchids

Merry Gardens
Camden, Maine 04843
exotics; list free, culture booklet $1

Norvell Greenhouses
Dept. 5-g
318 South Greenacres Road
Greenacres, Washington 99016
exotics

Oakhill Gardens
Route 3
Box 87C
Dallas, Oregon 97338
sedums and sempervivums; list 10¢

George W. Park Seed Co., Inc.
Greenwood, South Carolina 29646
*seedsman, including gesneriad, begonia, and other houseplant
seed*

Plaza Nursery and Flower Shop
7430 Crescent Avenue
Buena Park, California 90620
bromeliads

Al Saffer & Co., Inc.
130 West 28th Street
New York, New York 10001
large selection of general supplies

Shaffer's Tropical Gardens
1220 41st Avenue
Santa Cruz, California 95060
orchids

Spring Hill Nurseries
Tipp City, Ohio 45366
seedsmen

Fred A. Stewart, Inc., Orchids
P.O. Box 307
1212 East Las Tunas Drive
San Gabriel, California 91778

Stokes Seeds, Inc.
Box 548, Main Post Office
Buffalo, New York 14240

or

Stokes Seeds, Ltd.
St. Catharine's, Ontario
Canada

Talnadge Fern Gardens
354 "G" Street
Chula Vista, California 92010
bromeliads and ferns

Tinari Greenhouses
2325 Valley Road
Huntingdon Valley, Pennsylvania 19006
African violets

Martin Viette Nurseries
Northern Boulevard (25A)
East Norwich, Long Island, New York 11732
hardy perennials; no mail order; catalog 50¢

Wayside Gardens
Mentor, Ohio 44060
bulbs, tubers; culture book/ catalog $2, refundable with order

Whistling Hill
Box 27
Hamburg, New York 14075
gesneriads; catalog 25¢

White Cloud Farm
R.R. 3
Carthage, Missouri 64836
African violets

Mrs. Rosetta White
1602 N.W. Third Street
Abilene, Kansas 67410
begonias

Wilson's Greenhouse
Ozark, Missouri 65721
African violets, episcias, begonias

Wood's African Violets
330 Dixon Road
Unit 2105
Weston M9R 1S9
Ontario, Canada
list 15¢

Irvin Wurthmann
5602 Theresa Road
Tampa, Florida 33615
bromeliads

Wyrtzen Exotic Plants
165 Bryant Avenue
Floral Park, New York 11001
gesneriads, begonias; plants sold at house only

Rudolf Ziesenhenne
1130 North Milpas Street
Santa Barbara, California 93103
begonias, begonia seed

Index